D0899002

Spectral Shakespeares

Reproducing Shakespeare: New Studies in Adaptation and Appropriation

Reproducing Shakespeare marks the turn in adaptation studies toward recontextual-ization, reformatting, and media convergence. It builds on two decades of growing interest in the "afterlife" of Shakespeare, showcasing some of the best new work of this kind currently being produced. The series addresses the repurposing of Shakespeare in different technical, cultural, and performance formats, emphasizing the uses and effects of Shakespearean texts in both national and global networks of reference and communication. Studies in this series pursue a deeper understanding of how and why cultures recycle their classic works, and of the media involved in negotiating these transactions.

Series Editors

Thomas Cartelli, Muhlenberg College
Katherine Rowe, Bryn Mawr College

Published by Palgrave Macmillan:

The English Renaissance in Popular Culture: An Age for All Time
Edited by Greg Colón Semenza

Extramural Shakespeare
By Denise Albanese

The Afterlife of Ophelia
Edited by Kaara L. Peterson and Deanne Williams

Spectral Shakespeares: Media Adaptations in the Twenty-First Century
By Maurizio Calbi

Spectral Shakespeares

Media Adaptations in the Twenty-First Century

Maurizio Calbi

SPECTRAL SHAKESPEARES
Copyright © Maurizio Calbi, 2013.

First published in 2013 by
PALGRAVE MACMILLAN®
in the United States—a division of St. Martin's Press LLC,
175 Fifth Avenue, New York, NY 10010.

Where this book is distributed in the UK, Europe and the rest of the world,
this is by Palgrave Macmillan, a division of Macmillan Publishers Limited,
registered in England, company number 785998, of Houndmills,
Basingstoke, Hampshire RG21 6XS.

Palgrave Macmillan is the global academic imprint of the above companies
and has companies and representatives throughout the world.

Palgrave® and Macmillan® are registered trademarks in the United States,
the United Kingdom, Europe and other countries.

ISBN: 978–0–230–33875–3

Library of Congress Cataloging-in-Publication Data is available from the
Library of Congress.

A catalogue record of the book is available from the British Library.

Design by Newgen Knowledge Works (P) Ltd., Chennai, India.

First edition: September 2013

10 9 8 7 6 5 4 3 2 1

Contents

Illustrations

Acknowledgments

Spectral Shakespeares began to materialize when I spent a six-month leave as Visiting Fellow at Columbia University, New York, in 2010. I owe primary thanks to Jean Howard for inviting me and acting as a wonderfully gracious host throughout my stay. Due to financial cuts to education in Italy, it is not easy for members of staff to be temporarily relieved of teaching duties and dedicate themselves exclusively to research. It is also for this reason that I want to thank the University of Salerno, and the School of Modern and European Languages and Literatures in particular, for consenting to a much-needed sabbatical. While in New York, I had the opportunity to talk to Tom Cartelli about this project. I am grateful to him for believing in it as well as for his patience, encouragement, and intellectual honesty and integrity. We share a passion for food, Italian culture, and media Shakespeare, so we share a lot. Tom also suggested that the book could be an appropriate addition to the Palgrave *Reproducing Shakespeare* series, which he coedits with Katherine Rowe, whom I also want to thank for encouragement and support. Brigitte Shull at Palgrave Macmillan has been a model editor, and I am grateful to her. I am also indebted to a number of people who contributed to making my stay in New York intellectually challenging, or helped to create an environment conducive to research: Louise Yelin, Caryl Phillips, whose fictional and nonfictional work I immensely admire, Ashish Avikunthak, whose films are so inspiring, Alan Stewart, Naomi Lieber, James Shapiro, Jonathan Gil Harris, Stef Craps, John Archer, Andras Kisery, the staff at the New York Public Library for Performing Arts, and the staff at the Columbia University Library.

Draft versions of some of the chapters were presented as papers at the Italian Association of English Studies conferences in Bari (2007) and Rome (2009); the "Shakespeare and His Contemporaries: Performance and Adaptation" SCAENA conference in Cambridge (2008); the "Rewriting,

Remixing, and Reloading: Adaptations Across the Globe" Adaptation Studies Association conference in Berlin (2010); the European Shakespeare Association conference in Pisa (2009); and the Spanish and Portuguese Association for the Study of the English Renaissance SEDERI conferences in Almagro (2008), Valencia (2009), and Sevilla (2012). Versions of other chapters were offered as seminar papers at meetings of the Shakespeare Association of America. I would like to express my sincere thanks to Amy Scott-Douglass, who worked very hard, and with incredible results, to coordinate a much-crowded "Shakespeare Spin-Offs" seminar in Washington, DC (2009); Mark Thornton Burnett, who led the "Shakespeare and World Cinema" seminar in Chicago (2010), and D. J. Hopkins, who coordinated the "Shakespeare and Hollyworld" seminar in Boston (2012). Both the SEDERI conferences and the SAA seminars have proved to be ideal forums for intellectual debates and much else besides. I profited from the detailed feedback provided in these contexts and enjoyed the stimulating conversations that developed afterwards *in praesentia* or in various media formats. These conversations continue to happen, and I treasure the exchanges with Mark Thornton Burnett, Richard Burt (who is always so generous with sharing his work), Clara Calvo López, Rui Carvalho Homem, Juan Francisco Cerda, Rebecca Chapman, Melissa Croteau, Pilar Cuder-Domínguez, Peter Donaldson, Berta Cano-Echevarria, Manuel José Gómez Lara, Keith Harrison, Ana Saez-Hidalgo, Alex Huang, Doug Lanier ("O my friend"), Courtney Lehmann, Zenón Luis Martínez, Michel Alfredo Modenessi, Amy Scott-Douglass, Paola de Pando Mena, Juan Antonio Prieto Pablos, Mark Robson, Greg Semenza, Jesús Tronch Perez, Rafael Núñez Vélez. Each and every book has a *conditio sine qua non*. Without the help, support, and exemplary academic work of these friends/colleagues, this book could not have been written.

I have learnt greatly from papers submitted to the "Re-Mediating Shakespeare in the Twenty-First Century" seminar, which I co-convened with John Joughin (European Association for the Study of English conference, Turin, 2010); the "Media Shakespeare: Appropriation Reconsidered" seminar, which I had the honor to co-convene with Doug Lanier (European Shakespeare Association conference, Weimar, 2011); and the "Shakespeare and the Media at the Beginning of the Twenty-First Century" seminar, which I led in Stratford-upon-Avon, and which was part of the International Shakespeare Conference program on "Shakespeare as Cultural Catalyst" (2010). Participants in these seminars included Anna Maria Cimitile, Antonella Piazza, Maria Izzo, Stephen O'Neill, and Anne-Marie Costantini-Cornède; Aneta Mancewicz, Mariangela Tempera, Reme Perni, Laura Campillo Arnaiz, Clara Calvo, and Ángel-Luis Pujante; Christie Carson,

Yong Li Lan, Christy Desmet, Simon Barker, and Martin Orkin. This is not just a list of colleagues and/or friends. I appreciate each one of them in different ways and for different reasons. The seminars were also the starting point for further intellectual exchanges and collaboration. Martin Orkin, in particular, has been a reference point for me for years, both because of his challenging work and because of his argute e-mails. The International Shakespeare conferences in Stratford-upon-Avon are rare events. I also associate these conferences with thought-provoking conversations with Pascale Aebischer, Deborah Cartmell, Rob Conkie, John Drakakis, Ewan Fernie, Ton Hoenselaars, Peter Holland, and others.

I want to thank my colleagues in English and North-American Studies at the University of Salerno (Italy), Linda Barone, Michele Bottalico, Mikaela Cordisco, Flora de Giovanni, Siria Guzzo, Marina Lops, Antonella Piazza, and Eleonora Rao, not least for tolerating my obsession with bringing this book to completion. I also want to thank the students of the "Literary Rewritings and Media Re-visions of Shakespeare" module here in Salerno for being ideal students. Over the years the classes have benefited more and more from the presence of Erasmus students from all over Europe. They have been a pleasure to teach, and often a lifeline. I am also grateful to Italian colleagues, with whom I discussed ideas related to this work on various occasions. Oddly, I meet some of them abroad more often than in Italy, for reasons that are too difficult to elaborate here. They include Maria Cristina Cavecchi, Iain Chambers, Maria Teresa Chialant, Rossella Ciocca, Lidia Curti, Marina de Chiara, Simonetta de Filippis, Maria Del Sapio, Carla Dente, Laura Di Michele, Serena Guarracino, Maddalena Pennacchia, Katherine Russo, Mariangela Tempera, who is always so kind in answering queries about Shakespearean material, Paola Pugliatti, Alessandra Marzola, Marilena Parlati, Tiziana Terranova, and Jane Wilkinson. A special "thank you" to Marina Vitale: she is the person to whom I have been sending drafts of my work for years, and this since I was one of her BA students at the University of Naples "L'Orientale." She has always been an inspiration to me.

Some former fellow MA and PhD students and colleagues at the University of Essex crossed over to the status of close friends a long time ago, and have stayed there since. Their work and friendship have had a profound impact on my intellectual and personal life: Jerry Brotton, whom I often meet unexpectedly, and with whom I have been talking about spectrality and hospitality for years; Silvana Carotenuto, who knows just about everything there is to know about specters and Derrida; John Joughin, who senses where I am going with my thinking and writing better than anybody else; Peter Hulme, whose intellectual style, integrity, and sense of friendship

I greatly admire. In a book that talks about spectrality, it would be only too easy to refer to the traces left on my work by people who are no longer with us. It is with hesitation, therefore, that I mention here the work of Francis Barker, Stephen Speed, and Jacques Derrida.

Quoi du reste? What about the rest? There is not much else to acknowledge except, indeed, the rest, which, if the argument of this book is in any way convincing, is just about everything there is that matters: I dedicate this book to Sue, who has read the manuscript, made suggestions, and shared this experience with me. Like me, she just about survived it.

* * *

All citations of Shakespeare's works are from Stanley Wells and Gary Taylor, eds. *William Shakespeare: The Complete Works*. 2nd ed. Oxford: Clarendon Press, 2005. An earlier version of parts of Chapter 1 appeared as "Ghosts, Burgers and Drive-Throughs: Billy Morrisette's *Scotland, PA* Adapts *Macbeth*," *Anglistica* 12.1 (2008): 39–57. This material is reprinted here by permission of the journal. A slightly different version of Chapter 4 was published as "This Is My Home, Too": Migration, Spectrality and Hospitality in Roberta Torre's *Sud Side Stori* (2000)" in *Shakespeare* 7.1–4 (2011): 16–34. The online version of this article is: www.tandfonline.com/doi/full/10.1080/17450918.2011.557505>. It is reprinted here with the permission of Routledge, Taylor & Francis. Chapter 5 is a revised version of an article that appeared as "Shakespeare in the Extreme: Addiction, Ghosts, and (Re)Mediation in Alexander Fodor's *Hamlet*" in *Literature/Film Quarterly* 39.2 (2011): 85–98. The material is reprinted here by permission of Salisbury University. I am extremely grateful to film director Alexander Abela for sending me a working copy of *Souli* in DVD format as well as production stills, and for answering questions about the film. Material from *Souli* is here reproduced with the permission of the director. I want to thank Charles Hunter, managing director at Mudlark, for permission to reuse tweets from the *Such Tweet Sorrow* performance, and reproduce images related to the performance. Last but not least, I am grateful to John Wyver for permission to cite from his *Illuminations* blog, and for talking to me about Twitter Shakespeare in person and via e-mail.

Introduction: Shakespeare, Spectro-Textuality, Spectro-Mediality

> There is then *some spirit.* Spirits. And *one must* reckon with them.
> One cannot not have to, one must not not be able to reckon with
> them, which are more than one: the *more than one/no more one* [*le
> plus d'un*].
>
> —Jacques Derrida, *Specters of Marx*

In *Specters of Marx* Jacques Derrida often draws attention to what he calls the "Thing 'Shakespeare'" (22). This is not a "Thing-in-itself" and/or a reservoir of essential, original and immutable meanings but, rather, an indeterminate ensemble of spectral and iterable marks. It is a "Thing" that, "like an elusive specter, *engineers* [*s'ingenie*] a habitation without proper inhabiting"; moving "in the manner of a ghost, . . . it inhabits without residing" (18).[1] The French philosopher also underlines that the "Thing 'Shakespeare'" lends itself to an infinite series of permutations and yet remains irreducible to, and in excess of, each of these permutations (22). It is translatable *and* untranslatable. (The immediate context of Derrida's ruminations is the multiplicity of translations into French of Hamlet's "The time is out of joint.") To be more precise, this "Thing" cannot be *properly* translated. In the language that will be adopted in the course of this book, it cannot be translated, adapted, or remediated without remainders, which are not necessarily *textual* remainders (at least not in the restricted sense of the word "textual") but are often mixed with media "matter." This translatability/untranslatability is the (aporetic) law of its survival as a "Thing," a sign and symptom of its life as irreducible living-on.[2]

Although Derrida's remarks on what may be called Shakespearean "spectro-textuality" touch upon crucial issues such as the "hauntological" (51) status of "Shakespeare" and its (uncanny) afterlife, his work on spectrality has not received the attention that it arguably deserves in Shakespeare studies. It has had even less of an impact on analyses of filmic versions of Shakespeare or adaptations of the Bard in other media, and this in spite of the fact that Derrida's reflections on "spectro-textuality," not only in *Specters of Marx* but in many other texts, often combine with cogent inroads on the spectrality of cinema and, more generally, the media, or, as he prefers to call them, "teletechnologies" (Derrida and Stiegler, *Ecographies* 35–39).[3] One of the purposes of this book is to redress this imbalance, which is not, I hope, a Hamlet-like attempt to "set it right" (1.5.190)—to establish, that is, a Derridean framework as *the* appropriate framework to approach media adaptations of Shakespeare.[4] The book argues that Derrida's notion of spectrality—and the uncanny articulations of temporality and spatiality that this spectrality entails—is relevant to an understanding of the increasingly heterogeneous and fragmentary *presence* of "Shakespeare" in the increasingly digitized and globalized mediascape of the beginning of the twenty-first century, a proliferation of multi-mediated "manifestations" of the Bard that succeeds what in retrospect may appear to be the relatively placid Shakespeare-on-film boom of the end of the twentieth century.[5] As a critic and/or consumer one is struck by—indeed, haunted by—the sheer multiplicity of this presence. The book registers this multiplicity by speaking of "Shakespeares" (in the plural), and thus adopting Richard Burt's argument that in contemporary mass media culture there is "not a stable, locatable whole that can be subsumed under the heading of a single 'Shakespeare'" ("Introduction" 3).[6] Moreover, by combining "Shakespeares" with "spectral," the book intends to clarify that the word "Shakespeares" is not a pluralization of the same entity, a plurivocity that leaves "Shakespeare"—its ontological status or its functioning as a cultural icon—unaffected. There is, then, to paraphrase the epigraph of this "Introduction," some Shakespeare; there are Shakespeare*s*, "*more than one / no more one*" (Derrida, *Specters* xx), and these Shakespeares take place in a variety of forms and media. Indeed, as I have begun to outline, the contemporary production of Shakespeares (also in languages other than English), a production that combines with a wider transnational circulation of Anglophone and non-Anglophone versions of the Bard, includes not only "traditional" media such as film and TV that have themselves undergone a process of digitalization, and whose artifacts are often repurposed and reformatted for the DVD and, more recently, Blu-ray market[7]; it also involves the online digital platforms of so-called Web 2.0. It is on these platforms, to provide examples almost at random so as to give a sense of the almost infinite variety of Shakespeare's afterlife, that scholarly editions of the Bard such as the *Internet Shakespeare Editions*, databases and archives of a more academic kind such as the *Shakespeare Quartos Archive*, *Staging Shakespeare* and

Designing Shakespeare: An Audio-Visual Archive 1960–2000, coexist with web-based interactive performances like the multilingual *HyperMacbeth* by the Italian artist dlsan or Herbert Fritsch's *Hamlet X*; video streaming websites such as *Shakespeare Performance in Asia* and *The Space*, hosting a significant number of Shakespearean performances; online samples of Karaoke Shakespeare and Hip Hop Shakespeare; Shakespearean apps for iPad, podcasts, and blogs with Shakespeare-related material such as *BardBox*; online games with Shakespearean components like *Mabinogi*; the relatively recent but exponentially expanding phenomenon of YouTube Shakespeare, or the inception of Twitter Shakespeare.[8] All these Shakespeares—and podcasts are no exception[9]—materialize on screen, whether this be the "traditional" cinematic screen of theatrical viewing, the increasingly wider and higher-resolution "small screen" of TV, the moveable screen of iPods, iPads, cellular phones, and portable DVD players, or the multitasking screen of those "very puzzling things" that are called computers (Winthrop-Young 186, 195), a medium, according to some media theorists, that encapsulates, simulates, and rewrites *all* other media, threatening them with obsolescence.[10] Therefore, if there is "Shakespeare" after Shakespeare on film, to refer to the title of a recent special issue of *Shakespeare Studies* dedicated to contemporary trends in Shakespearean remediation, it is "Shakespeare on screens" (Osborne 48).[11] Additionally, this is a "Shakespeare," according to one of the contributors, Douglas Lanier, that inherits the experiments with visual languages from the Shakespeare films of the 1990s as well as the collateral effects—some would say damages—of these experiments: in particular, the marginalization of the Shakespearean word, the undermining of "the notion that Shakespeare's essence is to be found in the particularities of his language" ("Mutations" 106).[12] The screen Shakespeares that appear at the beginning of the third millennium—and this label includes the perhaps residual category of cinematic or celluloid Shakespeare—are thus, according to Lanier, predominantly visual and "definitively post-textual" (106). [13]

I return to the question of visuality, the post-cinematic and the multiplicity of screens as part of a reading of Klaus Knoesel's *Rave Macbeth* (2001) in chapter 6; in chapter 3, I develop the notion of touch as a "medium" that competes with both the visual and the written through an analysis of Alexander Abela's *Souli*, an adaptation of *Othello*. For the moment, I want to suggest, in very general theoretical terms, and also in order to begin to clarify my approach to Shakespearean spectrality, that the materialization of Shakespeare through multiple screens does not emblematize a "move from medium-specific content toward content that flows across multiple media channels" (Jenkins 243), a shift toward content that is independent from, or even indifferent to, "any specific delivery mechanism" (243). It does not implement, that is, some kind of "convergence Shakespeare" as part of a wider media convergence. Notions of media convergence such as Henry Jenkins' aptly criticize the identification of media with narrowly conceived technical entities, but they do so by ultimately reinscribing a "humanist" paradigm. This is a paradigm whereby the inert materiality of "delivery technologies" (13), or the streaming of media content, need to be continually reanimated and/or reassembled by the active "liberal" subject/consumer—sometimes the collective subject/consumer of "participatory culture" (3)—, a subject that remains sovereign and present to itself in spite of its repeated interfacing with (new) media environments. In short, in approaches to media convergence such as Henry Jenkins', soul keeps on forming motionless (technical) matter. Moreover, and relatedly, given the fact that in our current mediascape Shakespeares not only appear on screens, but often appear to *happen* on screen, I want to propose that the multiple presence of the Bard is not synonymous with the reduction of hypermediacy to the "real time" of immediacy.[14] As I show throughout the book, but especially in chapter 7, in connection with a "live" performance of Twitter Shakespeare, the hypermediacy that structures from within each individual remediation of Shakespeare does not erase itself to pave the way for an immediate—multiple—access to "Shakespeare," or to allow the user/consumer to experience "Shakespeare" *as it is*, without the intervening *différance* of spectral or media remainders.[15] *Spectral Shakespeares* takes media convergence (or at least Henry Jenkins's version of it) and "real- time Shakespeare" to be idealistic constructs: they somehow resist and/or reverse, but do not effectively re-mark and displace, a technophobic framework whereby screen Shakespeare, and media Shakespeare more generally, are a simulacrum of the "real," a secondary, degraded and even perverse version of the "original," with Shakespearean spin-offs playing the role of derivatives of derivatives.[16] The instances of spectral Shakespeares included in the book suggest, instead, that the status of Shakespeare is "hauntological," a furtive mode of inhabiting without *properly* residing that simultaneously blurs any clear-cut distinction "between actual, effective presence and its other" (Derrida, *Specters* 40)—for instance, the distinction between the presence of the "original" and its spectral media simulacrum—*and* frustrates rigid notions of media exceptionalism, while inviting reconsiderations of media convergence.[17] As to the latter, as I argue in much more detail in the course of the book, and especially in my analysis of *Rave Macbeth* in chapter 6, these instances point to a disquieting overlapping—what may be called an *uncanny* convergence—of media, temporalities, and places.

The book selects a relatively small number of film, TV, and web adaptations of Shakespeare's tragedies from the vast array of screen Shakespeares that permeates our mediascape at the beginning of the twenty-first century. It chooses the term "adaptation," among the panoply of terms available to refer to the afterlife of Shakespeare, partly because of its plasticity as a term (for instance, its ability to signify both process and product [cf. Hutcheon esp. 6–22]), but mostly because, as Margaret J. Kidnie has recently argued, it is a term that designates a dense area of problematization: it not only concerns the belated transmission of texts but also impinges upon the fundamental ontological question of the nature and identity of "the work" itself (to use an expression Kidnie favors [7]).[18] *Spectral Shakespeares* focuses on twenty-first-century adaptations that have been less frequently discussed, and which broadly fall into the category of experimental or oppositional adaptations (Lehmann, "Film Adaptation" 75–78): Alexander Abela's yet to be commercially distributed *Souli* (2004), in which doctoral student Carlos's search for the tale of Thiossane is reframed as an adaptation of *Othello* that also reflects on the global circulation of the Shakespearean text as a template for construing the alterity of the other (chapter 3); Roberta Torre's *Sud Side Stori* (2000), an Italian revision of both *Romeo and Juliet* and *West Side Story* set in a Southern Italian city rife with racial and cultural conflicts (chapter 4); Alexander Fodor's self-proclaimed "extreme" version of *Hamlet* (2006), a simultaneously naive and trenchant low-budget experiment that finds its natural habitat, like many other twenty-first-century Shakespearean adaptations, in the urban environment of a youth culture replete with sex, violence, drugs, and music (chapter 5); Klaus Knoesel's technically innovative *Rave Macbeth* (2001), set in a rave club, a film that tells the story of young ambitious rave dancer and drug-dealer Marcus and his girlfriend Lidia (chapter 6); *Such Tweet Sorrow*, a five-week long, highly interactive Twitter-based online performance that utilizes the whole gamut of social media platforms to remake *Romeo and Juliet* (chapter 7). The book also examines adaptations that have already attracted considerable critical attention but are worth reconsidering not least because they emblematize significant, if perhaps diametrically opposed, trends in contemporary Shakespearean adaptation: Kristian Levring's Dogme95 *The King Is Alive* (2000), a filmic adaptation of *King Lear* in which the survival of a group of tourists stranded in the Namibian desert is inextricably interwoven with the survival of the Shakespearean text as well as with the fate of cinema itself (chapter 2); Billy Morrissette's *Scotland, PA* (2001) (which I read alongside Peter Moffat's inventive BBC retelling of the Scottish play as cookery drama [2005] in chapter 1), a film set in a burger joint whose irreverent take on Shakespeare is far removed from Levring's Northern European austere textual and cinematic aesthetics, and which explores the "deep and black desires" (*Mac.* 1.4.51) of two self-declared underachievers,

Joe "Mac" McBeth and his wife Pat, against a background of conspicuous consumption.

In all these twenty-first-century adaptations, "Shakespeare" is simultaneously material *and* evanescent. Like the ghost in *Hamlet* that Jacques Derrida continuously evokes in his work on spectrality, "Shakespeare" is "here," "here," and then is suddenly "gone" (1.1.123), even though this disappearance often turns out *not* to be an absence. Moreover, its "comings and goings" cannot be "ordered according to the linear succession of a before and an after" (Derrida, *Specters* 39). Its time is the time of "*the non-contemporaneity with itself of the living present*" (xix) (Derrida's emphasis), a time that is "out of joint," the time "without *certain* joining or determinable conjunction" (18) of anachrony. Put differently, the "Thing 'Shakespeare'" (22) does not so much appear as *re*-appear ("What, has this thing appeared *again* tonight?" [*Ham.* 1.1.19]) (emphasis added). Its first time is irredeemably the second time of repetition, a coming back that frustrates the supposedly linearity of time and puts the "original" under erasure. In *Such Tweet Sorrow*, the very first professional performance of Shakespeare on Twitter, this is literally so. As I show in chapter 7, the language of *Romeo and Juliet* emerges for the first time in the form of a *re*-tweet of a tweet sent to one of the characters by a "follower," a re-tweet containing the words: "Within the infant rind of this sweet flower / Poison hath residence, and medicine power" (Laurence Friar, 13 Apr. 7:21 p.m.).[19] Yet the first time of Shakespeare *as* the second time of repetition does not exclusively concern the appearance of the language of the "original." As many Shakespeare-on-screen theorists have noted, film adaptations are not unidirectional transpositions of Shakespeare from one medium to another (e.g., from page or stage to screen); in the language of this book, they cannot relate to the adapted text without conjuring up processes of remediation through which Shakespeare has already been consumed, reprocessed, and recycled.[20] "Shakespeare" never appears as such. If cinema, according to Derrida, playing the part of himself in Ken McMullen's *Ghost Dance* (1983), is "the art of allowing ghosts to come back," in its screen manifestations "Shakespeare" comes back without ever having been purely *itself*.[21] It is "always-already mediatised" (Burnett and Wray 2006: 8), enmeshed in a multidirectional rhizomatic field of mediality that makes it fundamentally "impure." For instance, the *Hamlet* of Alexander Fodor's *Hamlet* is Shakespeare's *Hamlet* just as much as Michael Almereyda's *Hamlet*; the *Romeo and Juliet* of Roberta Torre's *Sud Side Stori* is not only Shakespeare's *Romeo and Juliet* but also, at one and the same time, Baz Luhrmann's *William Shakespeare's Romeo + Juliet* and Jerome Robbins and Robert Wise's *West Side Story*, and so on. In fact, even in the example from Twitter Shakespeare I have just used, what may read like the language of the "original" is always-already a "mediation of a mediation" (Bolter and Grusin 59), subject to the "aphoristic" 140-characters constraints of Twitter as a medium and other conventions, and taking place at the point of intersection of multiple forms of mediality.

It is by pursuing the wider implications and ramifications of this spectral logic that the book intends to contribute to current debates in adaptation studies, performance theory and media theory. First of all, it underlines what has often been argued in post-fidelity adaptation studies but warrants repeating here in connection with the specific material included in the book, namely that these twenty-first-century Shakespearean adaptations are *not* an unproblematic re-presentation of a fixed and stable entity that somehow authorizes—and pre-exists—the process of adaptation. Each of these adaptations, to refer to work by Thomas Cartelli and Katherine Rowe that usefully brings Joseph Grigely's analysis of "textualterity" to bear on the field of adaptation studies, is "a reframing of earlier framings" (26); each articulates itself "as one of a series of texts that plays variations on a *work* which is not reducible to a single authorized version" (27). The potentially infinite series of variations by means of which the work is "*ontologized*" (Grigely 110) (his emphasis) bears witness to the status of the work as an *irreducibly* unfinished entity. Strictly speaking, and by definition, the work does not precede its variations in a clearly identifiable way. (Indeed, one may want to speak of the work as an entity that is "hauntologized" through its variations). Moreover, the potentially endless proliferation of these variations also inhibits any "future" actualization of the work in the modality of a presence that is present to itself. To adapt to this context a "classical" Derridean formulation, one may argue that the work repeatedly—and spectrally—differs from itself and defers itself (*Margins* 13). As regards the theoretical problematics of adaptation, what matters is that the "original" work, when seen in these terms, does *not*, and can *not*, offer a secure and stable ground for the process of adaptation. This does not apply exclusively to so-called loose adaptations. For instance, the "extreme" version of *Hamlet* analyzed in chapter 5 keeps the language of the "original" more than any other adaptation examined in the book, and also retains parts of the dialogue between Polonius and Reynaldo, which is not frequent in contemporary media adaptations of *Hamlet*. Yet, it not only turns Polonius and Reynaldo into Polonia and Reynalda but also offers its own version of a bad quarto by transforming the exchange between these renamed characters into an erotic lesbian game of seduction. Adopting W. B. Worthen's work on the vexed relationship between text and performance ("Performativity"),[22] but giving it a slightly more "deconstructionist" inflection, I argue that in this and other such "extreme" scenes the language of the "original" emerges—or, rather, *re*-emerges—as a retroactive spectral effect of a process of adaptation/surrogation that supplements the source and forces it to interact with other intertexts, in this case a visually luscious soft porn movie with film *noir* overtones. In effect, many twenty-first-century adaptations, and not only the ones I include in the book, from Greg Salman's *Mad Dawg* (2001) to Ralph Fiennes's *Coriolanus* (2011), from Roysten Abel's *In Othello* (2003) to Ashish Avikunthak's *Dancing Othello* (2002), from Don Boyd's *My Kingdom* (2001) to Liz Tabish's YouTube *A Cinematic Translation of Shakespearean Tragedies* (2008), show a similar process at work.[23] They do not only emblematize "an iteration that...invokes and displaces a textual 'origin'" (Worthen, "Performativity" 1104); they also articulate a process whereby the "original" is (retroactively) produced and re-marked as that which is being surrogated, and just as it is being surrogated, which confounds the boundaries between "before" and "after," "cause" and "effect," "inside" and "outside."[24] In my analysis of Kristian Levring's *The King Is Alive*, which, like Alexander Fodor's *Hamlet*, incorporates a considerable number of lines from the "original" (chapter 2), I develop this type of understanding of adaptation as retroactive production but in connection with the specificity of a film that repeatedly exhibits the fragile and "impure" status of the Shakespearean text through a character's attempt to (re)write Lear "by hand," the often botched rehearsals of this half-remembered script, and a performance that is never brought to completion. The chapter shows that this adaptation is neither a reproduction nor a selective interpretation of the "original"; it recreates *Lear* as that which is *essentially* an ensemble of fragments, and makes it interact with the "fragmentary" aesthetics of Dogme95. It is a re-creation that (retrospectively) reduces *Lear* to a "poor, bare, forked" script (3.4.101), an "unaccomodated" spectral "thing" (100) haunting the film characters with all the force of a memory that has never been fully present, and offering a life that is less *and* more than life—what the chapter calls, utilizing Derrida's work on the spectral logic of "autoimmunity," a radically ambivalent "autoimmune" life.[25]

* * *

Ramona Wray has recently argued that there is "a wealth of...Shakespearean filmic initiatives that unfold in languages other than English" that "have slipped under the radar of mainstream criticism" (279, 280). The book includes analyses of two twenty-first-century examples of these non-Anglophone "filmic initiatives," Alexander Abela's *Souli* and Roberta Torre's *Sud Side Stori*, first of all to contribute to the construction of what Mark Thornton Burnett calls "a more representative and ethically responsible Shakespeare [on film] canon" ("Applying" 114); second, and perhaps more significantly, to show that these two adaptations address in an exemplary way the unequal transactions between the local and the global that implicate "Shakespeare," and that they do so without reproducing a clear-cut opposition between the local and the global: they repeatedly suggest rearticulations of the global through the local and vice versa without losing sight of the asymmetry governing these transactions. For instance, *Souli* repeatedly draws attention to these asymmetric interactions (chapter 3). In particular, it intervenes in what it sees as the "vociferous" circulation and transmission of the Shakespearean word on the global stage by developing a multilayered rhetoric of silence. Like *The King Is Alive*, it combines an emphasis on bare life—this time the life of fishermen in Southern Madagascar—with the reduction of the Shakespearean text to a bare, almost wordless script. This is an *Othello*-like script that allocates (colonially inflected) roles and spreads trauma, playing itself out to its tragic conclusion with all its spectral force, almost as if it was fate itself. Yet the film also shows how this Shakespearean script is forced to cohabit with the vicissitudes of the "traditional" untranscribed African tale of Thiossane, a tale that undoubtedly bears the mark of the local but is not a pure uncontaminated "origin," and that the Othello-like character, Souli, refuses to circulate in a written form, pointing to alternative "spectral" modes of transmission such as touch or even telepathy. As this uncanny cohabitation develops, the Shakespearean script is itself re-marked and partially displaced. It re-emerges as something *other than* an emblem of the reiterative Western appropriation of the alterity of the exotic Other. It re-presents itself, albeit tentatively, as a language of the future that simultaneously inscribes threat *and* chance. This also indicates, once again, the complexity of the temporality of the process of adaptation. In Abela's film *Othello* is an adapted text, retrospectively produced as a bare but powerful spectral script. But it also re-appears as a text *yet to be adapted*, and perhaps inadaptable: the film gestures toward further migrations across spatial and temporal boundaries that may silently infiltrate global circuits of communication, also by virtue of the idiosyncrasy of their modes of articulation. *Sud Side Stori* equally engages with the asymmetric global/local nexus by presenting a local Italian variation of the *Romeo and Juliet* story, and setting it within the context of the global trade in human flesh, which is significantly conducted in English (chapter 4). In this film, which oddly blends gritty neorealist cinematographic techniques with the artificial style of the musical, the two "star-cross'd lovers" ("Prologue" 6) become Toni Giulietto, a Sicilian rock singer who dreams of escape, and Romea Wacoubo, a beautiful Nigerian prostitute who falls in love with him when she sees him standing on his balcony playing the guitar. One of the most remarkable aspects of the film, in terms of its contribution to an understanding of both the process of adaptation and the global/local nexus, is that it does not simply include the translated textual body of Shakespeare's *Romeo and Juliet*; rather, it produces this body as a series of fragments that *remain* to be translated in the so-called target language (i.e., they are not in English but they are not quite in Italian either). This draws attention to translation, and the translation of Shakespeare in particular, as an unfinished process, a process that does not necessarily reach its aim or destination. "Shakespeare" remains a "Shakespeare-*in*-translation," a spectral entity that inhabits without *properly* residing. Its vicissitudes thus become inextricably intertwined with the fate of the migrant(s) expounded in the film, especially Romea but also the similarly displaced, metaphorically homeless "native" Toni Giuletto: they are migrants who *remain* foreign, and whose foreignness interrogates not only notions of cultural homogeneity that deeply affect the "two households" ("Prologue" 1) represented in the film (i.e., the Sicilian and the Nigerian community), but also "liberal" understandings of hospitality as toleration, integration and assimilation—what may be called, after Derrida, "hos(ti) pitality," a conditional hospitality that uncannily approximates hostility ("Hostipitality" 3). By articulating a perturbing kind of foreignness that stays in transit, and making it work on a number of interrelated levels, the film also puts pressure on the idea that there is a clearly identifiable "foreign Shakespeare," and that it can easily be distinguished from a "native Shakespeare."[26] In this sense, *Sud Side Stori* is a perfect illustration of Richard Burt's polemical point that recent Shakespearean adaptations "significantly blur if not fully deconstruct distinctions between the local and the global, original and copy, pure and hybrid, indigenous and foreign, . . . *English and other languages*" ("Glo-ca1i-zation" 15–16, emphasis mine). It is one of the book's arguments that the blurring or deconstruction of these dichotomies does not diminish—in fact, it enhances—the ethico-political impact of this and other adaptations.

Souli and *Sud Side Stori* forcefully respond to the "out-of-jointedness" of the now. They raise with particular urgency ethico-political issues that affect the present, and make them coextensive with self-reflexive "formal" concerns. The other adaptations examined in the book attend to ethico-political issues in a less compelling way, with the partial exception of *The King Is Alive*,[27] but they are all characterized by a high degree of self-reflexivity. This takes a variety of forms. For instance, *Scotland, PA* and the BBC *Shakespeare Retold Macbeth* often bring an allegorical and metadramatic dimension to bear on the multiple forms of incorporation they foreground while adapting *Macbeth* (chapter 1). In particular, in these adaptations the incorporation of the flesh of the nonhuman animal allegorizes adaptation as a "voracious" reiterative process of inclusion (and not only of Shakespearean material), but one that does not fail to leave out various types of remainders that inexorably come back to haunt. Klaus Knoesel's *Rave Macbeth* also displays awareness of its status as an adaptation, and the precariousness of this status (chapter 6). It creatively responds to the indeterminate, uncanny reiterative structure of Shakespeare's *Macbeth* by incorporating the "sound and fury" (5.5.26) of the languages of rave culture, and identifying them as essentially reiterative, self-consuming, and addictive performances: the obsessive beat of techno music, the incessant trancelike bodily movements of the dance ravers, the repeated ingestion of ecstasy (i.e., an updated version of the "insane root / That takes the reason prisoner," 1.3.82–83). These languages metonymically, if obliquely, point to the film's own status as an addition to a series of adaptations of *Macbeth*, a supplement (in Derrida's sense) that inscribes itself in a chain of *Macbeth*-like stories subjected to the law of iterability that is also a principle of replaceability. More generally, the film's adoption and relentless exhibition of these media languages bear out Peter Donaldson's argument that in Shakespearean films, and especially contemporary films (at least since media-saturated Baz Luhrmann's *William Shakespeare's Romeo + Juliet*), "media themes rise to the level of subject matter, vying for attention with and sometimes supplanting the story line of the source play" ("Bottom" 23). Donaldson usefully adds that the pervasive presence of media themes and practices in these films does not necessarily imply a movement towards meta-cinematic self-reflexivity, "a narrative exclusively concerned with *cinema*"; it often inaugurates "journeys *across* media" (23, his emphasis).

Spectral Shakespeares builds on Donaldson's argument, and often explores the "journeys *across* media" activated by the adaptations under investigation, from the ironic inclusion of an episode from the *McCloud* TV series as a black-and-white melodramatic version of *Macbeth* in *Scotland, PA* to *Souli*'s poignant foregrounding of "corporeal" media; from the persistent use of rock music to recycle crucial scenes from *Hamlet* in Fodor's adaptation to the repeated deployment of a transnational mélange of sounds and dancing styles in *Sud Side Stori*. But it is especially in the final two chapters of the book, in connection with adaptations such as *Rave Macbeth* and *Such Tweet Sorrow* that make cross-media consciousness their *raison d'être*, that I pursue these "Shakespeareccentric" trajectories at length (Burt, "Introduction" 5),[28] while extensively engaging with Derrida's remarks on the "irreducible spectral dimension" of the media (*Specters* 53) as "out-of-joint" iterative technologies that delocalize and dislocate. It is also in these chapters that Derrida's remarks are brought to bear upon aspects of recent media theory (chapter 6), or understandings of social media, especially Lev Manovich's and Mark B. Hansen's (chapter 7). Chapter 6 argues that in *Rave Macbeth*, which is the very first feature-length film to be shot on a Sony's 24P-1080 digital camera, the continuous shift into a self-reflexive mode is facilitated by the spectral presence of Hecate, a "supernatural" character who is simultaneously inside and outside the cinematic frame, both chief drug dealer and media savvy. In the film the main cinematic screen often doubles as Hecate's gigantic screen that emulates a computer or video screen; it contains and is contained by this "supplementary" screen that also splits into separate "windows" competing for attention. Facing this huge screen with his remote control, Hecate replays clips of events that have just taken place before the start of the film; he cuts from one scene to the next and then moves back to the "real time" of the diegesis to play events "live," as they happen; he goes as far as to "rewind" the action back to the beginning and pause it so that he can reappear on the "main" cinematic screen and have a tête-à-tête with one of his "human" emissaries, drug-dealer Dean/Duncan. This reiterated phantasmagoric performance, in the course of which the "main" screen is often reduced to an optional "window" on Hecate's screen, recalls the rhizomatic, "paratactic, and smooth space of digital compositing," the additive juxtapositions typical of a post-cinematic mode (Shaviro 78); it suggests the extent to which the cinematic—and, by extension, cinematic Shakespeare—includes and is haunted by what it announces as its future, and perhaps its future erasure.[29] As pointed out earlier, all the adaptations included in this book embody elements of self-referentiality. *Rave Macbeth* goes further than any of them in staking out its position within its mediascape, and contributing to current debates on media convergence. It marks in advance its (potential) circulation, distribution, and consumption across multiple media platforms. As I show in detail in chapter 6, the film repeatedly supplements *itself*: it rearticulates itself as a film *and* a version of itself in DVD format with menus and scene selections[30]; it re-presents itself as a film *and* a music video without dialogue, with its 14,000 dance ravers and the appearance of renowned DJs such as DJ Tomkraft; it recasts itself as a film *and* a video game or even a theatrical performance, especially when it chooses to end with all the "human" characters coming back from the dead and lining up on what is a simulacrum of a bare seventeenth-century stage, standing there as if waiting for applause and/or to be selected for another rerun of a virtual *Macbeth*-like role-playing game. Therefore the film *does* envisage, from within the cinematic medium, a scenario of media convergence, but one of uncanny coexistence of media forms, each haunting the other, and thus points to the lack of absolute translatability across media. Moreover, in the course of its "Shakespeareccentric" media journeys that simulate and "theorize" convergence, the film also returns to the basic question of what may be called, after Derrida, "the medium of the media themselves," a medium that "spectralizes" (*Specters* 50–51), and uncannily juxtaposes this question to the pharmacological logic of the life-enhancing/life-threatening "medium" of drugs.[31] It shows the interimplication of the experience of drugs and the experience of mediality. Marcus's repeated ingestion of ecstasy, a chemical, "artificial" substance that replaces the "[natural] potions and poisons of yesterday" (Hecate's words), inscribes the addicted body in a temporal and spatial frame which is that of the "automaton, . . . technics, the machine, the prosthesis" (Derrida, "Faith and Knowledge" 51). It promises the re-emergence of a "natural" body—ecstasy is synonymous with "happiness"; it "melts . . . inhibitions away" (Marcus's words)—but through processes of acceleration and deceleration that divide, dislocate, and "spectralize" the present in much the same way as the iterative processes of what Derrida calls "teletechnologies" (Derrida and Stiegler 35–39). As a synthetic, prosthetic "technology," ecstasy "slows down and speeds up everything all at the same time" (Marcus's words). It offers "a maximum of life," but this is a life, like the life inscribed in the "phantom structure" of archival and media technologies, that "already yields to death" (39). Because of the body's insertion into what is in effect a "life-death" differential structure of temporization and spacing (Derrida, *Margins* 13), the (addicted) subject—the only subject there is—is also shown to be unable to pose as a "virtual" incorporeal point from which it can fully grasp and/ or master vision, or dispassionately "consume" media images, as if from a distance. Utilizing the uncanny dynamics of safety/unsafety of the "original" play (Royle, *How to*, 88–105) and extending it to the field of mediality, the film repeatedly marks this position as one of unsafety, and is trenchantly ironic about the hubristic attempt by Marcus (who also stands in for present and future spectators, users and consumers) to occupy it, in spite of his body's imbrication in the prosthetic technologies of media and drugs. It thus exposes what is perhaps the core fantasy of the humanist subject as a disembodied, transcendent, and autonomous subject of vision, a fantasy that can be summarized with words by art historian Caroline Jones: "an intact body deliriously magnified by technology. . . . but neither rewired nor obstructed in its access to reality by electronic media themselves" (97) as it freely moves across flows of media "content."[32]

Chapter 6 is crucial to the book's understanding of media Shakespeares as not only irremediably self-referential artifacts, or sites of self-allegorizing movements across competing media, but also as articulations of a self-reflexivity that extends to the experience of mediality itself. It leaves open the question of whether "being-on-drugs" (Ronell 3)—in particular, the logic of the *pharmakon* and the process of iterability this implements—is intimately related to the question of mediality, beyond the specific example of this, and perhaps other, adaptations of *Macbeth*.[33] In more general theoretical terms, and especially in the last two chapters, *Spectral Shakespeares* often works with the notion of the inherently spectral experience of mediality as exteriorization of life by means of technological prostheses (in an extended sense), a process that makes life, and not only "human" life, what it is by displacing and supplementing it.[34] The book emphasizes this aspect also in order to establish a dialogue with recent, philosophically inflected media theory which claims, for instance, that "in addition to naming individual mediums at concrete points within... history, 'media'... also names a technical form or formal technics, indeed a general mediality that is constitutive of the human as 'biotechnical' form of life" (Mitchell and Hansen ix); "media" designates, that is, a fundamental "operation of exteriorization and invention" (xiii) that makes humans "'essentially' prosthetic beings" (xii) while providing "an environment for the living" (xiii).[35] This dialogue with recent media theory also informs my reading of a sample of social media Shakespeare, *Such Tweet Sorrow* (chapter 7), an online Twitter-based adaptation of *Romeo and Juliet* that also entailed, as it developed over a period of five weeks in 2010, journeys across the whole gamut of Web 2.0 social networking platforms, including YouTube, AudioBoo, Yfrog, Twitpics, Tumblr, Spotify, and Facebook. In fact, the chapter shows that this Twitter experiment is not only an updated dramatization of the story of two "star-crossed lovers"; it is also a mise-en-scène of Twitter as a medium and the other social media it incorporates: Juliet's coming of age coincides with her increasing expertise in the use of Twitter and other social media; the formulaic pre-Juliet Romeo of the "original" becomes a character who "shuts up his windows" (*Rom.* 1.1.136) to the world of social media, temporarily refusing to join Twitter to then quickly become addicted to the medium; Friar Laurence (here Laurence Friar), when he is not too high because of the "flower" (2.2.23) of cannabis, meditates upon the social uses of Twitter to reach out to young people and thus stop the feud; Mercutio is a compulsive twitterer who continually engages with the audience of "followers" and easily shifts from one (social) medium to another, which shows that he is not only a boisterous character but also an emblem of the highly interactive and cross-media characteristics of the performance as a whole. To mention once again the argument developed by Peter Donaldson in relation to media-oriented Shakespearean films, *Such Tweet Sorrow* is also a media allegory whose "theme" is the "ferment in communications technologies" ("Media" 61). Yet the "rapidly shifting mediascape" (61) to which Donaldson refers to pursue his analyses has itself rapidly shifted. In order to attend to this shift, chapter 7 includes recent work on social/ new media by Lev Manovich and Mark Hansen who claim, respectively, that "we have moved from *media* to *social media*"

("Practice" 319) (Manovich's emphasis), "a new media universe" that "is not simply a scaled-up version of twentieth-century media culture" (319); and that we are witnessing "a widespread mediatic regime change,...a change in the vocation of media and mediation themselves" ("New Media" 180–81). As to the modes of articulation of these new media configurations, Manovich argues that in the new universe of social media "*content, news,* or *media*" are often "tokens used to initiate or maintain a conversation" (326, his emphasis); in order to understand the dynamics of social media, their function as tokens is more important than the "matter" of the conversation, a conversation that is also significantly "distributed in space and time": "people can respond to each other regardless of their location, and the conversation can in theory go forever" (*sic*) (327). In a similar vein, but in the course of a complex argument about the dissociation of media and technics in what can perhaps no longer be defined our *media*scape, Hansen maintains that "what is mediated by Web 2.0 is less the content that users upload than *the sheer connectivity*" (180, emphasis added); that in social media "connectivity emerges as an end in itself, distinct from the actual sharing of... (traditional) media content" (181). As it engages with these theories, chapter 7 suggests that if *Such Tweet Sorrow* is a media allegory, it is more specifically an allegory of the production of connectivity that materializes under the regime of social media: to be is to be on line at all times, a making contact "by distributing (traces) of [oneself] on many-to-many computational networks" (181), and this over and above any (media) "content" one happens to share. Yet the chapter also argues that there are aspects of this Twitter adaptation that run counter to the principle of connectivity, or contribute to its aesthetic rearticulation. In *Such Tweet Sorrow* "Shakespeare" is irrevocably transformed by means of its interaction with the languages of social media and, more generally, its insertion in a number of "citational environments" (Cartelli and Rowe 29–34) belonging to youth culture, including music, film, sport, and—again—drugs: Laurence Friar tweets Shakesperean lines as he smokes weed; the deaths of Mercutio and Tybalt take place in the midst of riots following a football match; Laurence Friar's instructions to Juliet regarding the "vial" (4.1.93) take the form of an acrostic posted on the Electric Kool-Aid Café website. But this radical (media-oriented) "Shakespeareccentric" journey alternates with a movement *back* to "Shakespeare," a "Shakespearecentric" movement whose outcome is the emergence, or re-emergence, of "Shakespeare" as an ensemble of spectral remainders. These ghostly traces are not a shadowy presence. They are not simply "tokens" in a "conversation" between one character and another, characters and followers, or among followers; they are not interchangeable with a vernacular tweet, a picture on Twitpics, or an audio file on AudioBoo, as the logic of Manovich's argument would make them to be. Especially as the online performance moves toward its tragic ending, the power of Shakespearean spectrality—the remainders of the "original" language of *Romeo and Juliet*; the constraints of its (endlessly recyclable) plot; the logic of the *pharmakon* informing the play—reasserts itself. It forces *Such Tweet Sorrow* to reconsider and interrogate the conventions of Twitter as a medium as well as the principle of connectivity itself, and this in order to be effective as a performance: we thus witness the tweet that does not reach its destination; the emphasis on an offline mode or, alternatively, on a random and/or inattentive access to Twitter as its online spectral equivalent (i.e., being online as if in the "borrowed likeness of shrunk death," 4.1.104). More generally, we are made aware of the full redeployment of Twitter as a medium working as a veritable *pharmakon* (i.e. "poison" *and* "medicine," 2.2.24), reducing "the separation of monads, infinite distance, the disconnection of experiences, the multiplicity of worlds" (Derrida, "Aphorism Countertime" 420) but also, at one and the same time, proliferating the disjunctions, dislocations and separations that it is supposed to preempt. Put differently, chapter 7 shows that *Such Tweet Sorrow* creatively responds to the spectral effect of that extended aporia that goes under the name of *Romeo and Juliet*—the oxymoronic entanglement of love and death, cure and poison, friend and foe, fate and chance—by implementing a self-reflexive media aporia of its own that experiments with the potential erasure of Twitter as a medium and the connectivity it affords. To a significant extent, it rewrites Twitter as an *asynchronous* medium that marks the essential impossibility of any "real-time" communication and transmission, or any unproblematic convergence of media or "tweeple," a medium that thus turns out to be replete with those "contretemps-traps" to which Derrida draws attention in his "aphoristic" reading of the "original" *Romeo and Juliet* (419).

* * *

Like the examples of "Shakespop" Douglas Lanier admirably analyzes in *Shakespeare and Modern Popular Culture*, the adaptations studied in this book, and perhaps especially *Such Tweet Sorrow* as a novel form of remediation of Shakespeare on social media platforms, raise questions about "what constitutes the essential or authentic Shakespeare"; "how far we are willing to extend the name 'Shakespeare'" (9). From the perspective of Margaret Kidnie's recent work on the "problem" of adaptation, these are not just trite questions that belong to the pioneering phase of adaptation studies, obsessed by issues of fidelity. As she puts it, "the arguments that continue to spring up around authentic and adaptive Shakespeare [do not] represent a critical or theoretical dead-end" (9). In fact, these arguments remain essential, and precisely because the boundary between (what Kidnie calls) the work and "adaptation, or what is 'not the work'" (7), are fundamentally porous and unstable. For Kidnie, there is no "*a priori* category that texts and stagings are production *of*" (9); the (dramatic) work does not precede, and cannot ground, "production." As she further explains, "the work, far from functioning as an objective yardstick against which to measure the supposed accuracy of editions and stagings, . . . continually takes shape as a *consequence* of [textual and theatrical] production" (7). Thus, for Kidnie, the radical ontological instability of the work calls for a pragmatic policing of boundaries that is implemented by "communities of users who accept, reject, or more often, debate as genuine a new print edition or a particular theatrical enactment" (7). Kidnie's theoretical position resonates with some of the arguments developed in this book, especially her emphasis on the fact that discussions of specific adaptations of Shakespeare cannot but result in reflections on the "nature" and identity of the (Shakespearean) work itself. These reflections lead to a number of paradoxes as regards the temporal unfolding of the work, such as the one she identifies when she argues that the work "takes shape as a *consequence* of production" (7) (Kidnie's emphasis). *Spectral Shakespeares* frequently turns to these uncanny temporal paradoxes. As mentioned earlier, it often speaks of the (retroactive) production of the "original" as that which is displaced and reformatted (especially but not only in relation to Fodor's *Hamlet* and *Such Tweet Sorrow*); it underlines the (retrospective) creation of the "original" as an ensemble of fragments (in connection with *The King Is Alive*), or a *corpus* that remains to be translated (in relation to *Sud Side Stori*). Yet the book is skeptical about the preponderance of the role Kidnie attributes to interpretive communities, and the effectiveness of such role, in providing "checks and limits" (7) on the work—the work as "an ongoing process" (6); "a process without an origin" (7)—and especially as one moves from the relatively specialized field of the production of textual instances of the work such as textual editions to the realm of performance and media adaptations.[36] From the perspective of this book, the proliferation of Shakespeares in contemporary media culture goes hand in hand with the exponential increase, fragmentation and dispersal of so-called interpretive communities, which is also to emphasize their metamorphosis into communities that can no longer be thought of in terms of "the schema of identity" (Derrida and Stiegler 66), or the idealistic notion of a (human) subject present to itself: these communities are often multifaceted online communities; they are perhaps no longer "communities" but "network[s] without unity or homogeneity" (66) in which "disidentification, singularity, rupture" prevail over "the solidity of identity" (67) that arguably governs *any* notion of community, including the concept of interpretive communities.[37]

Spectral Shakespeares thus stays with what Kidnie calls "the simple answer" to the question: "How...can one distinguish the work from its adaptation?", to wit, that "one *cannot* absolutely separate the two" (30) (Kidnie's emphasis). To adopt the language of information theory, and in particular theories of the feedback loop, the book sees adaptation as some kind of output that is fed back into the system (i.e., "Shakespeare") as input, an operation that does not render the system homeostatic but, rather, causes "the distinction between [input and output]," work and adaptation, to "break...down," so that "a looping circularity overtakes a strictly linear flow" (Clarke 168).[38] Or, to refer to Derrida once again, and specifically to the remarks he makes in relation to his reading of *Romeo and Juliet*, the singularity of the work is "worked, in fact *constituted*, by the possibility of its own repetition (readings, indefinite numbers of productions, references, be they reproductive, citational, or transformative)" ("Strange Institution" 69, emphasis added). Thus, the (Shakespearean) work—what Derrida calls in *Specters of Marx* the "signature of the "Thing 'Shakespeare'" (22)—cannot be clearly or absolutely separated from its afterlife. It takes place as a necessarily contaminated "entity," in that it is structured from within—and "de-structured"—by reproducibility and iterability. Its first time is inextricably intertwined with the second time of repetition; its time is the anachronistic time of spectrality. To use Derrida's words, the work is an event that "comes about as impurity—and impurity here is chance" ("Strange Institution" 69). In terms of the arguments developed in this book, this chance is the chance of survival of the "Thing 'Shakespeare.'"

The media adaptations analyzed in *Spectral Shakespeares* bear witness to the survival of this "Thing." They are idiosyncratic, often inventive, forms of "countersigning."[39] They also show—and re-mark—the "virtue" of impurity in many different ways: they mix the remainders of Shakespeare's language with the languages of other media in ways that are reciprocally illuminating; they make old media uncannily overlap with new media, a process that Richard Burt may call a "dialectic of reanimation and de-animation" (*Film and Media* 29); they repeatedly pull "Shakespeare" into the gravitational orbit of youth cultures, or make it cohabit with non-Anglophone cultures; they sometimes go as far as to make the (spectral and impure) law of iterability into their *modus operandi*, a process that extends from the thematic level to the level of mediality. Moreover, whenever these "Shakespeareccentric" movements turn into "Shakespearecentric" journeys, what emerges is a language that is always-already mediatized. Or, alternatively, we witness the ghostly reappearance of *what counts* as the "original" within specific contexts. This is a comeback of an "original Shakespeare" as prosthetic media/spectral effect, often associated with the "spirit" of the archaic: the old-fashioned reel-to-reel tape recorder in Fodor's *Hamlet*; the music track by *Gill* Shakespeare in *Scotland, PA*; the *passé* conventions of the silent movie in the balcony scene of *Sud Side Stori*. Perhaps more significantly, not only do these adaptations testify to the survival of the "Thing 'Shakespeare'" and re-mark the chance of impurity; as part of their wide-ranging self-reflexivity, they also draw attention to the process of adapting Shakespeare as an unfinished business and, by implication, to the fluidity of their own boundaries.[40] This takes many different forms. At times, these adaptations point to future forms of remediations that they often partially include and/or simulate: *Souli*'s emphasis on manifold migrations of stories involving nonconventional "spectral" media; *Such Tweet Sorrow*'s tongue-in-cheek experiments with self-erasure as part of its rearticulation of the potentialities of Twitter as a medium; *Rave Macbeth*'s presentation of the spectral return from the dead of the main characters, ready to be redeployed. At other times they conjure up spectral figurations of "Shakespeare" that allegorize a demand for supplementary revisions: the "animal Shakespeare" of the BBC *Shakespeare Retold Macbeth*, a "Shakespeare" that is metaphorically sliced, cooked, and served up *à la carte* to hungry customers but remains as yet indigestible; the undead corpse of Hamlet's father in Fodor's *Hamlet*, a restless spectral entity that keeps on coming back as a reminder of the unplaceability of a (textual) *corpus*; the body-in-translation of a "migrant Shakespeare" that never quite reaches its destination in *Sud Side Stori*.

Thus, one of the most idiosyncratic aspects of these adaptations is that they stress the irremediably unfinished character of the process of adaptation: they look to the future while inscribing and re-marking it in advance, which is not a way of predetermining, or programming, what is yet to come but, rather, a way of signaling the urgency of an opening. Put differently, they enact an uncanny spatio-temporal logic whereby what is "out front, the future, comes back in advance, from the past, from the back" (Derrida, *Specters* 10). This is a logic whose spectrality is accentuated by the fact that they are media manifestations of Shakespeare in which the different media involved regularly put into play forms of reciprocal haunting that further dislocate spatio-temporal boundaries.[41] As it explores early twenty-first-century media adaptations that do not properly end, and whose boundaries are exceedingly porous on many different levels, *Spectral Shakespeares* suggests that "Shakespeare" is a "Thing" that keeps on coming back, an uncanny, multilayered mediatized body that is repeatedly on the point of vanishing only to reappear elsewhere and in different (media) formats. It is a spectral "Thing" whose "survivance," like the "survivance" more generally described by Jacques Derrida in the latest of his posthumously published seminars, is largely a kind of untimely, out-of-joint, de-canonized and low-brow "survivance" without "superiority,...supremacy or sovereignty" (*Beast and Sovereign II* 131), the kind of "survivance" that may frustrate any cohesive interpretive gathering, but one that does not fail to leave its mark on contemporary media culture.[42]

CHAPTER 1

The State of the Kitchen: Incorporation and "Animanomaly" in *Scotland, PA* and the BBC *Shakespeare Retold Macbeth*

In an interview with Jean-Luc Nancy, Jacques Derrida underlines the dominant "carnivorous" and "sacrificial" structure of the human subject: "The subject does not want just to master and possess nature actively. In our cultures he accepts sacrifice and eats flesh." Playing on the double meaning of the French word *chef* (i.e., *chef* as the head of the kitchen; *chef* as the political head of a state), he adds: "The *chef* must be an eater of flesh (with a view, moreover, to being 'symbolically' eaten himself)" ("'Eating Well'" 114).[1] Derrida's somewhat elliptic—almost Freudian—observations suggest that sovereignty, including sovereignty over one's self, has to do with eating the "other," and that this incorporation—a "symbolic" operation when the human animal is involved; a "real" *and* "symbolic" one in the case of the nonhuman animal (112)—is by its very nature made of repeated performances.[2] Like each and every act of violent foundation, incorporation is not achieved once and for all, not least because it is irresistibly haunted by the specter of that which is being incorporated. Moreover, as Derrida parenthetically remarks, it is potentially reversible.

Derrida's comments on incorporation, combined with his rigorous problematization of the distinction between the human and nonhuman animal, especially in his latest work,[3] inform this chapter's reading of two adaptations of *Macbeth*: Billy Morrissette's *Scotland, PA* (2001), premièred at the Sundance Film Festival, and Peter Moffat's *Macbeth* (2005), directed by

Mark Brozel and first shown as part of the BBC *Shakespeare Retold* TV series.[4] These adaptations arguably take their cue from the play's many references to food, animals that prey and are preyed upon, banqueting and hospitality, and creatively transform them. They also enter into dialogue with scenes from previous adaptations in which one or more of these elements play a prominent role, such as Ken Hughes's *Joe Macbeth* (1955) and William Reilly's *Men of Respect* (1990).[5] They repeatedly foreground incorporation and its uncanny effects. The chapter argues that incorporation operates on a number of interconnected levels: it indicates, for instance, the conspicuous consumption of the flesh of the animal, the symbolic ingestion of the "sacrificial victim," and the inclusion of media material. It shows that incorporation is inextricably bound up with these adaptations' frequent shift into a self-reflexive mode, and so much so that it often allegorizes the multifaceted ways in which they engage with the adapted text.

Billy Morrissette's *Scotland, PA* is set in a small town in 1970s rural Pennsylvania. In this film Pat (Maura Tierney) and Joe "Mac" McBeth (James LeGros) work for Norman "Norm" Duncan (James Rebhorn), the owner of a dowdy burger restaurant, Duncan's Café. Pat and Mac are both frustrated in their jobs, and this is exacerbated by the fact that, after the dismissal of the diner's dishonest manager, Douglas McKenna, Duncan announces that he will promote his son Malcom (Tom Guiry) to the role of manager, even though Malcom is more interested in being a rock musician than in his father's business. The two self-proclaimed "underachievers" conspire to murder Duncan to gain ownership of the restaurant. The BBC *Shakespeare Retold Macbeth* centers around the world of Duncan Docherty's classy restaurant and explores its dark corners. It emphasizes the process of cooking, serving, and—last but not least—disposal of food. The witches become garbage collectors. Macbeth turns into Joe Macbeth (James McAvoy), an ambitious Scottish head-chef whose fundamental contribution to the success of the restaurant is not properly acknowledged. As to Lady Macbeth, she becomes Ella Macbeth (Keeley Hawes), a glamorous manageress who impeccably presides over the establishment's dining room. The Macbeths' resentment intensifies when Duncan's diner is awarded "three big Michelin stars," as the witches/garbage collectors had predicted, and Duncan (Vince Regan) reveals that he will leave the restaurant to his son Malcom (Toby Kebbell), a former vegetarian who does not appear to have cooking "in his blood."

Both adaptations draw attention to acts of incorporation from the very beginning. *Scotland, PA* opens with the three witches-turned-hippies sitting on a Ferris wheel in what looks like a disused Carnival Fair. They smoke dope, eat from a bucket of fried chicken, and "dis-member" the textual body

Figure 1.1 The witches as garbage collectors.

of the first scene of *Macbeth*: "It was foul... The fowl [i.e., the chicken] was foul... and the Fair was fair... Foul's fair... the Fair is foul." Yet the consumption of pieces of fried chicken seasoned with remainders from Shakespeare's play does not seem to be part of a healthy diet. Indeed, this (double) incorporation *repeats* on the female witch, as the two male witches clarify: "She's having a spell... Oh God, *so* dramatic." As Thomas Cartelli and Catherine Rowe remind us, in this context "having a spell" means "feeling queasy and disoriented (because you ate bad chicken)" (114). But it also irresistibly suggests a conjuring of another medium within the cinematographic medium. More specifically, "having a spell" also means the evocation of the American television police series *McCloud* within the film: the opening sequence ends with the inclusion of an extended black-and-white excerpt from the 1972 *McCloud* episode "The Park Avenue Rustlers," a TV *repeat* in which a well-dressed quasi-corporate "bad guy" (Eddie Albert) is brought to justice by detective McCloud (Denis Weaver), who pursues him by hanging beneath the helicopter in which he is trying to escape.[6] Placed as it is in such a prominent position, the sequence is undoubtedly significant, and works in a number of different ways. It is, first of all, one of the versions of "the battle... lost and won" (*Mac.* 1.1.4) within the film and, more generally, of the tumultuous state the witches in *Macbeth* call "hurly-burly" (3). It is, moreover, a visual "pre-diction." It is some kind of visual foretelling of events that takes place *before* the actual meeting between the hippies and Mac, and that uncannily connects with subsequent scenes, maybe also by virtue of the mere fact that these scenes involve a series of "Mc"s: for instance, the public humiliation of Manager Douglas *Mc*Kenna, caught out embezzling money from the diner's till, which whets Mac's appetite for his post; or, more generally, detective *Mc*Duff's relentless, if quirky, pursuit of the would-be small-town entrepreneur Joe "Mac" *Mc*Beth.[7] Perhaps more importantly, the inclusion of the *McCloud* excerpt draws attention to the film's typical way of proceeding. It shows that the film self-reflexively folds medium within medium, unashamedly exhibiting not only its impure, hybrid status as a film but also its joyous inability to relate to Shakespeare without conjuring up processes of remediation of the Bard—in this case, televisual remediation—of which it is of course part.[8] The *McCloud* sequence is arguably a remediation of Shakespeare in at least two interconnected senses. It remediates (i.e., it provides a remedy for) the "sickening" surplus-enjoyment one indulges in when misspelling and chewing, as it were, bits and pieces of the Shakespearean *corpus*.[9] It does so by re-presenting *Macbeth* in a different medium; by offering, that is, a condensed shortened version of *Macbeth* as a melodramatic black-and-white detective show depicting a world in which "fair" is indeed "fair" and "foul" is indisputably "foul," a world where one might still be unable "to find the mind's construction in the face" (1.4.12) but where criminals are brought to justice without much of a hint of ambiguity.[10] The sequence is of course placed in ironic quotation marks, and this becomes even clearer when it is repeated later on in the film. This time we are inside the local police station, and we see the sleepy police officer Eddy being so immersed in watching this episode of *McCloud* that he hardly pays any attention to Anthony "Banko" Banconi's potential revelations about the Mcbeths' involvement in the murder of Duncan.[11] This scene implies that believing that the black-and-white TV excerpt is an effective or definite remediation of *Macbeth*—or, indeed, that *Scotland, PA* as a whole exclusively belongs to the genre of the police serial—is equivalent to occupying the same foolish position as Eddy, a passive consumer who is under the spell of a TV screen and ignores whatever exceeds its frame. In short, the inclusion of the *McCloud* sequence is an ironic and partial release from a bodily and textual extra-enjoyment, a release that "lies like truth" (5.5.42).[12]

The opening of Peter Moffat's BBC *Macbeth* immediately introduces us to liminal domain of waste that haunts acts of conspicuous consumption.[13] It is this domain that the witches-turned-garbage collectors mainly inhabit. We are offered a view of a rubbish tip swept by wind and crowded with seagulls.[14] Parked right in the midst of this tip is a red lorry adorned with discarded children's toys. Inside the lorry the three garbage men eat their sloppy sandwiches, mixing day-to-day conversation with lines from Shakespeare's play.[15] After a while, they start talking about the (ungrateful) task they are about to perform: "scooping up the debris" after the "hurly-burly" of a day in Joe Macbeth's kitchen is "done," nauseating left-overs that include "bones and guts, fish-heads, knob ends of the black pudding, skins of haggises." It goes without saying that these leftovers are what allows them to "look into the seeds of time" (1.3.56), and predict—in an inescapably equivocal way—a bright future for Macbeth and Billy/Banquo's sons. The three men do not fail to pass sarcastic class-inflected comments on the posh restaurant "Duncan Docherty" as well as on its head-chef Joe Macbeth, the "kitchen warrior," the "cooking brave heart." The belch one of them emits at the end of the sequence underlines the sarcasm.

Yet the ironic import of the opening sequence can be fully appreciated only by juxtaposing this sequence with the "primal scene" of Joe Macbeth at work in the kitchen, a scene in which he articulates some kind of foundational logic of cooking as absolute incorporation of the nonhuman animal. In this scene "brave" Macbeth's "brandished steel" (1.2.16–17), with which he "carve[s] out his passage" (1.2.19) until he faces the rebel Macdonald, becomes head-chef Joe Macbeth's sharp kitchen knife and cleaver; Macbeth's honorable "unseam[ing] of the rebel from the nave to th' chops" (1.2.22) turns into Joe Macbeth's equally honorable slicing and dicing of a pig's head.[16] The atmosphere in Macbeth's kitchen is that of male camaraderie, extremely jovial and relaxed: just before Joe performs the dissection of the pig's head, all the kitchen assistants are singing a well-known old tune, The Ronettes' "Baby, I love you!" What follows is part of the speech Joe delivers as he performs his "anatomy lesson"—his "execution" (1.2.18)—before his staff:

> First rule in a kitchen: respect...See this animal [takes the pig's head in his hands]...this animal was noble, highly intelligent, feeling...It died for us, never forget that...First off with the ears [cuts off the pig's ears]...then you want to cut down the front of the face...Get a cleaver [cuts off the rest of the pig's head]...Now this is everything: ears, cheeks, tongue, brain...no waste: *that*, in a word, is respect. Anybody can make it in the kitchen, if they've got the guts and the passion.

From Joe's perspective, therefore, "respect" for (what he calls) the animal paradoxically means the latter's utter disappearance through repeated acts of incorporation ("no waste").[17] It coincides with the absolute consumption of a creature that willingly sacrifices itself ("it died for us") for the sake of the (re)construction of a carnivorous virile human subject. This subject can be called "virile," following Derrida's definition of the human subject as carno-phallogocentric ("'Eating Well'" 113), first of all because the dissection is performed before an all-male audience; second, because the pig's

Figure 1.2   Joe's anatomy lesson.

head is clearly gendered in the feminine, as shown by the fact that Ronnie, one of the kitchen assistants, puts emphasis on the words "Baby, I love you!" (from the song by The Ronettes) as he lays down the animal's head on the table. Derrida also underlines that the dominant schema of the carno-phallogocentric subject is fraternal. And, indeed, in Macbeth's kitchen, it is the lifeless gendered body part of the animal that allows the temporary creation of a potentially horizontal fraternal bond between men ("Everybody can make it in the kitchen"). In short, (gendered) MEAT appears to make a (fraternal) TEAM (i.e., MEAT's anagram).

Leftover food—the outcome of the daily "hurly-burly" in both the kitchen and the restaurant—accumulates in the "dark alley" that runs alongside the classy restaurant, which is the place the witches regularly frequent. This constitutes a reminder of the impossibility of bringing to fruition the project of absolute consumption of the animal. In other words, in spite of what Joe enunciates, there is, indeed, waste. This combines with the striking images of mountains of rubbish in the opening sequence to suggest that "man" cannot quite come back to "himself" through the incorporation of the animal without leaving traces of this process in the form of food remains or other leftovers. Significantly, just before the meeting between the garbage collectors and Macbeth and Billy/Banquo, we are shown a wheelie bin rolling down the "dark alley." This bin nearly crashes to death Macbeth and Billy, who are returning from a drinking session in a pub. Printed in capital letters on the bin is the word MEAT. One thus witnesses here, perhaps in an oversimplified and unsubtle way, the graphic representation of the lability of boundaries: what remains from the act of incorporation refuses to stay in its place and comes back to haunt.

Joe Macbeth's is a *visceral* kind of cooking. It requires "guts and passion."[18] (This is what Malcom lacks, according to his father Duncan. Having been a vegetarian for a year, Malcom "needs transfusion.") It is a visceral kind of cooking also in the sense that it involves using cheap cuts of meat that are usually discarded and turning them into something that is no less than sublime. In the speech cited earlier, Joe mentions pig's ears, cheeks, tongue, brain, which are served with the fancy name of "pork assortments," but the restaurant menu also offers black pudding and all kinds of offal and innards, including bone marrow, calves' liver, lamb's heart, and so on. Joe Macbeth's dealings with the (dismembered) corpses of animals define his being. As to Mac in *Scotland, PA*, his cooking of burgers and fries cannot be defined sublime by any means. Nonetheless, as James R. Keller points out, his "appetite, hobbies, decorating taste and profession are all predicated upon the slaughter of animals... Dead animals adorn the walls of [his] house as well as his table" (42).[19] He is addicted to meat and a purveyor of addiction, since it is on this that his livelihood, and later his drive-through, depend. His being is nothing but being carnivorous.

While establishing the "core of being" of the two main male characters, *Scotland, PA* and the BBC *Macbeth* also surmise that violence against the nonhuman animal and violence against the human animal are inextricably bound up with each other, and that in fact the former is the precondition for the latter. In both adaptations the immediate context for the decision to murder Duncan is the latter's announcement that he will leave the restaurant to his son Malcom. But ambition, frustration or the perceived sense of injustice are unable to turn into murder, they seem to suggest, without the addictive murderous dealings with animals the two lead characters are already engaged in. This is perhaps clearer in the BBC *Macbeth*. For instance, when the restaurant is awarded three Michelin stars, Ella Macbeth incites Joe to murder not only by stressing the fact that he does all the hard work and the executive chef Duncan reaps all the glory; she also insists that Joe's expertise in the kitchen constitutes the appropriate preparation for the "deed": to Ella, her husband is always-already "a knife man."

The preparation, serving, and consumption of the flesh of the animal thus pave the way for the murderous "deed." Moreover, the murder of Duncan is itself an act of symbolic incorporation that is predicated upon the transformation of the human animal into something that is less than human. In the case of *Scotland, PA*, it is "chance" that largely seems to "crown" a clumsy Mac, without much of "[his] stir" (1.3.142–43): he inadvertently pushes Duncan in the fryolater after the witches/hippies suddenly appear on the kitchen's counter. The repeated shots of Duncan with his hands tied behind his back, and protruding from the fryolater in which the rest of his body "deep fries," suggest that he has in fact become what Mac had threatened to turn him into: a "big ugly French fry," the kind of junk food that the witches, who inhabit the time of anachrony, were already eating before the event. The BBC *Macbeth* goes even further than Morrissette's film in making Duncan's murder closely resemble an act of symbolic anthropophagy. On the night of the award Joe cooks "a feast" of a lifetime, a banquet fit for a king for the executive chef Duncan and his guests, who give the latter a standing ovation for a meal he once again has not himself cooked. Joe wants Duncan Docherty "to eat the meal of his life" (i.e., "the dog's bollocks," as Billy glosses it), the irony of it being of course that this is the last supper he will consume. Or, rather, to use words from *Hamlet*, Duncan will soon be once again "at supper," but "not where he eats but where a is [symbolically] eaten" (4.3.19–20) and feasted upon by "knife man" Joe.

It is worth recalling in this context the Lacanian distinction between the Symbolic Father as the agent of prohibition and the Father-*Jouissance*, a corrupted position divested of moral authority which is Lacan's intriguing reworking of the primal father in Freud's *Totem and Taboo* (*Totem* 201–8). As Slavoj Zizek explains, underneath the Father as the apparently neutral placeholder of the Law, there lurks another Father, the *Père-Jouissance*, the Father who enjoys too much, "the obscene, uncanny, shadowy double of the Name of the Father," an "excessively *present* father, who, as such, cannot be reduced to the bearer of a symbolic function" (*Enjoy* 180). *Scotland, PA*'s Duncan mostly remains, in Lacanian terms, a Symbolic Father, the incarnation of prohibition, a prohibition that is often class bound, as shown by his snide remarks about Scotland's "white trash." He forbids his son Malcom to wear long hair and pursue his career as a rock musician. He is an agent of prohibition also in the sense that he refuses to acknowledge Mac's contributions to the running of the restaurant. Yet there is undoubtedly some kind of perverse enjoyment in denying him advancement, especially as he is also willing to share with the McBeths his plans to improve the restaurant. As far as the BBC *Macbeth*'s Duncan Docherty is concerned, his narratives of symbolic transmission—"My father taught me, and I taught you, Joe"—as well as his nostalgic memories of his poor childhood in Ireland constitute an attempt to cover up the fact that he is, in Lacanian terms, a *Père-Jouissance*, a Father who can hardly be said to be devoid of enjoyment.[20] In effect, in this *Macbeth*, Duncan does not bear "his faculties so meek" (1.7.17). He has not been "so clear in his great office" (18). He is certainly not "Lord's anointed temple" (2.3.67), and does not possess a "silver skin" (112) either. He is reverentially called "the old man," but he drives a Mercedes, wears an

Armani suit, and complains about the fact that his big wallet spoils the line of his trousers. Moreover, he repeatedly, and unashamedly, flirts with Ella Macbeth. On the night of the award, after Ella ironically smears his apron with blood in order to turn him into "the real thing," a real chef, "hot and bloody, straight from the stove," he addresses her as follows, with his typical vulgar humor: "You know what I love about this woman? She has massive bollocks." In short, Duncan is not only a sham but also, quite simply, a pig, a human figure but not quite.[21] The slaughtering of Duncan, therefore, uncannily recalls the dissection of the pig Joe performs in the scene to which I referred earlier. It is in fact its metaphorical transformation.[22]

Eating up the corpse of what is less—or more—than human does *not* bind individuals together, which is unlike the Freudian narrative of *Totem and Taboo* these adaptations nonetheless recall. In *Scotland, PA* it leads to the reproduction of hierarchical relations in the newly furbished restaurant with a drive-through window, as signaled, for instance, by the scene in which Pat teaches Robert, the employee whose name she carelessly and repeatedly forgets, how to spin and pump from the ice-cream machine to produce a "beautiful cone," which doubles the earlier scene in which the Assistant Manager Douglas McKenna was condescendingly teaching *her*.[23] Another upshot of Duncan's murder is the destruction of the long-standing bond between the new head of the restaurant and his closest male friend Anthony "Banko" Banconi, which will eventually result in the latter's murder. In one scene a puzzled and suspicious Banko asks Mac why he has never mentioned to him the idea of the drive-through. In the next scene we see Mac sitting in a semidarkened room in a gloomy mood, and somberly announcing to Pat that "Banko is a problem," a colloquial version of Macbeth's "Our fears in Banquo / Stick deep" (3.1.50–51). The TV commercial Mac is watching, which advertises "The Prince Spaghetti Company," and which shows a mother at a window calling out "Anthonyyy!" (also Banko's name) and then a young lad in shorts running back home presumably to be fed, only confirms his fears, in that it visualizes the possibility that one day his "sceptre" may be "wrenched with an unlineal hand" (3.1.63–64); that one of Banko's heirs, an Anthony at the head of some "Prince Spaghetti Company" may take over his empire of burger and fries.[24]

In the BBC *Macbeth* one of the effects of the symbolic incorporation of Duncan is not so much the reproduction of the discrepancy of power between employer and employee as the creation of a stronger sense of hierarchy, which undermines the (potentially) horizontal bond between men in Joe's kitchen as well as Joe's intimate relationship with Billy/Banquo. For instance, after a furious argument with Billy over the most appropriate way of serving a dish, Joe asserts his despotic power as head of the restaurant before all the kitchen assistants in the following way: "*I* run this kitchen. *Mine* is the only voice." To Billy, this means the obliteration of "respect," the "first rule in the kitchen," as Joe himself had stressed earlier on. Moreover, in both adaptations the murder of Duncan has a profoundly negative impact on the special relationship between the new heads of the restaurants and their respective "partner[s] of greatness" (1.5.11), a relationship the act of incorporation was supposed to cement. In both this is often signified by a communication breakdown, and the male partner is being blamed for it: "What's wrong? Why won't you talk to me?", Pat complains to Mac; Ella echoes her when she stresses that they "were together once," and then Joe stopped "talking to [her]." We also witness a swapping of roles between the male and female partner in terms of agency, with the female partner increasingly confining herself, or forced to confine herself, to a private space. The BBC *Macbeth* offers recurring shots of Ella in her apartment repeatedly washing her hands. We also see her standing in front of the mirror while strenuously applying makeup to her face in an effort to hold on to her public persona, and singing Janis Joplin's "Mercedes Benz," which conjures up the image of Duncan driving the German car. Even when in the public space of the restaurant reception, she carves out for herself a "private" enclave, and starts talking to customers about the most private of experiences (i.e., the fact that she had lost her baby after only three days).[25] Her next appearance in a public space coincides with her suicide: after smearing her face with a crimson red lipstick, she lets herself fall off the building that houses the restaurant.

In *Scotland, PA* the brief conversation between Mac and Pat about Banko being "a problem" not only marks the inception of Mac's paranoia but also the beginning of a shift in the relationship between the King and Queen of burgers and fries. It is, more generally, a turning point in the film, which unashamedly begins to "cannibalize" the atmosphere and the typical characteristics of the film *noir*.[26] After the exchange with Mac, Pat appears to be deeply affected by his somber mood. As she walks out of the semidarkened room, she briefly looks at her hand. From this moment on the (inexistent) grease burn that symptomatizes her corporeal involvement in the "deep frying" of Duncan becomes one of her major concerns. It repeatedly drives her down to the local chemist's where the pharmacist and his assistant—Morrissette's version of Shakespeare's doctor and waiting-gentlewoman—somehow reluctantly supply her with larger and larger quantities of ointment. Moreover, her facial expression as she looks at her hand provides a condensed version of the play's lines concerning a murderous deed that fails to bring about its desired effects: "Naught's had, all's spent, / Where our desire is got without content. / 'Tis safer to be that which we destroy / Than by destruction dwell in doubtful joy" (3.2.6–9). It is in this oxymoronic state of "doubtful joy" that she survives, but only just. Confined to the private space of her new middle-class home, endlessly waiting for Mac to come back from his expeditions, she starts chain-smoking and drinking to excess. In Shakespeare's *Macbeth*, the title character reassures his wife, who asks him what it is "to be done" (3.2.45) about Banquo, with these words: "Be innocent of the knowledge, dearest chuck, / Till thou applaud the deed" (45–46), and then launches into the "Come, seeling night" speech. This is mostly an appropriation of Lady Macbeth's earlier "Come, thick night" speech (1.5.49–53), a speech that connotes *her* determination to act. Similarly, in *Scotland, PA* Mac becomes more and more secretive, withholding from Pat information about his murderous plans, mistakenly believing that he is doing this in order to protect her, which robs her of agency and drives her insane: "Everything's going to be all right. I'm going to take care of *everything*, Pat. I'm going to take care of *you*."

* * *

Taking as his starting point the scene of *Macbeth* from which I have just quoted, Nicholas Royle observes that "the word 'done'... repeats, reverberates, resounds like a knell, summoning strange kinds of communication between one speech or scene or character and another" (*How to* 99). He argues that,

> *what* is done is apparently never completely or purely done. The murder (or assassination) is not just something that happens and is then all over and done with. However much Lady Macbeth might want to claim that "what's done, is done,"...the doing of the deed in a sense never ends... [T]he crime is at once something that cannot be "undone" and yet also (in its haunting enormity and after-effects) something that carries on happening. (98–99)

And, paradoxically, one tries to prevent it from "happening" by making it happen over and over again; one tries to escape from the deleterious effects of the "deed" by performing it over and over again, as if "things bad begun" could "make strong themselves by ill" (3.2.56). Both *Scotland, PA* and the BBC *Macbeth* respond to the "original" by adopting a compulsive spiral-like logic of reiteration of their own, a logic of "strange things...which must be acted, ere they may be scanned" (3.4.138–39) but inexorably "return / To plague th'inventor" (1.7.9–10).[27] More specifically, they implement a logic of repeated murderous deeds that fail to be effective as acts of full incorporation, and therefore produce (bodily) remainders that relentlessly come back to haunt. It is through this logic, moreover, that these adaptations continue to explore and problematize the border between the human and the nonhuman animal.

In the BBC *Macbeth* the removal/incorporation of Duncan, the head-chef who enjoys too much, does not result in the spread of enjoyment in Joe's kitchen. Quite the contrary. Like in the Freudian narrative of *Totem and Taboo*, the not-quite-so-human primal father re-presents himself as guilt (204–5). As far as Joe Macbeth is concerned, guilt takes on quite specific material forms. For instance, in an emblematic sequence after Duncan's murder, which takes place two-thirds of the way through the film, we are shown Duncan looking down on Joe from inside a photographic frame. This is a gaze Joe cannot bear: it turns the milk—he is, after all, or was, as this adaptation repeats, "full o'th' milk of human kindness" (1.5.16)—that he has just taken from the fridge into blood. We are also shown the extent to which Joe's daily routine has metamorphosed into a nightmarish experience: the kitchen's atmosphere is dismal; Joe hardly talks to his staff; at the end of the sequence we see a frying pan filling up with blood, with two pieces of chicken that remain uncooked. This combines with many other similar articulations of guilt. Duncan repeatedly comes back to "plague" (1.7.10) Joe, and he does so in the form of body parts of animals, which shows that the "animal" into which he has been "translated" through the act of murder has not been fully incorporated. In Shakespeare's *Macbeth*, as Royle argues, "what is done is never completely and purely done" (*How to* 98). In this adaptation, after the death of the "old man," Joe keeps on making mistakes. What is done, that is, is never *properly* done. It is *under*done or *over*done. In one scene, we see a piece of liver that is left in the pan for too long and thus becomes inedible.[28] In another scene, a customer sends back to the kitchen what he claims is an uncooked piece of lamb. At this point Macbeth storms into the restaurant, beats up the customer and kicks him out. It is, after all, *his* restaurant: "Get the hell out of *my* restaurant."[29] After this, he enjoins the other customers to eat: "What are you looking at? *Eat!*" Faced with this injunction, they cannot but choose to leave the restaurant.

In *Scotland, PA*, while Pat experiences seclusion and feels that her hand is gradually turning into a less-than-human extraneous body part, Mac starts "roving and ravaging the open spaces that now seem too small to contain his appetites" (Lehmann, "Out" 246). Indeed, to him, the whole of Scotland, PA becomes an extension of Birnam woods (i.e., the place where he regularly goes hunting with his male friends), a wilderness where he keeps on exercising his killer instincts. By now Mac *is* only in so far as he is *after* something or somebody.[30] He feels that he is being pursued, like an animal, as Lt. McDuff's murder investigation puts increasing pressure on him. He therefore relentlessly pursues, which does not appease his appetite. He becomes "a threat to mammals everywhere" (Keller 41). In one scene we witness the juxtaposition between the unconscious body of a drunken Banko being carried into McBeth's house and the lifeless body of a deer shot by Mac being carried on one of his friends' shoulders.[31] Once the visual connection between the dead body of the deer and Banko is established, a connection which is reinforced by the fur hat that Banko wears, we are prepared for the next step: Mac's murder of his best friend, which symbolically replaces the body of the nonhuman animal with the body of the human animal. But this symbolical substitution is itself preceded by the consumption of the corpse of the deer.[32] Through this and other scenes the film suggests that one cannot incorporate the flesh of the animal without somehow turning into the animal one incorporates; without metamorphosing, that is, into a hybrid creature that is likely to lose sight of the distinction between the human and nonhuman animal and is thus more likely to kill. In short, we are continuously invited to associate the consumption of meat with murder.

In Shakespeare's play Macbeth keeps on doing the deed, or having it done on his behalf, also in order to prevent the royal couple from "eat[ing] [their] meal in fear" (3.2.17).[33] Mac keeps on "producing"—and symbolically consuming—dead human bodies, including that of the non-Shakespearian character Andy, the homeless guy who is initially blamed for Duncan's murder, not in order to eat in peace (or not mainly), but in order to keep the drive-through safe, a business that is founded upon the violent symbolic incorporation of Duncan, and that offers for consumption the potentially unhealthy "greasy" corpse of the animal in the form of meat.[34] Given the uncanny connection between violence against the human and violence against the animal the film stringently develops, especially in its second half, it should come as no surprise that the murder investigation becomes more and more a confrontation between the carnivorous culture of Scotland, PA and the vegetarian culture of the outsider Lt. McDuff (Christopher Walken). This is a conflict, to Mac's increasingly paranoid eyes, that is nothing but a class-bound division between the "better half" and the lesser half of society, a division no cash flow can hope to bridge.[35] Coming back home drunk after the murder of Banko, and after another trip to Birnam woods to consult the witches, Mac finds McDuff there with Pat, and addresses him with pungent irony:

> What brings you here?...Don't tell me. You're gracing our humble home with a vegetable dish of some kind tonight, a little tidbit to show us how the other half lives...I meant *better* half...No, you don't think that. *That*

> would be mean, and you don't think mean thoughts... just *us* vicious car-
> nivores can think mean thoughts [he strokes a stuffed mountain cat].

This same speech also contains an oblique threat to "big daddy McDuff and
all the little McDuffs," a "mean" and "vicious" thought only a predatory
carnivore such as Mac is supposedly able to entertain.[36] When Mac next
meets the hippies in his restaurant, "big daddy McDuff and all the little
McDuffs" come up in the conversation, a conversation in which they are
trying to decide what Mac should do. Significantly, the discussion takes
place while Mac is cooking burgers for the three hippies who are starving ("I
could eat a horse"; "I could eat a cow"; "I could eat a pig"), as if to remind the
viewer once again that murder is linked to the preparation and consumption of meat. One of the male hippies suggests: "Mac should kill McDuff's
entire family." The other one strongly disagrees: "Oh that'd work... about a
thousand years ago... These are modern times. You can't go around killing
everybody." The female hippie simply interjects: "Or can you?", and looks
intensely into Mac's eyes. After a while she takes on a male voice and adds:
"I think we have to go straight to the source of the problem."

The "source of the problem" is of course McDuff, who is by now absolutely certain of the McBeths' guilt and has asked them to report to the police
station in the morning. But it is worth stressing the highly self-reflexive and
allegorical nature of this scene. It is a scene that reflects (or pretends to
reflect) on the possibility of altering the Shakespearean "source," at least
as regards the final phases of the film ("These are modern times. You can't
go around killing everybody"). Most significantly, it self-consciously hints
at the "problem" that *Scotland, PA* shares with its Shakespearean "source":
the performance of the deed produces uncanny after-effects that one can
(attempt to) magic away only by performing the deed over and over again.
Can one go around killing everybody? Moreover, can one put an end to the
uncanny iterative structure that governs both the film and its "source"? It is
thus also a scene that raises metadramatic questions about endings; about
how to bring the performance *as such* (and not just the repeated performance
of the deed) to a close. The hippies crave for an answer to these questions
just as much as they crave for the burgers that Mac is about to serve. And so
does the viewer.

In *Scotland, PA,* the "source of the problem"—Lt. Ernie McDuff—seems
to be aware of the "problem" of the ad infinitum reiteration of the murderous deed. During the final confrontation on the roof of the restaurant,
he warns a self-assured Mac, who is pointing a gun at him: "So I'm next
but after that it looks like you have to kill Malcom... and then Donald,
because Donald is coming after you." Mac recognizes the genre from within

which the Lieutenant speaks, a genre that forcefully prescribes his demise as a small-town criminal: "This is not an episode of Columbo...I'm not gonna break down, hand you the gun, get waltzed out of here between a couple of good-looking cops with my head bowed down." Unfortunately for Mac, there are no bullets in the gun he has seized from the local policeman Ed. At this point, he seems to resign himself to be, after all, a character in an episode of a detective serial; to be "tied" to the "stake" of generic constraints: he raises his hands, which mirrors the gesture of surrender by the "bad guy" in the *McCloud* episode. But this is not the end. Not unlike Macbeth, he resolves that, "bear-like," he "must fight the course." (cf. "They have tied me to a stake. I cannot fly, / But, bear-like, I must fight the course," 5.7.1–2). Mac attempts to escape *from* the constraints of the detective serial (i.e., the *McCloud* episode as a black-and-white version of *Macbeth*), which reproduces in an inverted form the witches' initial ironic escape *into* the genre. Unlike his *McCloud* counterpart, that is, Mac doggedly tries to exceed the detective serial's "pre-scripted" outcome and decides to react, odd as his reaction may seem. He yawns to distract McDuff's attention, perhaps to signify the tiredness of the detective serial's conventional solution. This allows him to keep on fighting with the only weapon left, a weapon that seems appropriate for his role as a purveyor of potentially unhealthy, murderous eating practices: a meat burger, with which he tries to inject portions of lethal *jouissance* into McDuff's mouth. After McDuff bites his hand, which shows that vegetarians, too, can stick their teeth into the flesh of the (human) animal, Mac runs downstairs in pain, and appears uncertain about what to do. He looks up and is himself distracted by the apparition of the witches who are sitting on the restaurant's neon sign bearing his name. This gives McDuff the opportunity to jump from the roof onto him, which causes Mac to meet a gruesome death: he ends up impaled on the steer horns that adorn his car.

The "course" that Mac fights thus ends with death. He moves from the field of constraints of the detective serial to another, a field of constraints called *Macbeth* that requires his death.[37] This does not mean that the "original" reasserts its rights. What we witness is the reactivation of the film's own logic of failed incorporation with which it creatively responds to *Macbeth*. To be sure, the final shot of Mac irresistibly invites the viewer to consider how much he resembles all the dead stuffed animals that embellish his house. It suggests that one cannot incorporate the animal and keep it safe inside one's self (as food), one's home (as grisly décor) or restaurant (in the form of mass-produced meat to be cooked and served) without it eventually coming back to haunt.

In the BBC *Macbeth* Joe is, in a more literal sense than Shakespeare's Macbeth, a "butcher" (5.11.35) who has indeed "supped full of horrors"

(5.5.13).[38] Near the end of the film, he fights in the restaurant's kitchen until "from [his] bones [his] flesh [is] hacked" (5.3.33) by the headwaiter Macduff. The "equivocation of the fiend, / That lies like truth" (5.5.41–42) involves, perhaps inevitably, an animal. The three garbage collectors had predicted that "pigs will fly before anything happens to [Joe]"; and that "pigs will drop on [his] head before [he is] harmed." In a way similar to Shakespeare's *Macbeth*, these words make Joe believe that he bears a "charmèd life" (5.10.12), and so much so that he bursts out laughing when he hears them.[39] Yet the illusion is shattered when pigs do indeed start flying; when, that is, a police helicopter lands on the building that houses the restaurant,[40] which is perhaps an intertextual reference to the *McCloud* episode included in *Scotland, PA*. This may not be a convincing denouement, but it ties in with this adaptation's repeated figurations of the haunting animal that does not stay still and keeps on crossing boundaries.

After Joe's death, the legitimate heir Malcom takes over the restaurant. He also becomes the host of the popular TV cookery program "Dining at Docherty," excerpts from which are self-reflexively included at regular intervals, as they mark the shift of power from one head-chef to another.[41] In the final sequence we see Malcom going out for a smoke in the alley by the restaurant after a hard day's work. We are also shown the three witches/garbage collectors sitting on the back of a lorry driving off. We finally see Freddie, Billy/Banquo's son, riding a bike, the same bike he was riding on the day of his father's murder, and looking enigmatically at Malcom. The film, therefore, does not *properly* end.[42] It allows us to imagine the basic features of another retelling, with Malcom turning into Duncan and Freddie turning into Joe Macbeth, a future retelling that is simultaneously a movement *back* to the beginning. In short, the BBC *Macbeth* doubles back upon itself and re-marks its uncanny iterative structure. It leaves out indeterminate spectral remainders that compulsively demands further revisions.

Scotland, PA also concludes by drawing attention to the indeterminacy of its ending. We are shown McDuff standing outside the newly refurbished diner, which has become the "Home of the Veggie Burger," with his little dog, eating a carrot and presumably waiting for customers who have not yet arrived and perhaps never will. The lack of customers functions as a trenchant ironic comment on the effectiveness of McDuff's establishment of a vegetarian order after the multiple incorporations of human and nonhuman animals. The film seems to suggest that one cannot eradicate incorporation, lethal as this maybe for oneself as well as a host of others, without also wiping out *jouissance*. In other words, the specter of incorporation remains.[43] It continues to make itself felt through its conspicuous final absence. It also comes back to haunt from the future (i.e., the film's present), a future that is saturated with burgers—and media images—to an extent that is unimaginable in 1970s Scotland, PA.

McDuff's refurbishment of the diner can also be read in allegorical terms as the ironically inflected attempt to reconstruct a new "home"—a veggie home—for Shakespeare. This "home" is meant to host an urban, mostly middle-class, edulcorated version of Shakespeare, a Shakespeare made of self-help meditation tapes that flatten out the rough "carnivorous" edges of the playwright's language, like the tapes McDuff listens to in his olive green car: "Do not toil in your troubles"; "Tomorrow is tomorrow. Tomorrow is not today." McDuff's attempt thus stands opposed to the McBeths' previous flashy revamping of Duncan's diner, a revamping that allegorizes the "deconstruction" of the soporific normative legacy of a class-bound Shakespeare.[44] In an earlier scene, which takes place after the death of Duncan, Pat reassures Malcom and Donald that as new owners of the diner they will "carry on [Duncan's] legacy" and "keep his name alive." No sooner does she end this speech than we are shown a montage of the dismantling and extensive refurbishment of the diner, the sign bearing Duncan's name being the very first item to fall prey to the McBeths' iconoclasm. Toward the end of the montage we see Mac and Pat in the garden of their new middle-class home, with Mac drinking a beer and Pat floating in a newly built above-ground pool: iconoclasm undoubtedly provides its moments of bliss. Significantly, the soundtrack being played throughout the sequence is "Beach Baby" by *Gill* Shakespeare, and by the time the montage ends Gill has clearly replaced William. Yet, as a way of responding to the adapted text, this iconoclasm is short-lived. As to the veggie *Macbeth*, the film's ending shows its shortcomings, and prefers to relegate it to a yet unspecified future. What we mostly witness instead, when the film shifts into a self-reflexive mode, are a number of selective incorporations driven by a bodily *jouissance* that frustrates any desire for the proper meaning of the "original": they are sometimes playful and verging on surfeit (as in the witches' "The fowl was foul"); sometimes satirical (as in the dismembering of the title of Shakespeare's play during Mac's meeting with the witches)[45]; sometimes governed by savage black humor (as in the image of Mac impaled on the "stake" that Macbeth is only tied to). These are *partial* incorporations that retrospectively produce *Macbeth* as an ensemble of remainders that are forced to cohabit and interact with 1970s popular culture, and in a way that is reciprocally illuminating. Given the open-endedness of *Scotland, PA*'s ironic conclusion, no restoration of order seems to be able to put an end to this process. The only remedy to the *jouissance* of incorporation appears to be the prospect of further remediations.

With these considerations in mind, I want to return for the last time to the "primal scene" of the sectioning of the pig's head in the BBC *Macbeth*, and read it now for what it tells us about this adaptation's interaction with what is being retold. When interpreted allegorically, and seen within the context of the wider logic of incorporation the film cultivates, the scene suggests that slicing, dicing, cutting up the "animal Shakespeare" ("noble, highly intelligent, feeling...it died for us") with a view to serving it up to customers/audiences—Shakespeare à la carte—emblematize adaptation as a process of selective and partial incorporation of that which cannot be fully consumed. This "anatomy lesson," effective as it may be, does not fail to generate remainders. Not unlike the processes of partial incorporation and remediation exhibited by *Scotland, PA* in its self-reflexive mode, the production of remainders of "Shakespeare" in the BBC *Macbeth*—the production of "Shakespeare" *as* (spectral) remainder—may be the mark of true "respect" for the Bard. It may be no less than what allows the "Thing 'Shakespeare'" (Derrida, *Specters* 22) to remain "young in deed" (3.4.143). It may be no less than the precondition for the survival of "Shakespeare" as "anima-nomaly."

CHAPTER 2

Shakespearean Retreats: Spectrality, Survival, and Autoimmunity in Kristian Levring's *The King Is Alive*

In the "Exordium" to *Specters of Marx*, Jacques Derrida elaborates on the enigma encapsulated in the expression "to learn to live" ("*apprendre à vivre*"), an expression that describes "a strange commitment." It is simultaneously impossible—"[t]o live, by definition, is not something one learns. Not from oneself, it is not learned from life, taught by life"—and necessary—this "wisdom . . . is ethics itself" (xvii–xvii).[1] To learn to live, Derrida suggests, can only come from the other; more specifically, it can only come "from the other at the edge of life." It is, he adds, "a heterodidactics *between* life and death" (xviii, emphasis added). Because of the irreducible trace of alterity inscribed within it, to learn to live turns out to be a spectral, indefinite, and interminable process that exceeds any living present. It can only happen "between life and death. Neither in life nor in death *alone*" (xviii). In a sense, therefore, to learn to live is, first of all, to acknowledge, and bear witness to, the originary temporal structure of life as "*sur-vie*" (*Learning* 26), a living-on, a survival that does not wait for death and is not merely added on to a life that preexists it. It is to learn that life implicates ghosts; that it can only "*maintain itself* with some ghost, can only *talk with or about* some ghost [*s'entretenir de quelque fantôme*]." Put differently, learning to live corresponds to the uncanny aporetic process of learning to live *with* ghosts, "in the upkeep, the conversation, the company, or the companionship, in the commerce without commerce of ghosts" (xviii). One may want to add that these ghosts inescapably haunt the presence to itself of a supposedly "sovereign" self that endeavors to learn (how) to live; and that, in ethico-political terms, as Derrida emphasizes in the course of *Specters of Marx*, this dislocatory haunting—a spacing out of time and place—constitutes both a threat and a chance.

In this chapter, I want to argue that Derrida's remarks resonate with some of the key concerns of Kristian Levring's certified Dogme95 film *The King Is Alive*, a film whose very title points to the enigma of life and survival—and life *as* survival—and associates it with the equally complex multifaceted question of sovereignty, including the sovereignty of "Shakespeare" and the text of *Lear* in particular. Shot on location over a period of six weeks on three handheld mini-DV cameras and later transferred to "Academy 35 mm" film format (Roman 72), as prescribed by one of the rules included in Dogme95 "Vow of Chastity,"[2] the film focuses on a group of French, British and American tourists who find themselves in a life-or-death predicament—"a deadly serious situation," as one of the characters puts it—when their coach, directed to an unspecified airport and driven by a black character significantly called Moses (Vusi Kunene), runs out of gas in a diamond-mining ghost town in the middle of the Namibian desert. For the stranded passengers, to learn to live is, first of all, to learn to survive in the desert on a diet of canned carrots, boxes of which have been left behind by the German colonizers, and morning dew. But it is also, and more crucially, to learn to live in the company of ghosts of various kinds as they emotionally and intensely relate, or fail to relate, to each other as well as to their past in the "here and now" of the film. [3] Prominent among these ghosts, which paradoxically embody a sense of life that is more vital and material than physical survival, is the ghost of *Lear* and what it evokes in terms of radical "dis-adjustment" and bare life.[4] This is a ghost that the passengers "resuscitate" and keep alive—one of the senses of the film's title—through an awkward and patchy performance that also keeps *them* alive (or at least most of them) as characters who double as actors.

Initially, *Lear* is summoned into being by Henry (David Bradley), a former British actor whose current, demeaning job is that of reading inane Hollywood scripts, when he begins to perceive the inadequacy or incompleteness of alternative forms of survival. Sitting on a stage-like raised platform with Kanana (Peter Khubeke), the local character who has been living in the mining town since the Germans left, and who intermittently acts as a commentator,[5] Henry scrutinizes (what he sees as) the senseless activities of his fellow travelers: repairing a roof so as to collect morning dew; trying to attract the attention of planes that might fly over the abandoned town by means of a wing mirror reflecting the rays of the sun; playing golf; improvising dance steps, and so on. He reacts with the following caustic remarks: "Assholes...Fucking assholes...It won't be long before we'll be fighting each other over a drop of water...killing for a carrot." To Henry, whose position here coincides with that of the handheld camera moving in a series of "whip pans" from vignette to vignette, from character to character, his fellow travelers are all engaged in "some fantastic striptease act of basic human needs."[6] His assessment of the ongoing *reductio ad absurdum* almost inevitably leads to *Lear*, which is the "first absurd drama," according to the film director (Kelly 50): "Is man no more than this? It's good old *Lear* again...Perfect." In a sense, therefore, *Lear* is being (unknowingly) re-played before being properly played. As Cartelli and Rowe observe, "Henry discerns in the emerging configurations he witnesses from his seat beside Kanana much that is already established in the *Lear* script" (155).[7]

The following scene shows Henry at work on his project of "put[ting] on *Lear* out here, in this god-forsaken place, with all these lost souls." We see him sitting at his desk in one of the abandoned houses as he scrupulously writes down lines from *Lear* on sheets of paper precariously stuck together with plasters—the "rolls" he will eventually distribute to his "actors." The first lines we see him writing—and hear him speaking as he writes—are a compressed version of the lines, addressed to Edgar, and absent from the Folio, with which Edmund describes the disruptive effects on the socio-symbolic order of "these eclipses": "Death, dearth, menaces and maledictions against the King and nobles."[8] This is and is not *Lear*, and in more senses than one.[9] What Henry transcribes is "as much as he can remember of [*Lear*]," or even what he "think[s] [he] can remember," as he self-apologetically explains to Catherine (Romane Bohringer), a dark-haired young cerebral French woman who interrupts his writing session to ask if she can borrow a book. The actual extended rehearsal of Shakespeare's play, a rehearsal that never becomes a full-fledged performance, with the characters-turned-actors forgetting, mispronouncing (e.g., "have" or "leave" for "heave"; "facilitate" for "felicitate" in the abdication scene, 1.1.91, 75), or continually reiterating the lines that Henry imperfectly reconstructs from memory, only accentuates the uncanniness of this *Lear* of the desert. But if this *Lear* is not quite *Lear*; if it is, to use the word with which the Fool clinically registers the increasingly unsubstantial post-abdication status of the King, *Lear*'s "shadow" (1.4.213), the "original" *Lear*, on the other hand, cannot quite claim to be *itself*. As is well known, what frequently goes under the name of *King Lear* is a text that conflates versions (i.e., Q1 [1608], Q2 [1619], and F [1623]) that do not quite match one another, and are in fact stages in a process of revision. As Mark Thornton Burnett argues, the instability and multiplicity that "infects" the "original" makes *Lear* not just a text "that can be adapted but...a body of work for which there is legitimate [i.e., historical] precedent for *ghostly* reinvention" such as the one Levring offers in his film (*Filming* 115, emphasis added). If, that is, *Lear* lends itself to "desert(ed) appropriations," it is because "the authority with which it is associated is transferable, because the text has already been incarnated and reincarnated in *spectral* versions of itself" (116, emphasis added). In short, the adulterated and flawed versions of *Lear* in the film are shadows of shadows.

Yet Burnett may be slightly underestimating what he himself calls the "unpredictable...life" of *Lear* in the film (119). The chapter argues that this is a spectral life for which there is not necessarily "legitimate precedent," and that often exceeds "authority" (116) in more radical ways than Burnett's approach contemplates. But for the moment, I want to stress that the film's repeated exhibiting of the "impure" status of the play it includes is not only an ironic reminder of the (multiple) spectral supplement at the source. It is also part and parcel of the aesthetic project of *The King Is Alive* as a typical Dogme film that insists on a number of constraints—in this case, Henry's necessarily defective and partial version of *Lear*; the characters' lack of familiarity with the play or with anything that has to do with "literature or high culture" (Cartelli and Rowe 155); their helplessness as actors, aggravated by the harshness of their surroundings—to suggest that these constraints are in fact enabling, in that they generate fresh and unexpected meanings.[10] In particular, given the predominantly character-driven style of Dogme films, one could argue that these limitations are instrumental, to cite from "The Vow of Chastity," in "forc[ing] the truth out of [the] characters" who come into contact with the Shakespearean text.[11] This applies not only to characters who wholeheartedly embrace Henry's project, such as Gina (Jennifer Jason Leigh), a young blonde Californian woman who will play Cordelia, but also to those who are unwilling to join in, such as Catherine, who turns down Henry's offer to play Cordelia; or Charles (David Calder), who thinks that Henry's idea is "bloody ridiculous," and only eventually consents to play Gloucester when Gina agrees to have sex with him in exchange for his participation. One must add that these are unpleasant and unwelcome "truths"—they are the "ghosts" that each one of the characters endeavors to come to terms with. They can also be lethal, as is the case when Catherine's self-inflicted exclusion from the play turns into an uncontrollable Goneril-like jealousy leading her to murder Gina, Henry's favorite "daughter," with a dented poisoned can of carrots. But it bears repeating that the emergence, or re-emergence, of the uncomfortable "truths" that haunt the characters is inextricably bound with the idiosyncratic status of *Lear* within the film. In cultural and ideological terms, the relocation of *Lear* in the "nowhere" of the Namibian desert[12] is an antagonistic movement away from Western assurances. It bears witness, as Mark Thornton Burnett argues, to the film's conviction that "Shakespeare"—one of the kings of the title—can only be kept alive "in environments of disorientation and displacement" (*Filming* 113), "outside institutions and beyond the parameters of elite culture" (112). It is also a movement back in time whose aim is to rejuvenate the partially Anglo-eccentric postwar status of *Lear* as an apocalyptic and absurdist document (Cartelli, "Pain" 159–61), an emblem of a unredemptive journey toward annihilation, despair, and nothingness (Joughin, "Afterlife" 72), associated with the work of Jan Kott and Peter Brook, and, in the world of Shakespeare on film, especially with the latter's highly meta-cinematic 1971 version of the play (Scott-Douglass 258; Griggs 172–73). In more specific textual terms, this relocation amounts to a stripping down of *Lear*, a "shak[ing]" of its "superflux" (3.4.32) that not only parallels the "fantastic," metaphorical "striptease act" performed by the film's characters, but also allegorizes Dogme's programmatic dismantling of the cinematic apparatus, its attempt to force the "pomp" of cinema, especially in its Hollywood incarnation, to "take physics" (33), with the aim of reaching the "naked film."[13]

The King Is Alive thus shows us the remains of *Lear*. Yet, it is worth pointing out that the performances of *Lear* in the desert—both Henry's writing performance and the often botched rehearsals—are not merely partial reiterations of a fixed and stable entity that somehow preexists and authorizes them.[14] They are not even, in any simple sense, selective interpretations of an "original." They are (retrospective) *productions* of *Lear* as what is essentially an ensemble of spectral decontextualized fragments that draw attention to themselves as fragments, and that refuse to be part of—or to mourn—an organic textual whole, and this each time they come into being. In this sense, this *Lear* of the desert is in keeping with one of the Dogme *Manifesto*'s tenets, in that it privileges the "instant" of the fragment over and above the illusory homogeneity of the "whole," or the "work."[15] Put differently, the stripping down of *Lear* corresponds to the (repeated) appearance of an uncanny "poor, bare, forked" text (3.4. 101). It *does* reveal what Lear on the heath calls the "thing itself" (3.4.100). But this is not some kind of "thing-in-itself," an embodiment of essential, immutable, and unmediated meanings. It is a spectral, irreducible, and indeterminate "thing" that can be associated with what Jacques Derrida calls, in *Specters of Marx*, the "Thing 'Shakespeare'" (22), an "unaccomodated" (3.4.100–1) entity that continually crosses boundaries *and* triggers crossings of boundaries of various kinds. This is a "Thing" that inhabits these fragments without properly residing. Its first time is irremediably the second time of repetition (Derrida, *Specters* 10), as when *Lear* materializes before Henry's eyes in the form of a "re-play"; it appears only to disappear, but not without leaving behind indelible traces each time it emerges during rehearsals and/or outside rehearsals. Cohabiting with the anti-illusionist, "de-cosmeticized" naked "Thing" of Dogme cinema in ways that are reciprocally revealing, it relentlessly affects the positions of the characters.[16] It radically undermines any sense of self-possession—any sovereignty over themselves—they may have and spreads trauma. It forces them to embark on the exploration of roles they did not know they could play, or play to such an extent, and this should be taken both literally and metaphorically.

*   *   *

"I mean, the play...What's it about?", asks Ray (Bruce Davison), who is reluctant at first to participate in what he calls "party games" or "group therapy." His estranged wife Liz (Janet McTeer) replies by providing a fairly accurate summary of *Lear*, or at least a middle-class American version of it: "It's about a king who has three daughters...or maybe it's three. Anyway, he has a couple of kids. And he's old and he wants to retire, and he wants to divide his kingdom...So whoever says they love him the most gets the biggest share." Yet even Liz, who is the most diligent among the survivors in learning her lines, relishing her role as "the evil daughter" and "the real bitch" to upset her husband, is "a little bit confused" about the play. After overzealously delivering a conflated version of Goneril and Regan's declaration of love toward Lear without reading from the script, she tells Henry that she needs to know more about the part she is playing, "who [Goneril] is and where she is coming from."[17] Instead of explaining, Henry, who takes on the role of Lear after Ashley (Brion James) falls prey to delirium tremens in the middle of the first rehearsal of the abdication scene, launches into an incredibly effective and unusual rendering of the lines with which Lear rejects Cordelia, starting with "Let it be so. Thy truth then be thy dower" (1.1.108). This speech is interspersed with, and followed by, a series of reaction shots, so that the whole sequence forcefully makes the point, perhaps a little hyperbolically, that what we are witnessing, along with the characters attending the rehearsal, is the "thing itself"[18]: the play is not about its plot or the background of its characters, or at least not mainly; it is about letting *Lear* speak through one's self, or even letting it take possession of the self "doing" the speaking, and this in the here and now. This is in turn the precondition for the exploration of one's sense of displacement, dispossession, and "dis-adjustment."

Henry is of course not immune to these experiences, even though his initial hauteur may seem to suggest otherwise. In fact, his speech cannot but be related to a previous scene in which we see an already livid Catherine sneaking into his room and listening to what he has been recording on his dictaphone. We learn from this scene that he has been thinking about his daughter "more and more"; that he "should have done this a long time ago"; that he regrets his "mistakes." The *Lear* speech can thus be seen as part of the process whereby he endeavors to come to terms with the loss of his daughter. Indeed, in the light of this scene, his idea of staging the play acquires further, more personal meanings, as does his unrelenting pursuit of the project. For Henry, however, to learn to live with the ghost of his daughter through the re-enactment of *Lear* proves to be a process fraught with numerous paradoxes. In the scene just mentioned, for instance, Lear's speech undoubtedly gives him the opportunity to explore his sense of loss and nostalgically look back to a time prior to separation—he is on the brink of tears when he utters the lines: "I loved her most, and thought to set my rest / On her kind nursery" (1.1.122–23).[19] But the grafting of these lines onto a personal story does not entirely displace what the rest of the speech also, and predominantly, inscribes: a father's disclaiming of all "paternal care" (13). Can the re-enactment of a rejection that leads to loss (i.e., making one's daughter a "stranger to [one's] heart" [115] again) unproblematically become part of the process of mourning for this loss? To raise this question is not to argue that the meaning of the "original" inexorably reasserts itself in spite of Henry's transformative strategies of adaptation (in both senses of the word). It is to underline that once the "Thing 'Shakespeare'" penetrates into the "real life" of the characters of the film, it circulates in ways that are not necessarily predictable. It often exceeds consciousness. In other words, no matter how effective Henry's strategies are, they leave out an irreducible spectral remainder that recasts the scene as a scene that also involves desertion. As far as Henry is concerned, mourning for one daughter here (i.e., his "real" daughter) goes hand in hand with his inadvertent failing of another (i.e., his surrogate daughter Gina, whom we have previously seen in intimate conversation with him and affectionately leaning on his shoulder). It is not by chance that of all the characters attending rehearsal, Gina is the one who seems to be most affected by Henry's speech. She is literally moved by it: she is the only character who does not seem to be able to stay still as he speaks. When Henry ends his performance, we find her lying on the floor and in a pose that speaks of dejection and alienation from the rest of the group. Unlike the other characters, therefore, she does not merely listen to the speech; she silently *plays* "poor Cordelia" (1.1.77), and in a way that is more convincing than during the first rehearsal of the abdication scene, when she cannot bring herself to say "heave" (91). (She alternates between "leave" and "have," the latter being perhaps a citation of the inappropriate word the Cordelia-like figure uses in Jean-Luc Godard's *Lear*). In what is arguably an ex post facto visual paraphrase of "What shall Cordelia speak? Love and be silent" (62), she responds with her body to words that repeatedly inflict wounds upon her. This is not, one must add, the only time that she is psychically wounded or forced into an awkward position. In fact, as the film progresses, Henry's "unconscious" failing of Gina/Cordelia eventually, if indirectly, leads to her death. This reactivates, in circular way, a process of mourning that has in fact never ceased. In a very important sense, Henry's exploration of loss in this scene ("I loved her most, and thought to set my rest / On her kind nursery," 122) is not only a nostalgic looking back to the past but also a retrospective anticipation of the (mourning of the) future. This bears witness once again to the odd temporality of the "Thing 'Shakespeare'" informing the film.[20]

An integral part of the uncanny logic of desertion is Henry's blindness to the "deal" between Charles and Gina, a "deal" that is vociferously commented upon by other characters, including Charles's son Paul (Chris Walker). Since Gina really "want[s] to do the play," as she confesses to Henry in the course of the intimate dialogue mentioned earlier, she accepts to "perform" sex with Charles to ensure the latter's participation in the play as Gloucester.[21] She sacrifices herself sexually "for art" (as Charles ironically remarks) but, as is often the case with a film in which the boundaries between the "real life" of the characters and the fictive life of the play are continually renegotiated, she does so not only as Gina but also as Cordelia. Her act of "immolation" extends to the world of the play her Cordelia-like filial affection toward Henry that she has been developing. Gina's is thus also an unspoken gift of love from a "daughter" to a "father," perhaps another version of Cordelia's "Love and be silent" (1.1.62) that exposes (in both senses of the word) the "masochism" of these lines. In any case, it is an act that does not fail to implicate Henry. Henry's powerful performance shows that the play can be done, and that it can be done effectively. But the progress of the play turns out to be predicated upon, Gina's sexual "performance," at least partially.[22] The ending of the scene I have been commenting upon is an ironic reminder of this. When Henry ends his speech, Charles temporarily takes on the role of the director of the play: "Well, I thought that went very well." He then cynically asks: "Is that it?", as if to underline that he is immune to the spell Henry casts on his audience as well as on himself. Finally, he beckons with his eyes to Gina, who is lying on the floor, silently reminding her of the "deal." One can go as far as to argue that "Chronos who makes his generation dishes to gorge his appetite"—the mythological figure evoked by Henry's speech who replaces the "barbarous Scythian" of the "original" (1.1.116)—materializes before our eyes in the form of Charles. A corpulent version of Gloucester, Charles impatiently marks the time; he does not accept delay on what he has previously called "payment on delivery"; he metaphorically feeds upon a younger "generation."[23]

In the conversation with Gina that precedes Henry/Lear's rejection speech, Charles provides an updated version of Renaissance antitheatricality. He expresses his strong dislike for "this urge that people have to parade themselves"; people who impersonate "Sinatra or Elvis Presley," or "women who can't wait to get on TV to tell the world that they are shagging their husband's best friend."[24] To Charles, Henry's play does not escape the logic of the society of the spectacle, or even reality TV. It is a "farce" devoid of "dignity," nothing but a delusional strategy whereby one endeavors to avoid the "truth" of death, which is slowly but surely approaching. It is of course tempting to dismiss Charles's tirade altogether by interpreting it as the irrelevant—and hypocritical—ranting of a character who is irremediably affected by arrogance, *amour propre* and a Gloucester-like blindness with regard to kinship, as shown, for instance, by the fact that he repeatedly frustrates his son Paul's attempts "to get to know" him.[25] However, if the mixture of (sexual) cynicism and philistinism he exhibits in the dialogue with Gina marks him as an anti-Dogme type of character ("Is this not what you're supposed to do? Sacrifice yourself for your art?"), his critical assessment of superficial action disguising (itself as) truth undeniably resonates with Dogme's wider ideological and aesthetic critique of artificiality and fantasy, including "the cinema of fantasy" (Livingston 103–7).[26] It should therefore come as no surprise that in an interview Kristian Levring himself draws attention to the complexity of Charles as a character: "Charles is the baddy, of course. But the interesting thing about Charles is that everything he says is true. I heartily disagree with his cynicism. But the way he analyses the world is quite sharp." He adds that Charles and Catherine "are linked...they are part of the same family" (Kelly 212). They are of course part of a "family" that refuses to be part of *any* family, not least the "family" that reassembles around Henry's project, and which is itself, like in previous Dogme certified films such as *The Celebration, The Idiots,* and *Mifune,* a "dysfunctional family" (Mackenzie, "Manifest" 50), this time ridden with conflicts brought about or exacerbated by the specter of *Lear*.

Catherine is another example of a character who is mostly construed as unsympathetic but whose negative connotation does not dispel the dark shadow she intermittently casts upon Henry's project.[27] As mentioned earlier, she is the character to whom Henry first reveals his plan to put on *Lear* in the middle of the desert. She expresses her skepticism about it, even though her words also point to her intellectual kinship with Henry, which one may be tempted to call a "bond" (1.1.93): "*They* couldn't learn these things" (emphasis added). She doesn't recognize the play transcribed on the "roll" Henry hands out to her, keen though she is to guess ("*C'est Othello?*"). Nonetheless, her delivery of Cordelia's "I cannot heave / My heart into my mouth" (92–93) is clearly meant to be contrasted with Gina's subsequent botched delivery of the same lines during rehearsal. In spite of, or because of, her "natural affinity for Shakespeare" (Scott-Douglass 260), she turns down Henry's offer to play Cordelia.[28] However, her behavior is an act of resistance that is unmistakably structured from within by her spectral identification with the Shakespearean character. Like Cordelia in the "original" text, marking her difference from the "theatricality" of her sisters, she refuses to play a role to please her "father." Moreover, she refuses to do so by saying *nothing* to Henry: she hands back the roll, picks up one of his books, William Faulkner's *As I Lay Dying*, and abruptly leaves. This extremely complex and multilayered scene shows that Catherine deflates in advance what she construes as Henry's Lear-like hubris, as also exemplified by her trenchant question about authority: "Are you writing *King Lear* by hand?" To Catherine, Henry's transcription of the actors' part on individual rolls, as well as his apportioning of roles, are nothing but versions of the division of the kingdom in the "original" play; they are part of a senile and patriarchal love game ("Which of you shall we say doth love us most?," 1.1.51), or at the very least a condescending form of amusement, which announces, and will in fact produce, strife and rivalry.

Catherine further explores the "darker purpose" (1.1.36) underlying this love game when Gina, who cannot go to sleep and clearly sees Catherine as a surrogate elder sister, asks her to tell a story in French, a language she does not understand but is eager to hear. Reluctant to do so at first, Catherine offers a sexualized version of Henry's project. She speaks of "an old man...lost in the desert" who becomes so bored with himself that he comes up with the "crazy idea" of staging *Lear*. This "old retard" offers a part in the play to the "French chick," she continues, just because he gets "a hard-on at the thought of her tight little ass"; being turned down by the intellectual French woman, he then tries his luck with the "Yankee bitch," who enthusiastically accepts, not because she is in any way interested in Shakespeare but because she loves the idea of being in "a real play." (Failing to understand the story as well as the insults Catherine hurls at her, Gina earnestly applauds Catherine's performance. French is foreign to her, the scene implies, just as much as Shakespeare). As Cartelli and Rowe point out, there is hardly anything in the film that corroborates Catherine's story: Henry "gives little indication of harboring this particular [i.e., sexual] motive" (156). Yet on the whole the lack of evidence of sexual motive on Henry's part may be less crucial than the fact that Catherine's "fairy tale"—the expression she uses to summarize to Gina what the story was about[29]—conjures into being the

ghostly silhouette of "an old man" who enjoys too much, a figure who perhaps remains in the "textual unconscious" of the "original" abdication scene
but is undoubtedly an essential part of the spectral logic of Levring's film. As
shown in chapter 1, this father figure who enjoys too much can be associated
with the Lacanian *Père-Jouissance*, the "obscene uncanny shadowy double of
the Name of the Father" who "cannot be reduced to the bearer of a symbolic
function" (Zizek, *Enjoy* 180), an "anal father," according to Zizek, who is
"'*alive*' . . . *in his obscene dimension*," alive with enjoyment. This is the kind
of father who does not erase himself to become "the dead-symbolic father"
(143), a figure of symbolic authority, without leaving out a remainder of
enjoyment that haunts the realm of the Symbolic.[30]

It is of course Charles, much more than Henry, who incarnates the specter
of the *Père-Jouissance* in the film. Moreover, it is highly ironic that Gina, who
(unknowingly) applauds Catherine's evocation of the *Père-Jouissance*, is also
the character who repeatedly comes into contact with the surplus enjoyment
embodied by this figure, and is cruelly affected by it. In the scene in which
he exacts his sexual compensation, Charles continues to play Gloucester.
He is, however, a much more brazen version of the hearty Gloucester of the
beginning of Shakespeare's *Lear*. He is a Gloucester who enjoys the "sport"
(1.1.22) of "illegitimate" lovemaking without a blush, and boasts his masculine prowess: "I'm in pretty good shape, don't you think?", he asks Gina after
making love to her. Blindness is still very much one of his defining features:
if Gloucester fails to read properly Edmund's forged letter, Charles mistakes
Gina's faked pleasure for "passion": "That was fantastic . . . I have never seen
such a passion." After the lovemaking scene he talks incessantly while Gina
mostly lies naked on the sand with her face toward us, and hardly says a
word. This shows that Charles is oblivious to the fact that he has forced yet
another character into a position of degradation, not through a calculated
withdrawal, as is the case with his own son, but through obscene proximity.[31] Gina responds to her sense of "dis-adjustment" by taking refuge in the
Lear script.

As Charles contentedly sleeps, we see her rehearsing the speech by
Cordelia in which the queen of France addresses Lear who lies in bed "in the
heaviness of sleep" (4.6.19), and reproaches her (absent) sisters for their cruel
unkindness toward him, not just as a father but also as an old man ("Had
you not been their father, these white flakes / Did challenge pity of them.
Was this a face / To be opposed against the warring winds?," 4.6.27–29). She
speaks the first two lines twice, punctuating each word with a gesture of her
hand to get the rhythm right—this is, after all, the play she has sacrificed
herself for. Yet when she pronounces the words "white hairs," which stand
for "white flakes" in Henry's script, the camera moves away from her to offer

a close-up of *Charles*, with his "white hairs," lost "in the heaviness of sleep." Once again, the film shows that reiteration is not reproduction, and that it has to do with specters. In this case, as Gina reiterates Cordelia's lines, the speech doubles back upon itself to inscribe another scene, the uncanny reverse side of Cordelia's reproach: the scene of an old man's unkindness toward a younger woman, or even of a father's unkind abuse of a daughter. It must be added that if the scene is traumatic, it is not only because it resurrects the specter of the *Père-Jouissance*, but also because it points to the lack of a clear-cut distinction between a benevolent and a malevolent father, between a father who is "sinned against" and a father who is "sinning" (3.2.60).[32] The re-emergence of this scene causes her speech to come to a halt. After angrily throwing away the script, she mechanically repeats variations on the line "Was this a face?...Is this a face?...This is a face...Was this a face?...Was this a face to...?" Through her performance these fragments of *Lear* take on meanings they did not know, or did not fully know, they had. They begin to articulate alternative forms of compassion and reproach. They begin to speak *of* her; they begin to speak *her*; they begin to speak her incredulity toward the fact that her "face" could prompt men, and old men in particular, to debase her.[33] We are far away from Cordelia's speech, and yet we are

Figure 2.1   "Was this a face?"

still there, in the same uncanny place, as Gina explores, and protests against, her position of abjection within a patriarchal *dispositif* of bodies and identities. This is an exploration that proceeds through and against *Lear*, and that implicitly extends to her own previous tacit articulation of "Love and be silent" in relation to both Henry and Charles.[34]

Cordelia's compassion re-presents itself immediately afterwards, and in an unexpected way, as the camera follows Henry on a morning walk and borrows his eyes to discover a half-naked Catherine, with her back to him as well as us, washing herself and reciting "O dear father, it is thy welfare I care about." This misremembering of the "original" ("O dear father, / It is thy business I go about," 4.3.23–24), which arguably accentuates a daughter's concern for her father, is extremely significant. And so is the shift from one Cordelia to another, from a Cordelia who throws away the (patriarchal) script of *Lear* to a Cordelia who appears to have made the script her own, unbeknownst to all the other characters and to the director of the play in particular. It is almost as if this scene wanted to reconstruct one of the tenets of the *dispositif* of patriarchy that the spectral logic of the previous scene had radically undercut, above all by drawing attention to the intermixing of fathers and the disquieting contiguity of the (lean) Symbolic Father and the (corpulent) *Père-Jouissance*—what in Derridean terms may be called the uncanny proximity of the sovereign and the beast, "the one inhabiting or housing the other, the one becoming the intimate host of the other" (*Beast II* 18).[35] It is of course highly paradoxical that the character who is pivotal to the attempt to reactivate elements of the *dispositif* of patriarchy is the wayward "daughter" who has already refused signs of paternal affection, and even reinterpreted these signs as obscene request. When Catherine ends her speech, she senses the presence of somebody who has been listening to her words. She turns round and meets Henry's eyes. The expression on her face unequivocally speaks of hope, reconciliation, and repentance. A number of shots and reverse shots sustain the dramatic tension of this unspoken dialogue, until a disconcerted Henry decides to walk off. A close-up of Catherine ends the sequence, and we can hear her heavy breathing that symptomatizes her disappointment as well as her mounting anger. This is undoubtedly a silent replay—with inverted roles—of the initial dialogue between Henry and Catherine, itself one of the many revisions of the opening "primal scene" of *Lear* within the film. This time it is Henry who rejects Catherine's offer; he "disclaim[s] all [his] paternal care" (1.1.113) for one Cordelia and implicitly restates his allegiance toward his second choice, which, as pointed out earlier, is not entirely devoid of ambiguity. The endeavor to revive a compassionate relationship between a "father" and a "daughter" is thus short-lived. The shift from one Cordelia to another turns out to be not a movement forward but a movement *back* to a bitter exchange that re-marks division and paves the way for trauma. This "pro-re-gression," combined with Gina's questioning of her scripted role, suggests that the doubling of "daughters" does not indicate a widening of possibilities; it is, rather, an index of the extent to which the film sees the subject position of Cordelia as uninhabitable and unperformable. From this scene onwards neither Gina nor Catherine will speak as Cordelia ever again. After a number of sequences in which she recalls poor Tom, "grime[d] with filth" (2.2.172), with "all [her] hairs in knots" (173), frantically walking across the rehearsal space as if "the foul fiend follow[ed]" her (3.4.43), an increasingly distracted Catherine takes on the plot function of Goneril and poisons her "sister." As to Gina, forced into the position of Regan, she takes it upon herself to perform a metaphoric blinding of a foolish and already blind Charles/Gloucester, and this on the point of death: "You're an old letch... When you touched me, you made me want to puke... I thought I was going to crawl out of my skin." (Charles slowly absorbs Gina's poisonous words and then reacts by urinating upon her, putting on "fresh garments" [4.6.20], and hanging himself).[36] Gina *does* reappear as Cordelia, but as a silent Cordelia, a dead "prop" in Henry's arms as the community of survivors, with the exception of Catherine, gather around the fire to offer a final fragmented performance of the play.

In an interview with Richard Kelly, Kristian Levring underlines the "ordeal" the film characters go through to "'get' *King Lear*," to "start to hear these words and understand them" (Kelly 50). And, indeed, many scenes draw attention to the characters' "ordeal," which also arguably allegorizes Dogme's strenuous effort to breathe new life into a "Shakespeare" that seems to have disappeared from the cultural landscape, like the postapocalyptic Shakespeare of Jean-Luc Godard's *King Lear* or Kevin Costner's *The Postman*, along with the true spirit and naked truth of cinema. Amanda (Lia Williams), for instance, limits herself to quietly sitting in close proximity to Henry for most of the rehearsals. When she first practices her lines, outside the rehearsal space ("Ask thy daughter's blessing. Here's a night pities neither wise men nor fools," 3.2.11–13), her only audience is the black driver Moses, who expostulates as follows: "I cannot hear you." In his role as director of the play, Henry wants to hear her, too. To be more precise, he wants to hear *her*: "What I need is to hear *you*. Not the Fool, *you*." He thus affectionately lends Amanda his dictaphone, the precious technological supplement that stores his personal memories, to help her "find [her] own meaning" in the Fool's words. Like in the rejection speech, Henry implicitly stresses that the play is about its self-erasure as a play, as "a mystifying or irrelevant cultural monument," and its re-appearance as life, "a life that is worth living even in the harsh condition in which they find themselves" (Livingston 107). Just before the dialogue between Henry and Amanda, we see Ray struggling with Kent's lines: "This is nothing, fool" (1.4.127). He is about to give up ("I don't think I'm cut out for this stuff"), but Henry reassures him, and encourages him to "concentrate on the words and forget about the rest of us."[37] In the interview with Kelly, Levring adds that the characters' "ordeal" is also "a form of cure" (50). This is certainly the case with Amanda. The process whereby she finds "[her] own meaning" in the Fool's words is coterminous with her transformation from a self-effacing submissive wife to an assertive woman who finally adopts the Fool's prerogative to state uncomfortable truths: she gives herself the license "to anatomize the disabling brutality of her husband, Paul" (Cartelli and Rowe 159) as well as the sterility of their marriage.[38] Reacting to Paul's last desperate attempt to recast her into a position that makes her voice inaudible, she uncompromisingly declares: "I do mean what I'm saying. For once, I'm absolutely clear-headed about what I'm saying." The film stresses the interimplication of the two processes by allowing us to hear, in the scene that follows immediately afterwards, the lines that Amanda has recorded on the dictaphone, even though her spectral and disembodied voice is the kind of extradiegetic sound contravening the Dogme rule according to which "the sound must never be produced apart from the images or vice versa" (Trier and Vinterberg n. pag.).[39]

The outcome of the confrontation between Amanda and Paul is that the latter disappears into the desert only to re-emerge much later on as an almost speechless, shaven-headed Edgar-like figure who bears the mark of a double rejection, both his father Charles's and Amanda's. What is therapeutic for Amanda is thus toxic for Paul. More generally, the film characters' fraught encounter with the *Lear* script is simultaneously "a form of cure" (Kelly 50) *and* poison. As far as Gina is concerned, her "sacrifice" can also be read allegorically as an extreme form of the "ordeal" to which Levring refers. If one adopts this perspective, her sexual performance with Charles is no less than the *conditio sine qua non* for her first effective *vocal* performance as Cordelia, a kind of dreadful rite of passage. Yet Gina's vicissitudes also show that to "'get' *King Lear*" (Kelly 50) is not, in any simple sense, a "cure." It does not offer an unproblematic solution to her experience of dispossession. As mentioned earlier, her full immersion into the *Lear* script is, at one and the same time, an escape from trauma *and* what inexorably brings it back. As to Liz, who is the character that most consistently blurs the boundaries between the world of the play and her "real life," her performances throughout the film are also informed by the double-edged status of the *Lear* script. If to "'get' *King Lear*" is an "ordeal," she subjects herself to it with enthusiasm, but her eagerness almost immediately turns out to be tinged with bitterness: she soon admits to taking sadistic pleasure in playing the part of "the evil daughter," and especially "the real bitch" vis-à-vis her husband Ray, whom she repeatedly forces into the position of Albany. She clearly resents Ray before *King Lear* enters the scene, but it is only by acting as Goneril—during rehearsals *and* outside rehearsals—that she fully discovers the insidious power of taunting and the destructive potential of sexual jealousy. She continually exposes what she sees as her husband's upper-class "milky gentleness" (1.4.321) and repeatedly flirts with Moses/Edmond. After taking Moses to one of the abandoned houses, she confesses that she has "brought [him] here to piss [her] husband off." She subsequently evokes the specter of miscegenation and thus implicitly translates the "plague of custom" (1.2.3) that ostracizes "illegitimate" Edmond into the "plague" of racism that affects members of the group of survivors in their relationship with Moses.[40] She says to the black driver that he is "perfect" for her plan to arouse her husband's jealousy and adds that "white men don't like their wives being fucked by black men," which profoundly upsets Moses and causes him to humiliate her in return. What is most striking about Liz's performances is the sheer one-sidedness of her interpretation of Goneril—her Goneril, especially as the film progresses, is a defiant, strong-willed, and adulterous, or would-be adulterous, wife much more than an "evil daughter." (The role of "evil daughter" is of course reserved for Catherine and, in a much more surreptitious way, for Gina, who plays the good daughter but nonetheless brings to light the obscene underside of the "dear father," 4.3.23). In this sense, to "'get' *King Lear*" is to "get" something over which one has hardly any control. It is to be affected—or infected—by some kind of virus that one carries and blindly reproduces. However, this reproduction is not a reiteration of the same; if it is a repetition, it is one that responds to the spectral logic of iterability as (retrospective) attribution of identity *and* alteration/displacement. In more specific terms, Liz's selective interpretation of Goneril is a compulsion to repeat that also generates new forms of infection. It engenders meanings shot through with affect that are not contemplated by the "original." This is clearly the case when she makes visible the latent racism of members of the group, a form of violence to which she is not immune.

Through Liz's reiterations the "plague" of racism permeates this *Lear* of the desert. The film goes as far as to transform the honorable duel between Edgar and Edmond into a vicious racist attack by Paul at the expense of Moses. The connotation of the two Shakespearean characters varies accordingly: Paul is most unlike the Shakespearean character whose "tongue...of breeding breathes" (5.3.134) since he ideally bonds with the absent Ray and takes upon himself the task of "protecting" white women from the sexual "invasion" of the black man: "If you want to fuck our women, then you've got to fucking fight." (This brutal aggression is what triggers Amanda's reaction, which will eventually lead to Paul's expulsion into the desert). The (unlikely) construction of Moses as an embodiment of rampant black male sexuality is also the subtext of the rehearsal scene in which Liz as Goneril declares her shift of allegiance from Albany to Edmond ("I must change arms at home, and give the distaff / Into my husband's hands")[41] before giving the latter a favor and kissing him on the lips. Liz insists on repeating the scene and continually monitors her husband's reaction. As director of the play, Henry thinks that the scene is perfectly all right, but of course what matters to Liz is not so much her delivery of Goneril's lines as the extent to which her reiterated performance effectively works as "poison" for Ray. Overwhelmed by a jealousy that feeds upon the racial construction of Moses, Ray stands up, throws away the script and walks off into the desert. It is only when he starts wandering aimlessly in the desert that he "gets" *Lear* and offers a condensed and fragmentary performance as Kent, punctuated by a series of whip pans that blur the images and effectively convey his disorientation.[42] This is a Kent who treads the thin line between life and death, a Kent who addresses his (absent) "master" Lear ("Good Lord, sit here and rest a while"; "Hard by there is a hovel. Repose but there while I to this hard house—")[43] but whose lines speak just as much of *Ray's* own profound sense of "dis-adjustment" as well as his desire to put an end to it. This is a desire to "rest" that is ultimately a desire for death, as suggested by the reiteration of lines from 5.3, a refrain that sounds like a death knell: "My master calls me; I must not say no" (5.3. 298).

If Ray's "journey" (5.3.297) does not reach its deadly conclusion, it is because he discovers the body of Jack (Miles Anderson), an apparently experienced Australian traveler who plays a prominent role in the early stages of the film since he appears to be knowledgeable about how to deal with this "serious situation": he communicates in Swahili with Kanana and authoritatively enunciates the "five rules for surviving in the desert" before setting off to seek help from the nearest village.[44] That Jack's body is found not so far away from the mining settlement retrospectively proves his self-confidence as a would-be explorer ("I am the only one who stands a chance out there") to be a sham and his "five rules" to be inadequate if not risible.[45] Ray's reaction to this discovery—a bloodcurdling scream that quickly dissolves into hysterical laughter—can thus be interpreted as a symptom of the film's trenchant irony about the generic conventions of survival movies (Cartelli and Rowe 146), which is itself part of Dogme's wider pejorative assessment of "the superficial action and the superficial movie" (Trier and Vinterberg n. pag.).[46] It also functions, and still in a metadramatic way, as an implicit reassertion of his allegiance to Henry's project, even though the film often

shows that the "survival kit" called *Lear* that Henry distributes as an alternative to Jack's rules does not unequivocally situate itself on the side of life. In
other words, if there is life in Henry's "poor, bare, forked" *Lear* (3.4. 101),
it is the intensity of life as temporary reprieve from a death, a sense of life as
survival that confounds the boundaries between life and death.[47]

As the film draws to a close, the boundaries between life and death
become increasingly blurred. In the scene that follows Ray's return to the
settlement with the news of Jack's death, we see all the survivors sitting
motionless and silently in one of the abandoned houses, while Gina is lying
in another house in the throes of death. They seem uncertain about what
to do next, as if annihilated by their renewed awareness of an impending
doom. Indeed, "all" appears to be "cheerless, dark, and deadly" (5.3.266).
Lear is also silent. It temporarily stops speaking through the characters and
keeps still in spite of, or because of, Paul's attempt to offer a colloquial updat-
ing of Edgar/Tom o' Bedlam's poetic equivocations, a "little piggy" nursery
rhyme obliquely addressed to Amanda that only succeeds in irritating Liz,
who twice tells him to shut up.[48] Although they are clearly physically and
psychologically exhausted, they finally decide to give Jack a Christian burial
and thus perform their own journey into the desert, their stylized silhouettes set against a harsh and merciless background decidedly evoking the
atmosphere of scenes from Ingmar Bergman's *The Seventh Seal*.[49] They bury
Jack and, with him, any remaining notion of survival as physical subsistence
or involving mere diversions to "keep [their] spirits up," as enunciated in
Jack's rules. They return to the settlement to find Gina and Charles dead.
They collectively react to the signs of death surrounding them on all sides
by implementing a counterintuitive and largely "counter-narcissistic" logic
of annihilation. This can be associated with what Jacques Derrida calls the
"strange illogical logic" of autoimmunity, a logic "by which a living being
can spontaneously destroy, in an autonomous fashion, the very thing within
it that is supposed to protect it against the other, to immunize it against the
aggressive intrusion of the other" (*Rogues* 123).[50] In a sequence in which
the eccentric and estranging cinematographic style of this Dogme film
reaches its climax, the survivors compulsively destroy whatever is at hand;
in particular, they feed the flames of a huge bonfire with the corrugated tin
roofs that have previously been repaired to collect morning dew, and add
to this bonfire the wooden boxes of canned carrots that have been their
staple diet thus far. In short, they fight off death by accelerating it, as they
perform, in an autoimmune fashion, some kind of potlatch involving items
that may still help them defer "the promised end" (5.3.238). In a sense,
this is Dogme against Dogme; it is Dogme against the found setting and
props of Dogme, a Dogme cinema that finds its nakedness to be still too

"sophisticated" (3.4.100) and thus proceeds to trim it down ("Off, off, you lendings!" 102). The sequence also brings to a paroxysmal conclusion the "symbolic" process of transformation of survival items that has already been at work throughout the film, examples of which are the transubstantiation of water into Amanda/the Fool's repeated refrain "Court holy water in a dry house is better than this rain-water out o' doors" (3.2.10–11), or the inclusion of a food item such as a tin of canned carrots in Catherine's plot of jealousy and revenge. It is a process that also affects the function of the omnipresent bonfire: no longer simply a means of attracting attention, and keeping the survivors warm at night, in the film's last movements it becomes an essentially self-consuming prop, a kind of funeral pyre, located on the "naked stage" where the last performance of *Lear* takes place.

*   *   *

For Jacques Derrida, there is no community that does not "cultivate its own auto-immunity, a principle of sacrificial self-destruction ruining the principle of self-protection (that of maintaining its self-integrity intact), and this in view of some sort of invisible and spectral sur-vival" ("Faith and Knowledge" 51). It is worth adding, with the French philosopher, that "auto-immunity is not absolute evil. It allows for exposure to the other" (*Rogues* 152). It is true that it "opens the space of death" ("Faith and Knowledge" 51); and yet, "without auto-immunity, with absolute immunity, nothing would ever happen again" (*Rogues* 152). Derrida's description of the aporetic logic of auto-immunity comes very close to being a reading of the vicissitudes of the body politic in *Lear*, a play in which the "ab-solute" and hyperbolic decision by the sovereign (i.e., Lear's "darker purpose" 1.1.36) makes the body politic as well as the king himself immune to their own immunity, and in which the intensity of life turns out to be nothing but life being continually "usurped" (5.3.293), a spectral *sur-vivre* that uncannily coincides with a repeated, self-consuming, and certainly *not* "unburdened," "crawl[ing] toward death" (1.1.41).[51] In the final phases of the film, the survivors similarly activate "a principle of sacrificial self-destruction ruining the principle of self-protection" and thus recast their newly established imagined community as "auto-co-immunity" ("Faith and Knowledge" 51).[52] They collectively rephrase, and bring to a culmination, the autoimmunitarian impulse that structures from within Henry's decision to stage a play, and that re-emerges each and every time a character implicitly and/or explicitly draws from the "survival kit" whose name is *Lear*. For instance, as noted earlier in slightly different terms, both Liz and Amanda inject poison into the relationship with their respective husbands, which triggers near-death experiences, and yet they do so in the name of life and survival. This autoimmunitarian drive, a drive whose dramatization is also an oblique *collective* remediation of scenes of extreme vulnerability in the original play such as the storm scene, paves the way for the final performance of *Lear*. In this scene the remaining characters, with the exception of a guilt-ridden Catherine, gather in a circle next to the campfire to recite lines mostly from act 5 of the play, in a stupefied and yet almost hieratic pose. This highly charged and self-reflexive scene is not so much about the more or less appropriate delivery of lines, significant as the latter is. It does not attempt to encapsulate the essence of the ending of *Lear*. It is much more concerned, and in a metadramatic way, with the characters' spectral survival *through Lear*, as well as with the survival *of Lear* itself. To accurately attend to the question of survival, it is worth recalling that Derrida's aforementioned argument implies that spectral survival, a survival *in the name of which* autoimmunity operates, does not escape the logic of the autoimmune. It is a re-marking of the mechanics of a life that "only has absolute value by being worth more than life, *more than itself*" ("Faith and Knowledge 51, emphasis added), a life that is thus not clearly distinguishable from death. To Derrida, survival is itself aporetic; it is an inherently spectral "life-death" ("*la vie la mort*"), neither life nor death *as such*, above and beyond the opposition between life and death (*Beast II* 130).[53] In the scene in question, survival through *Lear* is first of all the characters' renewed exposure to the spectrality of the "Thing 'Shakespeare,'" a "Thing" that is not immune to the logic of the autoimmune: it does not guarantee life but, at one and the same time, it does not necessarily and/or unequivocally bring death when it takes over the life of the film characters.[54] Cartelli and Rowe underline the spectrality that informs this final performance of *Lear* when they point out that "the entire cast becomes...spellbound after discovering the poisoned Gina and the hanged Charles," and when they argue that "the same impulse that took possession of Henry [i.e., as regards his rejection of Cordelia/Gina while playing Lear] and moved *Lear* to speak through Ray outside the rehearsal space...takes hold of the rest of the cast" (163). They do not fail to notice that, more generally, the film characters are most often themselves when *Lear* speaks *through* them (159). However, they arguably underestimate the extent to which spectrality is bound up with survival, as well as the unpredictability of survival as "life-death." To refer to the lines that Ray as Kent repeats as he wanders in the desert, which are lines that are still minimally audible when the other characters perform their own allegorical journey, the final performance of *Lear* re-marks the characters' exposure to an irresistible spectral "call" by the "master" text to which they "must not say no" in order to continue to experiment with survival (5.3. 298). This is a call that makes them hostage to the "master" text but also reanimates them.

It is simultaneously threat *and* chance. To respond to this call is thus for the characters to re-enact, through *Lear*'s words, a "fictional" but no less intense life that is "an openness...to alterity and [the] event," a life that is also, at one and the same time, "an openness to the possibility of instant death and destruction." As Geoff Bennington continues to explain, commenting on Derrida's concept of autoimmunity, "a life that did not involve this openness would not be a life worthy of the name 'life'" ("Foundations" 241).

Amanda's "prologue"—her appropriation of the Fool's lines from 3.4.—self-reflexively points to the threat inhering in the characters' exposure to the alterity of the "Thing 'Shakespeare'": "This cold night will turn us all to fools and madmen" (73). The exchanges that follow Amanda's prologue emphasize, instead, the equally challenging but less destructive aspects of the characters' openness to alterity. They are dialogues, that is, that articulate the characters' belief in the possibility of learning to live with ghosts, with their own ghosts as well as with the ghosts of others through *Lear*. We thus see a contrite Liz speaking a version of Goneril's lines to come to terms with her own deceitfulness as regards both Moses and Ray, a deceitfulness that has caused strife and brought to the surface rivalry between men: "By the laws of war, thou need'st not answer an unknown adversary. Thou art not vanquished but cozen'd and beguiled."[55] (She addresses Moses as Goneril does Edmond in Shakespeare's play, but as she speaks, the camera shifts from Moses to Ray, so that we are made to understand that her speech includes her husband as an addressee). As to Moses, his speech is more clearly articulated as a confession ("As you have charged me, I'm guilty and have done much more"),[56] which can be interpreted as a belated acknowledgment of his willingness to play along with Liz's plan to make Ray jealous. He addresses this revision of Edmond's words to Paul, who replies with Edgar's conciliatory lines "Let's exchange charity" (5.3.157), and thus accepts to put an end to the race-inflected hostility that has characterized his relationship with Moses throughout the film. Yet Henry's bloodcurdling and inhuman "Howl, howl, howl" (232) epitomizes a shift of register. It recasts life as an openness to absolute destruction. His lines undermine an incipient sense of community as reciprocal exchange of words that is meant to assuage the traumas of the past: "You are men of stones. / Had I your tongues and eyes, I'd use them so / That heaven's vault should crack. She's gone for ever" (232–34) In other words, speaking of himself as himself *and* another, Henry/Lear reintroduces an autoimmune remainder within this newly established community. He does so by drawing attention to the ineradicable trace of alterity haunting and ruining the integrity of that self that is supposed to mirror the self-integrity of this community, as he painfully performs a form of mourning that can articulate itself only in so far as it instantly re-marks itself as interminable, a profound "dis-adjustment" with no solution. His second intervention in the scene ("A plague upon you, murderers, traitors all. I might have saved her; now she's gone for ever.—Cordelia, Cordelia: stay a little," 244–46) reiterates this different kind of learning to live with ghosts whereby self-possession is irremediably possession by another. To "speak what [one] feel[s]" (300) in order to connect or reconnect with one's self as well as others—Edgar's final recipe for survival after the disaster in Shakespeare's *Lear* that also arguably informs the dialogues preceding Henry/Lear's two speeches—is only a poor substitute for this radical sense of survival as "life-death," a spectral life "in the upkeep, the conversation, the company, or the companionship...of ghosts" (Derrida, *Specters* xviii) that puts under erasure any presence of the present and thus any teleology. And yet even the exchanges preceding Henry/Lear's speeches do not entirely situate themselves within a logic of redemption. There is no horizon of expectation that orients survival: one can easily imagine the characters speaking fragments from the play for an indefinite period of time in order to come to terms with a past that does not necessarily point to any future. It is for this reason that Ray/Kent's line "Is this the promised end?" (5.3.38) can only ever take the form of a question. Moreover, it *remains* a question, a question that cannot be properly answered. What we know about the "promised end" is that the film continuously insinuates suspicions about any sense of *telos*, and this at least from the moment when we are shown a black driver ironically called Moses leading a group of travelers through the desert "in a straight line to nowhere" (as the title of the second chapter of the DVD version of the film puts it). One may want to add in this context that if the film inscribes a spiritual dimension, as critics such as Mark Thornton Burnett have argued (*Filming* esp. 112–13, 121–22), this spirituality has to do with what Derrida calls a "desert-like messianism (without content and without identifiable messiah)" (*Specters* 28), a messianism that "has a curious taste, a taste of death" (169), in that it articulates some kind of "awaiting without horizon of the wait, awaiting what one does not expect yet or any longer" (65).[57] In Levring's film, it is precisely because of the lack of any horizon of expectation that the unpredictable happens. It is precisely because the survivors no longer *count* on being rescued, that salvation comes. It comes in the form of two truckloads of African people, which is the film's way of gesturing toward an inversion and displacement of the colonial trope of the white man saving the natives from themselves.[58] As they approach the campfire, we are shown the survivors' utter incredulity. We are then faced with a quick succession of flashbacks that allows us to have a glimpse of the survivors' former selves while on the coach to this "nowhere." We do not know what happens to them after being rescued. Kanana's voice simply tells us that "they're not here, now they're gone." What the series of flashbacks forcefully suggests is that the spectral silhouettes that we have just seen performing *Lear* are *more* substantial than the images of the tourists they have replaced. In spite of, or because of, their vicissitudes in the desert, they are alive. They have been animated by a ghostly "Thing" that is "poor, bare, forked" (3.2.101), and "forked" also in the obsolete early modern sense of "ambiguous, equivocal" (OED Def. 5). This is a fragmentary "Thing" that is made almost of nothing but exercises its powerful effects between life and death, marking the future in advance with the unpredictability of its survivance.

CHAPTER 3

Reiterating *Othello*: Spectral Media and the Rhetoric of Silence in Alexander Abela's *Souli*

What are you looking at? All the ghosts...
—Murray Carlin, *Not Now, Sweet Desdemona*

We keep doing this, don't we?
—Djanet Sears, *Harlem Duet*

Set in Ambola, a remote fishing village on the southwestern coast of Madagascar, Alexander Abela's *Souli* (2004) is the director's second experiment with a geographical, temporal, and cultural transposition of Shakespeare. Unlike its predecessor, *Makibefo* (1999), an adaptation of *Macbeth* also set in Madagascar that enjoyed a short theatrical run and subsequently circulated in DVD format, *Souli*, a film "freely inspired by Shakespeare's *Othello*" (as the end credits state it), has not yet been released commercially, in spite of positive responses when shown at international film festivals.[1] Mark Thornton Burnett has eloquently written about the "vagaries of global exhibition and distribution" in relation to both films, and how they have "slipped off the compass of mainstream attention," including Shakespeare-on-film criticism, "falling into the category of productions that... run the risk of remaining relatively anonymous" ("Madagascan" 240, 252). Thus, both *Makibefo* and *Souli*, and the latter in particular, bear witness to "a filmic world dominated by Hollywoodized versions of Shakespeare," and point to what is arguably a wider issue: the "inherent unpredictabilities of the Shakespearian filmmaking initiative" (251).[2] Employing categories of postcolonial theory such as transnationalism, migrancy and hybridity, Burnett also underlines that the composite dynamics of production, circulation, and reception are not only (what may be called) the "external border" of these films, but are also integral to them. These films, that is, inscribe within themselves—and highlight—these dynamics, and on a number of different but interrelated levels, without ever losing sight of the unequal transactions between the "global" and the "local." To give an initial sense of the presence of these aspects in *Souli*, one only needs to mention that the film is about the attempt by doctoral student Carlos to persuade the Othello-like title character, a self-exiled Senegalese writer who has decided to write only for himself, to circulate the "traditional" oral tale of Thiossane and thus reenter the "global" literary arena; or that part of the film's "Shakespeareccentric" plot concerns Mona/Desdemona's invention of an ice-making machine that could put an end to malignant Yann/Iago's lucrative monopoly over the export of lobsters for the global market.

In this chapter I return to the self-reflexive and allegorizing aspects that Burnett emphasizes in connection with Abela's Shakespearean production, but I restrict my focus on *Souli*. Building on Burnett's argument, the chapter argues that Abela's film develops and continually foregrounds a rhetoric of silence, a silence that is neither lack nor absence. A symptomatic sign of this is the fact that, as one of the very few reviewers of the film points out, the film characters are "all conceived as advanced practitioners of loaded but largely non-verbal communication" (Scheib 34). To be more specific, the film's dialogue is often subordinated to a form of communication that takes place in the interstices of speech, a quasi-telepathic *spectral* kind of communication that draws attention to the body, and the sense of touch in particular, as uncanny media.[3] The chapter also suggests that this rhetoric of silence articulates an ethico-political rephrasing, and even a radical interruption, of the asymmetric global/local nexus that governs the dynamics of cultural production, circulation and transmission within and without the film. Shakespeare's *Othello* is decidedly relevant to the articulation of this complex rhetoric. Like *The King Is Alive*, with which it shares an emphasis on bare life—this time the life of fishermen in Southern Madagascar—and a relocation of Shakespeare in non-Anglophone settings, Abela's adaptation is not only a transformation of the meanings of the "original"; it is also a radical (retrospective) *production* of *Othello* as a bare, spectral, almost wordless script, a script that allocates colonially inflected roles and traumatically governs the positionalities of the film's characters, and especially as the film relentlessly moves toward its tragic ending. Moreover, at one and the same time, it is a production of *Othello* that forces the Shakespearean text—and its exotic construction of alterity in particular—to cohabit with the competing claims of the "traditional", enigmatic tale of Thiossane. Thus, in this quasi-silenced film, the movement away from the Anglophone center corresponds to a kind of reduction/silencing of the Bard that does not erase the power of Shakespearean spectrality, the manifold ways in which the "Thing 'Shakespeare'" haunts. On the one hand, Shakespeare's *Othello*—in its spectral form—becomes part of what Souli (Makéna Diop), the most metadramatic of the film's characters, verbally and nonverbally associates with fate. In fact, as a stand-in for Othello, Souli is himself always-already inscribed in the West's appropriative writing of the exotic. On the other hand, as the relationship of reciprocal contamination between the Shakespearean story and the tale of Thiossane develops, *Othello* also emerges as something *other than* itself, and something *other than* the name for the repetition compulsion of colonially inflected traumas.[4] It also tentatively reappears, that is, as a language of the future—a re-marking of "Shakespeare"—that promises to turn death as well as the more general threat of radical "dis-adjustment" into the chance of survival or even redemption.[5] Once again, Souli's position is crucial, in that he not only refuses to deliver the "round unvarnished tale" (*Oth.* 1.3.90) of Thiossane; he also implicitly but forcefully points to spectral modes of transmission such as touch and telepathy that are an alternative to writing and communication (in their common sense meanings), and out

Figure 3.1   The characters of the film. From left to right: Mona, Yann, Abi, Carlos, and Souli. Production photograph, courtesy of Alexander Abela.

of sync with the "vociferous" presence of the Shakespearean word on the global stage.

We are only a few minutes into Abela's film when Souli's ghostly voice emerges, a voice that speaks from beyond the grave, and invites the viewer to "listen to the voice of this man who speaks with his notes,"[6] a man playing the flute (Ali Wagué) whom we have just seen riding a bike in the busy industrial port of Dunkirk with its foundries in the background.[7] This spectral voice subsequently addresses a "friend who speaks through others' voices," a friend whom we can retrospectively identify as Yann's young mistress Abi (Fatou N'Diaye). Souli's voice asks her to "shout louder than the winds," and "join [him] in telling this mysterious story," a "story" that is nothing but the film itself. This complex framing of the film plunges the viewer into the realm of spectrality, a realm, as Jacques Derrida observes, that not only frustrates commonsensical notions of identity but also problematizes dominant categories of time and space (*Specters* esp. 10–29). It is a device that allows the emergence of a multilayered sense of temporality, and even triggers a vertiginous process of mise-en-abîme. On the one hand, the "mysterious story" is a story safely confined to the past, something that merely waits to be retold. On the other, this is a past that slips into and affects the present, as testified not only by the survival of Souli's voice—a voice that will presumably disappear once the story is told—but also by the reverberations of the story on both the flute player, who "narrates" in the nonrepresentational language of music, and the "friend" Souli addresses, the friend who "speaks through others' voices" and "carries others' voices," including Souli's, and will probably take them into the future.[8] And, indeed, the coming into being of the multiplicity of voices embodied by Abi is strictly related to Souli's silent transmission to her of the tale of Thiossane at the end of the film, a tale that is part of the mysterious story that is the film. The beginning of *Souli* also rearticulates coordinates of space. First of all, it sets up an uncanny connection between Dunkirk and Ambola, the "traditional" village where most of the action takes place. Moreover, it insists that there is a lack of clear-cut distinction between these earthly sites and the "spiritual" location of the ancestors—here identified as the "spirits of the deep"—while simultaneously suggesting further reconfigurations of space, as notes and voices "travel," or promise to travel, across spatial boundaries in ways that undercut any rigid sense of location.

In terms of diegesis, the initial scene of *Souli* is of course a supplement to the film's finale: it shows that Souli's suicide is not an ending; it suggests that Abi, the unlikely "disciple" to whom Souli transmits the tale of Thiossane, almost telepathically and by means of touch, survives in unexpected ways, as does the extradiegetic character of the flute player who is intermittently visible in the course of the film, often conjured up by the appearance of Abi or by references to Thiossane. It is a scene that can be called "Shakespeareccentric," but, as is regularly the case with the "Shakespeareccentricity" described by Richard Burt ("Introduction" 5–6), the movement away from "Shakespeare" is also, at one and the same time, a centripetal movement toward "Shakespeare."[9] By highlighting the question of narration and the multiplicity of its forms, from voices to music, this scene touches upon significant structural features of Shakespeare's *Othello*. It obliquely reminds the viewer of the extent to which the Shakespearean text is dependent upon the telling of stories: stories about traveling; stories through which language unremittingly "travels" by means of displacement and sub-stitution, from Othello's reiterations of his "traveller's history" (1.3.138) with which he wins Desdemona (and Brabanzio) to Iago's "monstrous" produc-tion of lurid class- and race-inflected scenarios of polymorphous sexuality with which he seduces Othello.[10] More specifically, by associating the need, or even the compulsion, to narrate with forms of survival, Souli's voice can-not fail to recall the ending of *Othello*, when the Moor of Venice temporar-ily reacquires his power of narration ("Soft you, a word or two before you go," 5.2.347), and shows his concern about a *just* retelling of his story, its future "extra-textual" circulation and survival: "I pray you, in your letters, / When you shall these unlucky deeds relate, / Speak of me as I am. Nothing extenuate, / Nor set down aught in malice" (349–52). Yet, unlike Souli, Othello—an isolated black figure in a sea of whites—can only envisage a restricted circulation of his story, from a liminal location such as Cyprus to Venice, from the "margins" to the "centre."

*   *   *

The beginning of *Souli* thus foregrounds issues of inheritance, transmis-sion, and circulation. It also activates, perhaps more obliquely, an interplay between "Shakespeareccentric" and "Shakespearecentric" concerns that will remain a regular feature of the film. The "mysterious story" announced by Souli starts with a dissolve, as a shot of the ocean (i.e., the symbolic residence of the ancestors) merges with a shot of a forest, a panoramic shot of what the bodiless voice of Souli calls a "burning land." This introduces the viewer to the intersection of two journeys that equally bear the mark, albeit in differ-ent ways, of a "burning" desire: Carlos's journey to Ambola to meet Souli, which is the concluding segment of his long, seemingly idealistic, search for the tale of Thiossane, a coming-of-age oral tale he believes Souli knows but is unwilling to pass on; Yann's more clearly exploitative routine journey to the coast with his Land Rover to collect lobsters from local fishermen (including former author Souli), which will then be sold on the global market, a journey in which greed couples with his strong sexual passion for Mona, who has left him for Souli. Carlos's search is "Shakespeareccentric" but evokes signifiers of exoticism that are inextricably bound up with *Othello*, and unavoidably prompts questions about the significance of the connection between an unwritten tale and the endless circulation and remediation of "Shakespeare," and the story of Othello in particular, on the global stage. Moreover, the "bookishness" of his search paves the way for his transformation into a Cassio-like figure: in Shakespeare's play Cassio is, according to Iago, an "arithmetician...that never set a squadron in the field" (1.1.18, 21); in Abela's film Carlos (Eduardo Noriega) is a naive, unpractical and good-looking "proper man" (1.3.384) who, according to Buba, the local character who fools him into buying some stale beer, cannot even "build his own hut" (i.e., set up his tent on the beach), and thus becomes an ideal pawn in Yann's plotting.[11] When compared to Carlos's first appearance, the characterization of Yann is more clearly "Shakespearecentric." Yann (Aurélien Recoing) recalls, from the very outset, Shakespeare's villain, although he hardly ever poses, and is hardly ever seen, as "honest Iago" (294). Yann *does* love Mona/Desdemona (Jeanne Antébi), and perhaps "out of absolute lust" (2.1.291), or loves to repossess the "object" that has been taken away from him. He is a character whose quasi-colonial and patronizing attitude toward the natives, like the ones he carries to Ambola in the back of his van to fish for him, extends to all forms of alterity, including his black girlfriend Abi, a "city girl," and will ultimately find expression in his endeavor to "colonize" the psyche of Souli/Othello. In effect, his racially inflected brutality first emerges when he urges Abi to "get in the back" of the van he is driving to make room for the white man Carlos, which is an attempt to create a bond between white men over and against the body of a black woman. (Abi, however, refuses to oblige). As Mark Thornton Burnett points out, Yann's command to "get in the back"—and, one may add, especially when it is heard in the original French: *"Monte derrière"*—is part of the more general "economic" way in which the film "references the word of the 'original'" ("Madagascan" 242). More specifically, it is a compressed inversion and displacement of Iago's evocation of the "black ram...tupping [a] white ewe" (1.1.88–89). Yann, that is, fancies himself as the *white* ram having absolute power over a *black* ewe. One may argue that this is also part of his anxious compensatory response to an inversion/displacement that has already occurred—the fact that he has been sexually replaced by Souli.

The film insists on scenarios of substitution and displacement just as much as *Othello*, and similarly shows that the dynamic interaction of socioeconomic, erotic, and racial forms of substitution and displacement aggravates resentment and instigates traumatic mechanisms of psychological projection that eventually lead to violence. Soon after he realizes that Mona is "up to something"—he has been spying on her working with a local, Saikou, in a makeshift chemical laboratory—Yann warns Souli of the destructive potential of any attempt on Mona's part to add economic displacement to sexual displacement: "I won't give up my place so easily. Not a second time." He also "abuse[s] [Souli's] ears" (1.3.387) by raising the specter of Mona's deceitfulness ("Beware of her . . . she has deceived more than one"), and thus, by implication, of Souli's *own* future sexual displacement. By the end of this short conversation, which takes place on the veranda of Souli's hut, that Mona is "up to something" retrospectively acquires a sexual connotation it did not originally possess.[12] It is almost as if her agency—agency of whatever kind—has automatically become a sign of transgression that could simultaneously affect both Yann *and* Souli. In Shakespeare's play Iago exploits what he construes as Othello's lack of familiarity with the sexual habits of white women to pursue his plan: "I know our country disposition well. / In Venice they do let God see the pranks / They dare not show their husbands" (3.3. 205–7); in Abela's film the construction of Souli as a black outsider who ignores the "disposition" of white women is more implicit but no less forceful. Indeed, the scene on the veranda ends with Souli's psychological debacle. It does not go as far as presenting an exchange of vows between the "seducer" and the "seduced," as is the case with *Othello* (3.3. 463–72). Nonetheless, Souli's final silence remains a tacit, if provisional, acceptance of Yann's insinuations, a kind of silent pledge.

As far as the plot is concerned, there are arguably two turning points in the film, and they are both directly related to the threat(s) of displacement articulated in this scene. The first one is when Mona theatrically drops an ice cube in Yann's glass, which is a visible sign of her success at manufacturing an ice-making machine that could spell the end of Yann's monopoly over the lobster business. The second one is when Mona refuses to agree with Souli that Carlos is not the disciple he was waiting for ("Why don't you initiate him?"), which introduces a jarring tone in the "calms, . . . loves and comforts" (2.1.186, 195) of the interracial couple, and facilitates the work of Yann's immaterial "poison" (3.3.329). To a large extent, both scenes are "Shakespeareccentric," even though the second one is arguably less so, in that Mona's persistent request that Carlos be given a chance as suitable recipient of the tale of Thiossane recalls Desdemona's plea that Cassio be given a second chance as lieutenant. Moreover, they both hinge upon the agency of Mona, who is often a "Shakespeareccentric" character: if she is Desdemona, then she is the assertive, unprejudiced, and sensual Desdemona of the first act of *Othello*, or the "fair warrior" of the beginning of the second act (2.1.183). Paradoxically, these "Shakespeareccentric" turning points do not generate a further movement away from Shakespeare. In fact, they mark the uncanny re-emergence of *Othello* as a bare, spectral, almost wordless script that allocates, or even "pre-scribes," roles and inexorably drives the film toward a tragic ending.

Deeply affected by this re-emergence is the protagonist of Abela's film. Souli is initially positioned as the inverted mirror image of the Shakespearean Moor: if Othello presents himself as "rude" in his "speech" but nonetheless produces an alluring, seductive "traveller's history" (1.3.81, 138), Souli is an accomplished author who refuses to "deliver" the "round unvarnished tale" of Thiossane (90). The re-emergence of the "Thing 'Shakespeare'" predominantly means that Souli begins to "look to" Mona, and "observe her well" with Carlos (3.3.201). Surprised to find her in the company of Carlos at the impromptu party that will lead to the Yann-orchestrated "barbarous brawl" (2.3.165), he takes on the Othello-like "passive" spectatorial position of the jealous "supervisor" (3.3.400): he repeatedly watches Mona and Carlos talking to each other, which the subjective look of the camera construes as intimate whispering, and then he anxiously looks on as they dance together.[13] For Souli, Mona's (supposed) unfaithfulness means that "chaos is come again" (3.3.93). Yet in the film "chaos" has also to do with the ways in which the Shakespearean script infiltrates the vicissitudes of the story of Thiossane. That the bracelet—the film's "translation" of the handkerchief—ends up on Carlos's wrist not only "speaks against [Mona] with the other proofs" (3.3.446), and irremediably seals her fate; being a gift from Souli to Mona that inscribes a maternal genealogy in much the same way as the tale of Thiossane, its circulation also allegorically stands for some kind of "publishing" by Mona of what should have remained hidden and secret for Souli's lineage to be kept safe.[14] As Souli states in an earlier dialogue with Carlos, "divulging [the tale of Thiossane] would put the Koumba N'Diaye lineage at risk." We also learn from this dialogue that it was in order to protect his mother's lineage that he decided to withdraw from the Western literary world.

*   *   *

Mark Thornton Burnett underlines the "psychic dividedness" ("Madagascan" 242) that Souli inhabits, and relates it to the latter's transnational migration from Senegal to Madagascar that simultaneously empowers and disempowers him: Souli is clearly the leader of the community of fishermen in Ambola, and his "literary reputation and village status are mutually reinforcing"; yet "he fishes for Yann and is in his employ" (242). As Yann condescendingly declares: "I couldn't get by without you." However, I want to argue that the dialectic of empowerment and disempowerment is imbued with supplementary meanings. First of all, Souli is not just any character. As noted earlier, he is simultaneously "inside" the frame of the film *and* "outside" it as a ghostly voice embodying the power of narration, a position that cannot but have a bearing upon the role he plays "inside" the film.[15] Second, his repeated shifting between "polarized positions of inferiority and superiority" (242) inside the film combines with a radical sense of "dis-adjustment" that can hardly be interpreted only in psychological or sociocultural terms. I want to suggest that this "dis-adjustment" can be fully appreciated by associating it with the self-reflexivity of the film. Put differently, "dis-adjustment" is also the name for the way in which the Senegalese writer-protagonist looks at himself, as if from the outside, playing a part in an *Othello* script with a painful sense of déjà vu—a kind of looking back to *Othello* saturated with trauma. On the one hand, therefore, Souli appears to be utterly subjected to the Shakespearean script that "spectralizes" the second half of the film. In this compressed version of *Othello*, he does not even ask Yann for further evidence of Mona's unfaithfulness. He does not request him that "the probation bear no hinge nor loop / To hang a doubt on" (3.3.370–71). After the aforementioned dialogue on the veranda, the two male characters limit themselves to exchanging complicit looks and nodding in each other's direction. On the other hand, Souli seems to be metadramatically aware of playing a role in a script that is not of his own making, a script that disseminates deleterious constructions of alterity and exercises powerful constraints on the understanding of interracial relationships. In a sense, and paradoxically, his utter passivity uncannily doubles as the power of insight—his frequent poignant pauses, his facial gestures as well as his speeches pervaded by a sense of doom point in this direction.[16] Nonetheless, this metadramatic form of "power" does not stop him from compulsively acting out his Othello-like role to the very tragic ending. In other words, the film *does* attempt to re-mark the spectral remains of the *Othello* it incorporates so as to make them speak otherwise. But this is inseparable from re-enactment. And of course, this re-enactment is also the necessary prerequisite for Souli's narration of the "mysterious story" to take place, a narration that in its turn guarantees his transubstantiation into the realm of the ancestors.

To emphasize the re-emergence of a Shakespearean script that allocates roles is not, therefore, to deny the transformative rearticulations to which this script is itself subjected. The irreducibility of the "Thing 'Shakespeare'" has little to do with the permanence of the essence of the "original" (Derrida, *Specters* 22). In the second half of the film, as the characters re-enact the roles the *Othello* script prescribes, the "Thing 'Shakespeare'" takes on additional meanings it did not know, or did not fully know, it had. For instance, the late-night party during which local people and film characters congregate is followed by a number of scenes in which the characters' re-enactment highlights postcolonial problematics of various kind, including the issue of the economic, sexual, and literary appropriation of alterity. One such scene is the ostracization of Carlos, which results from his being (unjustly) accused of the rape of Abi. This of course echoes the dismissal of Cassio in 2.3, and is a reiteration of Souli's rejection of Carlos as a potential disciple earlier in the film. Moreover, in Souli's eyes, the (alleged) rape of Abi functions as "confirmation...strong" (3.3.327) that Carlos is "loose of soul" (421); it strengthens his conviction that the doctoral student is involved in a sexual liaison with Mona.[17] In terms of re-enactment bringing about additional meanings, it is especially worth contrasting the ways in which Souli and Othello react to the eruption of civic disorder that "frights" each of their respective locations "from her propriety" (2.3.168–69).[18] Woken up in the middle of the night by raised voices, and faced with a group of enraged local people attempting to restrain Carlos who is protesting his innocence, Souli does not pose as "honorary white" ("Are we turned Turks...? / For Christian shame, put by this barbarous brawl," [2.3.163, 165]).[19] He angrily dismisses what he calls "white men's justice," but in order to prevent further trouble he authoritatively tells Yann to "take [Carlos] back" with him the following day. He erects an impermeable boundary between whites and blacks; or, more specifically, between white men such as Carlos and Yann who perpetrate economic and sexual violence, and black men such as himself and his community who protect the body of the black woman and defy any further violation of it. In this process of redefinition of racial boundaries, Abi's position silently shifts, and somehow in spite of herself, from that of black, urban girl to that of an emblem of an always-already ravaged "Africa," a shift that paves the way for her role as recipient of the tale of Thiossane at the end of the film. One may want to add that Souli's assertion of blackness is a repetition with a difference—in fact, an inversion and displacement—of Othello's "I am black" (3.3.267), a line the Moor enunciates from a defensive position that is structured from within by Iago's pernicious constructions of alterity.

No matter how confused he is about what happened, Carlos instinctively believes himself to be innocent of the charge of rape. Indeed, it is Yann who beats up Abi and coerces her into accusing Carlos, and this is only the climax of his continuous brutal treatment of his girlfriend. (One of the film's most trenchant ironic aspects is that Abi asks for Carlos's forgiveness about her lie by giving him Mona's bracelet, which makes her an unwitting contributor to Mona's death). In a sense, therefore, there *is* rape, and it is through the French adventurer's repeated violations of Abi's black body that the film articulates, in an allegorical mode, its ethico-political concerns about postcolonial reincarnations of the colonial "scramble for Africa."[20] But the film is not only concerned with the economic and sexual exploitation of the "dark Continent" as well as with the ways in which they relate to one another. It also repeatedly draws attention to the literary and cultural appropriation by the West of African alterity. As Mark Thornton Burnett points out, Souli's decision not to publish any more is an implicit critique of the process whereby the postcolonial voice of the Other "is both commodified...and manipulated and misused" ("Madagascan" 251). Significantly, the film shows that this process of appropriation is simultaneously a taking hold of a textual *corpus and* a decidedly harrowing seizing of the body of an author. As Burnett adds, the film powerfully suggests "the bruising of Souli at the hands of the Western literary establishment," a "metaphorical" bruising that finds its "literary" and "physical" correlative in the representation of Souli's body as a "body...in pain" (251), and is an integral part of what I have been calling Souli's "dis-adjustment." Carlos is thus innocent of the charge leveled at him, but as a "figurative manifestation of the west's cultivation of the indigenous" (241), he is hardly alien to a process of appropriation that the film consistently identifies with a voracious violation of the *corpus*/body of the Other. In effect, *Souli* often casts doubts upon Carlos's pose as a naive doctoral student who is primarily driven by a disinterested love of knowledge. "Yeah, right": this is Yann's short caustic comment on Carlos's assertion that his ethnographic attempt to retrieve the tale of Thiossane has to do purely with his doctoral work on the Senegalese writer ("It's for my thesis"). Talking to Carlos and Mona on the veranda after lunch, and addressing the latter, Souli voices what is implied in Yann's sarcastic remark: "Don't you see, our friend here is eager to sign the preface of a best-selling tale." This upsets Carlos: "I simply wanted to persuade you to share something wonderful with the rest of the world." But it is especially in the final sequence of the film that the questioning of Carlos's motives more clearly becomes an exposure of his unwillingness to admit, even to himself, the nexus of (post)colonial power/knowledge in which he is imbricated. As Souli is about to die on the beach, Carlos rushes to the writer's hut and then feverishly starts leafing through the pages of the latter's unpublished manuscripts. Failing to find transcribed traces of the tale of Thiossane, he angrily brushes them onto the floor. (These are of course the same manuscripts that he had previously ecstatically admired in the aforementioned veranda scene). It is only at this point that he turns around, draws aside a curtain, and notices the "tragic loading of [Souli's] bed" (5.2.373).

* * *

With the white sheet covering Mona's body in its entirety, the film shifts back to its Shakespearean plot. And yet this white sheet irresistibly hints at what is missing from Carlos's search. It is a Shakespearean item but also arguably stands for the blank sheet of paper that inscribes the spectral *absence* of the tale of Thiossane. In the film the "Thing 'Shakespeare'" haunts, and part of this haunting has to do with the fact that it repeatedly contaminates, or threatens to contaminate, the Thiossane plot, as argued in connection with Souli's elaboration of a fantasy scenario impregnated with jealousy. The film also shows that the tale of Thiossane equally haunts, and this concerns not only Carlos. By making an absent, unwritten, and perhaps unwriteable, *African* tale interact with the *Othello* script, *Souli* forces an interrogation of the status of *Othello* as a Western inscription and appropriation of the alterity of the exotic Other. Not unlike what emerges from the African rewritings of *Othello* analyzed by Jyotsna Singh, the film shows the extent to which the Shakespearean text has historically become the "site for the production of troubled and contradictory colonial/postcolonial identities" (291) as well as a template for pejorative interpretations of the viability of interracial relationships; it underlines the difficulty of "*separat[ing]* the play from our colonial legacy of continuing racial conflicts" (299, Singh's emphasis). Singh also argues that "Europeans can turn their eyes from [the] spectacle of violence [in *Othello*]—and from the 'poisons' of racism in the play—through a disidentification with the black man" (291), but this is much more complicated for African readers or viewers.[21]

As mentioned earlier, for a metadramatic black character such as Souli, a character who plays a role in the *Othello* script but is also in an important

Figure 3.2   Uncanny transmissions. Courtesy of Alexander Abela.

sense a reader/viewer of this script, "disidentification" is synonymous with a re-enactment that produces supplementary "Shakespeareccentric" meanings and/or endeavors to make the Shakespearean script speak otherwise. However, as the film draws to a close, re-enactment seems to be increasingly less a matter of speaking. The ending of *Souli*, that is, intensifies the film's cultivation of silence. As far as Souli is concerned, he pursues his intermittent "writing back" to *Othello* while performing *Othello* by means of a re-enactment that is nothing but a further silencing of an already bare script. He performs the murder of Mona without saying a word. He does not even reply to the only words spoken in the scene, Mona's "what is going on?"[22] Learning from Abi that it was Yann who "set it all up," Souli walks steadily toward him as soon as he sees him getting off his boat, as if to engage in a fight and exact revenge. Unexpectedly, and again without saying a word, he launches himself on to Yann's knife and thus kills himself, which is a further undermining of the boundaries between activity and passivity typical of a metadramatic character who is simultaneously inside and outside the Shakespearean script. This final intensification of silence paves the way for the affirmation of the poetics of Thiossane, a poetics that offers the "challenge of the incomplete" (Chambers, *Culture* 174), in that it emphasizes opacity, the interval of the unsaid, the inassimilable remainder—what Souli calls, discussing the African tale with Carlos on the veranda, "the blanks between the words" ("*les blancs laissés par l'écriture*"), impervious to any ethnographic and logocentric attempt to "dis-cover" and decipher the true meaning of the alterity of Thiossane.[23]

The poetics of Thiossane informs and inspires the last scene of the film, a complex, multilayered scene encapsulating many of *Souli*'s concerns. In this scene, interspersed with shots of the flute player, we see Souli lying on the beach and about to exhale his last breath[24]; we watch him looking intensely at Abi, reaching out for her hand and nodding in her direction, as if to assert that she is the disciple he has been waiting for; we observe Abi's perplexed reaction and hesitation, which does not prevent her from taking hold of Souli's blood-spattered hand; we finally see her "shuddering at the point of what amounts to a psychic transmission of . . . inheritance" (Burnett, "Madagascan" 252). While on the veranda, Souli explains to Carlos that he does not "possess Thiossane"; it is, rather, Thiossane that "possesses [him]." In this final scene, trauma not only has to do with the physical wound Souli somehow inflicts upon himself; it also has to do with the fact that Souli is possessed by, and a hostage to, a tale that he is forced to pass on along with trauma. The way in which Souli and Abi relate to the tale as well as to each other compellingly recalls the "spectral" asymmetry of terms governing ethics as described by Emmanuel Levinas, an ethics as response to the alterity of the Other that undoes the subject and precedes consciousness.[25] In this sense, the poetics of Thiossane is also an ethics, a "po-ethics." To refer to Levinas's discussion of the ethical relationship, being possessed by Thiossane or inheriting it—being possessed by, or inheriting, a tale whose source is the M/Other—is an "exposure of the 'me' [*moi*] to another, prior to any decision...," an exposure whereby "a sort of violence is undergone..., a claiming of this Same by the Other." It amounts to "a traumatic hold of the Other upon the Same." It is "an assignation to respond, which leaves no refuge and authorizes no escape"(*God* 187).[26] Paradoxically, and in terms that are appropriate to interpret the scene, this "assignation to respond" is what "leaves me without speech" (174). It is an assignation to which the "subject," "unseated by the other..., cannot respond with words" (181).

The tale of Thiossane thus finally appears, but does not appear *as such*. It emerges as what is "translated" into another "language." It materializes as some kind of psychic flow that passes through bodies and finds its catalyst in the sense of touch.[27] If Thiossane embodies tradition, as the film repeatedly emphasizes, tradition as articulated here is *not* an uncontaminated point of origin and/or an embodiment of the genuine values of a self-contained ethnic community. Tradition is here irrevocably transmission and inheritance of what does not cease *not* writing itself, a configuration of spectral "blanks" (to use Souli's word) that refuses to be "colonised as pure silence, absolute lack" (Chambers, *Culture* 174) and articulates itself through the uncanny medium of the body.[28] Put differently, in this scene, which continuously negotiates the limits of the visible and thus of the cinematic medium itself, the spectrality of the unsaid reigns supreme. It is because of this spectrality—an irreducible marking of the in-betweenness of intervals dislocating speech and writing (in its common sense meaning)—that one can hardly contend that what we witness here is the communication of a tale, if by communication one means the transmission of a message from one preconstituted pole to another, from an addressor to an addressee who are fully present to themselves as subjects. Nor can one claim that contact by means of touch between Souli and Abi establishes a sense of immediacy or transparency. The limits of the visible are not supplemented, or not supplemented without remainder, by the close presence of touch. The film suggests that it is precisely because Souli and Abi are such unlikely partners—a self-exiled writer who refuses Western values and dreams of his ancestral home vis-à-vis a Westernized city girl with braided hair who fantasizes about escaping to Europe—that there is contact. By one and the same token, and to borrow from Derrida's work on touch, it is because of this *différance* that there is apartness in contact, that "contact never appears in its full purity, never in any immediate plenitude" (*Touching* 229).[29]

Mark Thornton Burnett argues that Abela's Shakespearean films "place under scrutiny the transmission and commodification of words in the global marketplace" ("Madagascan" 240). As far as Abela's adaptation of *Othello* is concerned, its silencing of Shakespeare—its tendency to reduce *Othello* to a bare script—is implicitly and explicitly, and especially through the performance of a metadramatic character such as Souli, a politically motivated intervention in the "vociferous" circulation and transmission of a Shakespearean word that, given the "historic association [of Shakespeare] with language" (240), comes to stand for the essence of Shakespeare *tout court*. More specifically, this silencing aims at disrupting the circulation and transmission of *Othello* as a text that predominantly signifies the appropriation of the alterity of the African Other, and that unceasingly appears to predetermine the range of meanings attributable to interracial relationships. The Western failure to discover Thiossane, as emblematized by Carlos's frustration, is strictly bound up with the vicissitudes of the Shakespearean script, in that it similarly marks an interruption of what the film sees as the repeated, traumatic (post)colonial appropriations of African alterity that are then circulated on the global stage. One must stress again that one of the most innovative aspects of the ending of the film is that this interruption does not posit, by contrast, the uncontaminated presence of an African origin; or, since this interruption also concerns Shakespeare, it does not formulate the "truth" of an African Othello, whatever this may be.[30] Some of the pronouncements by Souli, a migrant writer who adds exile to what Derrida would call a constitutive "originary" exile from a maternal language, and who is also the only character in the film who never speaks his mother tongue, are informed by a nostalgia for such uncontaminated origin, a compulsive desire to keep his mother's genealogy safe and intact.[31] But desire is not the realization of desire. What we witness in the final scene of the film is the irremediable transmission as "translation" of an origin; an origin, moreover, that is never quite itself before transmission/translation and in fact *constitutes itself* through transmission/translation. As shown earlier, this is an invisible, irreducibly spectral, ethically marked silent transmission of inheritance in which silence is not lack, an inverted mirror image of presence or full speech.

* * *

The interruption of the global circulation of Thiossane as one of the emblems of alterity does not mean that the tale does not circulate, or that it only circulates locally. The scene is punctuated by repeated shots of the flute player, a spectator/witness whose music combines with the diegetic splashing of the waves. It ends with the flute player walking along the busy port of Dunkirk, which shows that other locations and temporalities are implicated in this apparently restricted, spectral transmission taking place in a small African village. The appearance of the flute player at the end of the film cannot fail to recall his appearance at the beginning of the film, when we see him riding a bike in the same busy port and playing music while leaning against a metal grille, which is a prelude to the emergence of Souli's spectral voice. The film insists on this dizzying circular motion, which invites a re-vision of the beginning of the film in the light of its ending and vice versa. As mentioned earlier, at the beginning of the film Souli speaks as a voice without a body, which replaces the body without a voice of the ending of the film. His is a bodiless voice articulating itself as an invitation to "listen" ("Listen to the voice of this man, his words are his notes"), an invitation that concerns the implied spectator as well as Abi, a "friend" and disciple who "speaks through others' voices," and that finally extends to the ancestors. This is an ethical appeal to another, a call upon a host of others, that once again refuses to subscribe to the metaphysics of the "subject." It is yet another spacing out of presence that establishes a spectral flow of communication involving Souli, the implied spectator, Abi, the flute player and the "spirits of the deep," a re-marking of what the film sees as the dominant forms of global commu-nication and circulation of the word. This is a re-marking that unavoidably implicates *Othello*. The relationship of reciprocal contamination, or even haunting, between the story of Thiossane and the Shakespearean story, a relationship that asserts itself especially in the second part of the film, sug-gests that the vicissitudes of the two stories are inextricably linked to one another. Moreover, Souli is not just an heir to Thiossane who passes on this legacy to Abi. He is also an heir to Othello. More specifically, at the begin-ning of the film, he is an heir to the Othello who at the end of Shakespeare's play speaks to the future as he voices his concern about the survival of his story, even though he can only think of Venice as the most appropriate place for a retelling. As a voice from beyond the grave, Souli rephrases Othello's sense of the future and complicates the geographies of survival. More gener-ally, the beginning of the film envisages retellings that include, but are not limited to, Souli's "mysterious story." Given the spectral logic of *Souli*, these retellings are not even necessarily restricted to the medium of film. Abi is encouraged to "shout louder than the winds," to adopt a modality of com-munication that precedes and/or exceeds speech. She is also said to "speak through others' voices," not unlike Souli, which suggests that these retell-ings can take the form of psychic transmissions infiltrating the global flow of communication and situating themselves in the latter's interstices. In any event, these retellings are inextricably bound with Abi's migrations as well as with the peregrinations of the notes of the flute player, who breathes life into his instrument and acts as a guardian spirit toward Abi.[32] They are themselves, in fact, migrations that follow unpredictable routes. They engage the future and bear the mark of an ethico-political transformative potential. These retellings are also *Shakespearean* migrations. Among the "voices" Abi "carries" (as Souli puts it), there are the spectral voices of *Othello*'s marginalized female figures, including the voice of Bianca and perhaps that of Desdemona's maid Barbary, and especially the voice of Emilia, an Emilia who survives the tragedy and will, indeed, "ne'er go home" (5.2.204). The singular multiplicity of voices that Abi carries is a "pre-diction" of an inexorably hybrid, transmedial "Shakespeare" that will be subjected to continuous relocations and dislocations, a spectral "Shakespeare" that will not necessarily emanate from, or return to, the center.

The logic of the future implemented by the film may read as a utopic and idealistic gesture, and even more so if one recalls that the film itself has not yet been commercially released and has only enjoyed limited circulation within the circuit of mostly Francophone international film festivals. In sum, we are faced with the paradox of a silenced Shakespearean film that insists on silence and silent, uncanny modes of transmission to articulate its ethico-political stance toward global circuits of communication. But its being marginalized almost to the point of suppression within the multiple asymmetric *dispositifs* of power that go under the name of the "global" does not invalidate its stance. I want to end by arguing that even if a film such as *Souli* cannot imagine its own future (as distinct from its poetic and idiosyncratic imagining of future migrations), it shows at least awareness of its own utopic and or idealistic tendencies, and goes as far as to issue caveats against them. To best illustrate aspects of this, it is worth moving back to the ending of the film one last time. As it draws to a close, *Souli* pointedly excludes, on the one hand, any reestablishing of mastery in Ambola: there is no Cassio-like figure who takes over. By marginalizing Carlos, and with such trenchant irony, the film also ostracizes appropriative migrations from the "centre" to the "periphery." On the other hand, it cannot quite decide what to do with the Iago-like figure: we see Yann setting off on his boat after the death of Souli, and he never appears again.[33] The uncertainty surrounding the fate of Yann, a character whose brutalization and silencing of Abi is repeatedly emphasized, is an allegorical reminder of the ever-present threat of the reproduction of a variety of forms of "malevolent" appropriation and exploitation of alterity, and even of the latter's silencing or erasure. This is a threat that unceasingly inscribes itself within the multiplicity of chances that migration continues to provide.

CHAPTER 4

"This Is My Home, Too": Migration, Spectrality, and Hospitality in Roberta Torre's *Sud Side Stori*

> The question of translation is always the question of hospitality.
> —Jacques Derrida, *Of Hospitality*

Premièred at the *Mostra Internazionale d'arte cinematografica* in Venice and subsequently shown at a number of international film festivals around the world (London, Toronto, New York, Istanbul, and New Delhi), Roberta Torre's *Sud Side Stori* (2000) is one of the most distinctive experimental Italian films of recent years.[1] Combining neorealist cinematographic techniques with the artificial style of the musical (and echoing Jerome Robbins and Robert Wise's 1961 *West Side Story* in its title),[2] it offers a highly idiosyncratic partial retelling of Shakespeare's *Romeo and Juliet*.[3] Unashamedly exhibiting its status as postmodern pastiche (Jameson 16–18), and repeatedly, if implicitly, pointing to the politically transformative potential of this aesthetic style, Torre's film replaces "fair Verona" ("Prologue" 2) with an oxymoronic version of the Sicilian city of Palermo. It presents a cityscape that is at once gritty *and* oneiric, replete with realistic details *and* excessively stagy, thus bringing to the extreme the contradictory articulation of urban space in both Robbins's and Wise's film and Baz Luhrmann's *William Shakespeare's Romeo+Juliet* (1996) (Modenessi 65). Shakespeare's "star-crossed lovers" ("Prologue" 6) become Toni Giulietto (Roberto Rondelli), a local rock singer who is a pale imitation of the Italian King of Rock'n'roll Little Tony, himself a pale imitation of Elvis Presley, and Romea Wacoubo (Forstina Erhabor), a beautiful Nigerian prostitute who falls in love with him when she sees him standing on his balcony playing the guitar. Not unlike the relationship between Tony and Maria in *West Side Story*, the interracial passion between Toni and Romea exacerbates preexisting ethnic conflicts. It is opposed not only by the two lovers' "households" ("Prologue" 1)—respectively, Toni's three ugly aunties and Romea's closest friends Mercutia and Baldassarra—but also by the whole Nigerian immigrant community, including those African characters who run the racket of prostitution, and, more indirectly, by the local Mafia, in the person of the oddly named character Fred *'u scienziato* (Fred-the-scientist), who "protects" Tony (because he had an affair with his mother).[4] Indeed, ethnic conflicts pervade virtually all aspects of Palermitan life, from religious devotion to belief in magic, from popular music to culinary practices, from dancing styles to fashion, and are arguably even more pronounced than in *West Side Story*. Yet the film presents these conflicts only to ultimately expose the neurosis of cultural homogeneity that deeply affects, although in different ways, both the Palermitan and the Nigerian community.

Taking into account Derrida's reflections on spectrality in *Specters of Marx*, the chapter is an analysis of the disquieting presence of "Shakespeare-in-translation" in Roberta Torre's film, a presence that is simultaneously material and evanescent.[5] *Sud Side Stori*, the chapter argues, is a non-Anglophone adaptation of Shakespeare that does not simply include the translated textual body of *Romeo and Juliet*. It is not, moreover, an unproblematic re-presentation of a fixed and stable entity that somehow pre-exists—and authorizes—the act of translation. It is a reiteration that (retrospectively) *produces* and exhibits Shakespeare's *Romeo and Juliet* as an ensemble of spectral remainders, a series of indeterminate fragments that often remain to be translated in the "language of the other" (i.e., they are not in English but they are not quite in Italian either). These fragments, that is, are indicative of Shakespearean translation as a process that does not *properly* end. Furthermore, they are often remediated, decontextualized and forced to cohabit with the language of the body, music, and dance, or even with the conventions of silent films, in ways that are reciprocally illuminating and that point to re-articulations of "Shakespeare" beyond the constraints of *Romeo and Juliet*'s tragic plot. This chapter also aims to show that in Torre's film "Shakespearecentric" concerns—what counts as Shakespeare, which includes the multifarious ways in which *Romeo and Juliet* has been recycled in contemporary global media culture—and "Shakespeareccentric" concerns repeatedly interact with one another (Burt, "Introduction" 5). Particularly significant in this respect is the fact that *Sud Side Stori* often brings an allegorical dimension to bear on the issues of migration and hospitality it continually foregrounds, so that the response to the alterity of the body of the "other"/foreigner/migrant (i.e., especially Romea but also the similarly displaced "native" Toni Giuletto) becomes inextricably intertwined with the question of the incorporation of the "foreignness" of Shakespeare, a "textual body" that itself migrates from an Anglophone to a non-Anglophone context.

From the very outset, *Sud Side Stori* displays awareness of the global circulation of the story of the two star-crossed lovers, and not only by means of its unashamedly derivative title. For example, the handwritten opening titles recall the apparently unsophisticated end credits of *West Side Story*; the cartoonish animated image of a pulsating heart that appears in conjunction with the film's title is not only a generic parody of a love that knows no boundaries (and thus also of films based on *Romeo and Juliet*), but also, more specifically, of the obsessively present iconography of the "sacred heart" in Baz Luhrmann's *William Shakespeare's Romeo+Juliet*, which is perhaps already in itself a caricature of religious devotion (Modenessi 73–77; Donaldson 65–69). Moreover, at the beginning of the film we are shown an "anachronistic" video installation with six picture frames of various sizes and shapes containing "live" images of patron saints, including Saint Rosalia, patron saint of Palermo. These multiple frames are an unmistakable citation of the frame within the frame with which Luhrmann's film starts, and this becomes even clearer when a flashing light on Saint Rosalia's head attracts the viewer's attention to the central rectangular picture frame, which is the one that most closely resembles a huge TV screen, and which is just as kitsch as the retro TV in Luhrmann's film. However, when Saint Rosalia begins to speak from inside this "screen," global Shakespearecentric concerns are recontextualized and given a local inflection: she attributes the origin of the "grudge" ("Prologue" 3) between the Palermitan and Nigerian community to the Mayor's suggestion that she share her status as patron saint of Palermo with Saint Benedict, the son of black slaves who converted to Christianity.[6] The "translation" of Shakespearean references into a local idiom continues when we move "down below" (Saint Rosalia's words) and we are presented with the dead body of a woman reclining on a kitchen table.[7] This woman turns out to be Giuseppona-the-policewoman (*Giuseppona 'a sbirra*),[8] a busybody who greedily collects money for the annual celebration in honor of Saint Rosalia, and whose connection with the story of the two star-crossed lovers is probably that she is herself "star-crossed," an innocent victim of "fortune": she is dispatched by the local Mafia because they wrongly assume that she is involved in the (fake) death of Toni Giulietto. In addition to Saint Rosalia's, it is Giuseppona's spectral voice, which promises the audience to "tell the truth, nothing but the truth," that will play the role of Chorus: she will introduce the main characters—to her, Toni sings "like a donkey," and

Romea is a "black panther" and a "gazelle"—and provide a colorful commentary on "the fearful passage of [Toni and Romea's] death-marked love" ("Prologue" 9).

This description of the beginning of *Sud Side Stori*, with its double prologue, is indicative of the way the film more generally relates to its Shakespearean material. Not unlike the transnational postmillennial Shakespearean parodies that Mark Thornton Burnett explores in *Filming Shakespeare in the Global Marketplace*, in *Sud Side Story* "Shakespeare" functions as "a prompt rather than a model, a corpus of suggestions rather than a script to be replicated" (156). In fact, "Shakespeare" sometimes becomes a "pre-text" to address "with a particular urgency...some of the conflicted concerns of the contemporary era" (156). In an interview, Roberta Torre speaks of her movie in these terms: "I wanted to make a film on immigration and on the problems it inevitably brings, as this is something we are faced with today and will continue to be faced with in the future" (qtd. in Cavecchi 92–93). To Torre, immigration is nothing short of a "revolution." Her political and social concerns manifest themselves especially in her adoption of the conventions of documentary films that had already characterized her previous work, as well as in her use of largely nonprofessional actors. For instance, the film intermittently presents interviews with Nigerian women who talk about a non-Shakespearean kind of "traffic" ("Prologue" 12), the global trade in human flesh. They tell their real-life experiences as illegal immigrants: their arrival in Italy; their being forced into prostitution by local gangs of Nigerians who have seized their passports; their hard work to pay back a huge bondage fee; the brutality of Italian police as well as Sicilian men who never wash and are only too keen to prove their virility. These experimental—and oppositional—cinematographic techniques mark a movement away from Shakespeare.[9] Yet they are also instrumental in resituating the story of the two star-crossed lovers in a new context, a context intensely marked by illegal transactions, greed, violence and interethnic (as well as intraethnic) conflicts. In fact these techniques partially infiltrate the way in which the Shakespearean story is being retold: at times the Nigerian prostitutes who recount their real-life experiences as illegal immigrants are also the "characters" who are being interviewed about the relationship between Toni and Romea ("I know Romea very well. She works in the streets, just like me"; "He is a white man. He is not the right man for her," and so on). This suggests a blurring of the boundaries between "fact" and "fiction," but this blurring does not diminish the political impact of the migrant's story. It is not so much an end in itself as a symptom of the shifting and problematic status of the "real" in a film in which hostility toward the other is very much coextensive with "reality."

It is when the film shifts from a sober documentary mode to the highly artificial style of the musical—and the two modalities are often contiguous—that the migrant's story becomes more specifically a claim *not* to be merely a guest—and an unwanted guest at that—in the host country. This emerges most forcefully when we move from the public square, where we have witnessed a "fray" (1.1.114) between the African and Palermitan communities, with each community supporting its own religious icon, to *Vicolo Anello*, a shabby street in the market district of the *Vucciaria* adorned with clothes hanging from washing lines. (This is a note of local color but also a citation of the picturesque background to "Who Knows?", the song Tony sings on the eve of the dancing party in *West Side Story*). When we enter the Giulietto household, we find the three domineering "bloody harpies" (Toni's definition),[10] who have just played a prominent role in the march of protest in favor of Saint Rosalia, restating their allegiance to the patron Saint of Palermo against inappropriate innovations and talking about Toni—he is the "serious problem" they have inherited from their sister, who is a prostitute. As they are about to prepare lunch, the unexpected happens. Silence takes over this Palermitan cul-de-sac. After a while we hear some music in the distance as well as the beating of drums; we see three motionless, enigmatic black shapes and then a group of black women with suitcases who boldly announce: "We have just arrived from Africa." Dancing and singing to the rhythm of a music that defies categorization in terms of identity and belonging—a hybridization of hybrid transnational "traditions" such as ju-ju, reggae, and hip-hop—this group of women, whose leaders are Romea, Mercutia, and Baldassarra, repeatedly lays claim to a Palermitan home: "Street, sweet home, this is my home too." They threaten—or promise—irremediably to transform and "hybridize" what they lay claim to: "With our African colors [we will paint] your grey home." Not only do they undermine a sense of home that defines itself in relation to its outside/other; they also perform a reimagining of the boundaries of home that makes these boundaries limitless and meaningless: "Home is wherever the train stops." (This is even more effective in terms of the film's imaginary geography: one only needs to jump on a train to get from a clearly signposted "Africa" to an equally well signposted "Palermo," which is what Romea does when she reads the news about Toni's death later on in the film).

This flamboyantly staged arrival/invasion of the "other," which is one of the idiosyncratic elements of Torre's film when compared to films based on *Romeo and Juliet* that similarly emphasize ethnic conflict,[11] occurs in time (i.e., on a Sunday) and concerns a specific place (i.e., *Vicolo Anello*). But it also disrupts the sameness of empirical time, a temporality that unfolds as a linear succession and/or unproblematic repetition of present moments (as emblematized in particular by the cooking routine in the Giulietto house-hold), and calls for a rearticulation of space and the sense of "home." It is, in other words, an event in a Derridean sense, the chance irruption of the alter-ity of the other that exceeds customary configurations of time and space. Indeed, according to Derrida, who makes a distinction between "invita-tion" and "visitation" in his work on the notion of hospitality, the "other" who arrives "is not necessarily an invited guest." S/he is a "visitor...who could come at any moment, without any horizon of expectation,...with the best or worst of intentions" ("Hostipitality" 17).[12] In this scene of *Sud Side Stori* s/he is, more specifically, an *arrivant(e)* (cf. Derrida, *Aporias* 33), some-body who not only comes unexpectedly but also arrives more than once, an "extravagant...stranger" (*Oth.* 1.1.138) who is already part of the fabric of the city and yet keeps on re-presenting herself as an unbearably proximate "entity." As such, s/he triggers fears and stimulates desires.

Needless to say, the local residents, who look down from their balconies, mostly react to this event with hostility. The derogatory term: "Cannibals!" summarizes this hostility, and is coupled with fierce gestures, screaming and fainting. There are of course exceptions. Uncle Vincenzo, a 70-year-old ver-sion of the Shakespearean Paris, throws kisses at the Nigerian women and confesses that he has "lost [his] head" for Romea. (He will later kill himself when Romea, in love with Toni, refuses to exchange sex for money). As to Toni Giulietto, he looks puzzled but not hostile, and he is distracted by the sudden appearance on his balcony of the Rock Mayor. The latter is the film's incarnation of Prince Escalus. Unlike Officer Schrank, the Prince-like figure in *West Side Story* who perpetuates racism against the Puerto Rican community, the Mayor of Palermo articulates his multicultural creed by appealing to Toni's sense of civic duty: "Toni. Toni! This is your Mayor speaking. We must be the new men of tolerance and integration. Toni! Listen to me. These are the words of the future: tolerance and integration...inte-gration...integration." The film's tragic ending, with the death of two lov-ers who belong to different ethnic communities, shows by implication that there is no "future" for "tolerance and integration," at least not in the form of the "liberal," multicultural notion of hospitality promoted by the Mayor. In fact, "tolerance and integration" hardly ever materialize in the film, and are of course also opposed by the local Mafia who vociferously supports Saint Rosalia and go as far as to blow up the workshop of the sculptor employed by the Mayor to make the statue of the Black Saint. Yet this does not mean, as we shall see, that hospitality—the hospitality of love—does not take place.

Many of the scenes immediately following the unexpected appropriation of *Vicolo Anello* by the Nigerian women show that in this Southern Italian city there is no access to the "other" except through stereotypes that are so deeply ingrained in the fabric of the "real" as to become second nature—one of the ways in which the film registers the play's notion of fate. After Romea falls in love with a white man, this also applies to Romea's friends as well as to the whole Nigerian community. To illustrate stereotyping, the camera moves back and forth between the Giulietto household and Romea's household, so that the spectator is made privy to the nasty remarks each group of characters makes on the other. Mercutia and Baldassarra, lying in bed with Romea, observe that the Giulietto women are monstrously overweight because of all the food they eat, including *pasta al forno, salsicce, arancini di riso*; Toni's aunties, who are joined by Maria (Toni's eternal betrothed, an overweight version of Rosaline, affectionately nicknamed "the whale"), are similarly disgusted by all the unwholesome food they imagine the Nigerian women consume and, in particular, they wonder why they always eat bananas. This juxtaposition of sequences clearly functions ironically: unlike Romea, Mercutia and Baldassarra are themselves rather overweight, and the only characters who eat bananas in the film are the Giulietto women.[13] It is a juxtaposition that shows the extent to which the "fundamentalist" assertion of one's culinary/cultural identity blurs into uncanny proximity, a point further emphasized by the scenes in which both Romea's friends and Toni's aunties resort to witch doctors—one black, the other white—to try to keep the lovers away from each other, with equally disastrous results.

The uncanny proximity between the two communities is not synonymous with peaceful coexistence. In fact, the implicit or explicit acknowledgment of proximity can—and often does—reactivate aggressivity and violence, and this not only applies to what happens in Torre's film after these alternating sequences. But proximity is also what can give hospitality a chance beyond the rhetoric of integration. If Romea "connects" with Toni Giulietto—and, as we shall see, without exchanging words—on a night when she comes back home with her friends and sees him standing on the balcony, it is because Tony himself experiences his own form of migrancy/exile, what Derrida may call a "disorder of identity [*trouble d'identité*]" (*Monolingualism* 14).[14] When we first encounter Toni, he is, like the Romeo described by his father in Shakespeare's play, "private in his chamber" (1.1.135). He "locks fair daylight out, / And makes himself an artificial light" (136–37). In fact, not only is his room removed from "fair daylight," which is one of the symptoms of his being displaced in a sunny Southern Italian city such as Palermo; it is also crammed with the artificial signs of kitsch: an old-fashioned microphone, life-size cardboard cutouts of himself, Elvis Presley, Little Toni (an Italian version of Presley) and Marilyn Monroe, a red heart-shaped bed adorned with flashing lights, and so on. It is in this room that Toni "sings himself," as it were, in rhyme, starting like this: "[e]ven though I am not perfect, it is me,

Toni Giulietto." An embodiment of anachrony—and in this, perhaps, he is also not entirely dissimilar to the pre-Juliet Romeo of Shakespeare's play— with his 1950s hair style and satin clothes, he tells us that he feels like an unwanted "guest" or even a prisoner in the Giulietto household, and that his "life" with the "harpies" is "hell." He adds that they desperately want him to get married to Maria, which he sees as exchanging claustrophobia with claustrophobia. The son of a sailor and a prostitute, Toni is thus not at home. But he is also not at home with himself. The song's lyrics define his identity as a movement away, indeed a migration, from a narrowly defined sense of identity, even if the "local" he aspires to abandon always-already speaks of an intermixing of traditions: "*Piazza Kalsa* [i.e., the most extended Arabic quarter of Palermo] is too narrow for me, and the *Vucciaria* is even more so. America is waiting for me. My dream is to go away."[15]

If the female-dominated Giulietto household is a domain of "hos(ti)pitality" (i.e., hospitality as hostility) (cf. Derrida, "Hostipitality"), the male-dominated tavern *Da Zu Pippo* (Uncle Pippo's), an Eastcheap-like "place of orgies, perdition and lust" (according to Giuseppona's definition in voice-over), where Toni takes refuge more than once after his meeting with Romea, does not seem to provide a viable alternative. It is not that Toni is not welcome in this tavern, in which religious images, garlic and dried peppers vie for attention. Quite the opposite: as he comes in for the first time almost all the customers stand up to embrace and kiss him, and they are all concerned about his emotional state. But the greeting of Toni—the greeting of the "foreign other" Toni has in fact become, to these "friends" at least, by getting involved with a "foreign woman"—is, in a Derridean sense, *conditional*. It takes place, that is, "on condition that the host, . . . the one who receives, lodges or *gives asylum* remains the *patron*, the master of the household, . . . and thereby affirms the law of hospitality as the law of the household, *oikonomia*, the law of his household, the law of a place (house, hotel, hospital, hospice, family, city, nation, language, etc.)" (4, Derrida's emphasis). In terms closer to the film, the welcoming of Toni is predicated upon the reassertion of the Mafioso-style bond between men over against the body of women, and the foreign black woman in particular. It is to remind him of the "law of the place"—what may be called the Palermitan law of homo(sti)pitality—that one of the punters warmly encourages Toni to speak to the Priest (*Zu Prete*), the film's version of Friar Laurence, a complex character with glasses and a moustache who is less sympathetic toward Toni's predicament than the friar is toward Romeo in Shakespeare's play. *Zu Prete* speaks like a Dalek from inside his confessional, a giant bottle, and warns him against inappropriate liaisons: "Toni! That Romea will ruin you." To stress his point, he continues: "Toni. You are not black. Are you black,

Toni?" Later on, as if to (re)indoctrinate him into homosociality, he invites him to join the dance of the (male) odalisques ("Enter the magic world of the male odalisques; stay with your friends, we are your friends; come into our arms, and you'll be very happy"), a reworking of Mercutio's ostentatious drag performance in Luhrmann's film that is no less problematic in terms of sexual politics than the latter. More generally, the seedy tavern *Da Zu Pippo* functions as a reservoir of most of the homosocial energies of the film. It is in this tavern that Toni's homosocially induced nightmares occur. According to the homosocial logic of the place, being with a woman—and a foreign black woman at that—is tantamount to being a cuckold, which is signified by the fact that he suddenly finds himself with horns protruding from his head. After this "translation," which is perhaps evocative of Bottom's transformation in *A Midsummer Night's Dream*, Toni falls into a jealous trance and, Othello-like, fantasizes about "the act of shame" that Romea has "[a] thousand times committed" (*Oth.* 5.2.218–19): we are shown crudely realistic grainy sequences in which a sweaty Palermitan man in a sleeveless shirt repeatedly "consort'st"(*Rom.* 3.1.43) with Nigerian prostitutes, and these sequences are interspersed with shots of Romea as well as of her Nigerian pimp who articulates, in English, his own sense of *oikonomia*: "[f]irst pay and then play."[16]

Toni reacts to the Priest's rhetorical question "Are you black, Toni?" by switching to the realm of musical with the song "I Wish I Was Black," a song that is vaguely reminiscent of doo-wop with a light touch of gospel. His temporary transformation into an Othello-like figure is thus, in a sense, the phantasmatic fulfillment of a wish, but one that brings utter discomfort, not least because it resurrects the stereotypical association of blackness and jealousy and thus fails to facilitate the sealing of the relationship between the two lovers, which is what the song's lyrics had aimed at: "I wish I was black. I wish God was black, too . . . He would unite our hearts." In fact, even before this problematic transformation, at the very moment when Toni performs his number, the film identifies his wish with a politically debilitating form of appropriation: the chorus surrounding him is made of white men all blacked up playing fake saxophones, which recalls the dubious tradition of the minstrel show with its white impersonators of black characters.

This is not to argue that the film endorses the position of the Priest, or that its overall logic coincides with Anita's advice to Maria in *West Side Story*: "Stick to your own kind." It is to point out that, as far as Toni is concerned, the rearticulation of identity away from its oppressive local anchoring in a Palermitan "home" is a movement that does not unproblematically lead to the acquisition of a new (black) home. In a symmetrical but inverted way, Romea's route also bears witness to the fact that there is no end to wandering, and that identity remains in transit. Romea's liaison with Toni means, first of all, the interruption of the local/global economy of accumulation based upon the trading of human flesh. In a sense, this is her way of "steal[ing] love's sweet bait from fearful hooks" (Chorus 2.8). In other words, once she starts refusing to have sex with her customers, her love story with Toni finds itself at odds with what her Nigerian pimp (Dennis Bovell), singing and dancing to the rhythm of hip-hop, calls (in English) the "situation of [his] love story" (i.e., the accumulation of money). Unwilling to play the prostitute, and thus unlikely to pay back the huge bondage fee, which is her only chance of returning to her Nigerian home, Romea adds displacement to displacement. After the balcony scene, she underlines her difference from her community during the alternating sequences mentioned earlier, when her friends Mercutia and Baldassarra hurl insults at the Palermitan women, and vice versa. Significantly, she does so for the first time by reciting in Italian the lines Romeo delivers toward the end of the balcony scene in Shakespeare's play: "Love goes toward love as schoolboys from their books, / But love from love, toward school with heavy looks" (2.1.201–2). Mercutia and Baldassarra react with bewilderment ("What's the matter with her?"; "She is not well"), which emphasizes the strangeness of Romea's speech.

And strange, indeed, is the Shakespearean language she uses: she misquotes the lines more than once,[17] each time approximating the "proper" Italian translation, but never quite getting it right. By doing so, she draws attention to the spectral remainder of translation within "proper" translation that affects the boundaries of the so-called target language. Moreover, since she (mis)translates the speech more than once, Romea is also herself the "schoolboy"/"schoolgirl" she speaks of, a "schoolboy"/"schoolgirl" who is trying to learn. But since she is also a woman in love, proficiency can only mean a movement away from proficiency (i.e., away from "books" and "school"). This highly self-deconstructive moment of the film shows that translation never ends. It also implicitly underlines that "Shakespeare-in-translation" is not a fixed entity but, rather, a process that does not necessarily guarantee a safe return back "home," in terms of adequacy or restitution of meaning. It is worth adding that the film does not contrast a "bad" translation of Shakespeare with a "good" one. Later on, when Saint Rosalia, speaking from inside her picture frame as usual, repeats the "same" lines that Romea quotes and misquotes, she provides a different version in Italian of these lines[18] but ironically concludes her performance by asking the spectator: "Did you understand them?" This re-marks the strangeness of the presence of the textual body of Shakespeare in the film, an inassimilable "body" for which there is no "proper" translation. Since Romea articulates her singular in-betweenness—she is not Italian but not quite Nigerian either after her meeting with Toni—through her (mis)appropriation of Shakespeare's language, one can argue that the film establishes a parallel between the (textual) body of Shakespeare and the body of the migrant. They are both "bodies" that cannot be properly hosted until hospitality remains *conditional* hospitality (i.e., hospitality that takes place on condition that the "proper" boundaries between host and guest be maintained). One needs to add that the law of conditional hospitality—hospitality as fundamentally hos(ti) pitality—is inseparable from the law of "proper" translation, and that the latter law is nothing but the policing of the boundaries of the host's language to which the "guest" is endlessly subjected. As Derrida suggests, the "law of the host—tends to begin by dictating the law of its language and its own acceptation of the sense of words" ("Hostipitality" 7).

Like a specter, Shakespeare's language inhabits the film without properly residing.[19] On the few other occasions when Shakespeare's language in translation appears, the film similarly underscores its strangeness, the extent to which it crosses or exceeds the boundaries of the "proper" and/or oddly intermixes with other "languages." When Romea, after being forced to consult the black witch-doctor, shouts in the streets: "*O Giulietto, Giulietto, perchè sei tu Giulietto?*", she uses lines that appear unproblematically to correspond to "O Romeo, Romeo, wherefore art thou Romeo?" (2.1.75). Yet these lines are subjected to the law of *contre-temps*: they are uttered out of context at an inappropriate time, *after* we have been shown Toni reinventing himself "beyond" the family name "Giulietto" by singing and dreaming of escape. One last instance is toward the end of the film, when a journalist playing himself, like in Luhrmann's film, speaks the concluding lines of Shakespeare's play in the form of a news report. In this case the film underscores the uncanniness of a language that is infinitely malleable—it is always-already "translatable" into something else and remediated—and yet remains a "strange body" by means of which one medium (i.e., film) is set against another (i.e., TV), one style of doing TV against another.[20]

* * *

In an interview Roberta Torre speaks in damning terms of the rise to power of corrupt media-tycoon-turned-politician Silvio Berlusconi, with his commercial TV stations that endlessly promulgate the cult of the "body beautiful" and have in fact produced over the years what she does not hesitate to call a "veritable physical mutation" of the body, some kind of "homogeneity of the [Italian] species" (Interview by Barbara Palombelli" n. pag.). Commenting on the body politics of the film and its relationship with the Berlusconian "Age of Appearance," Mariacristina Cavecchi points out that

Torre "takes a stand against the modern imperative of physical beauty at all costs...by picturing real people, men and women, unattractive and full of faults, who are miles away from both the clones of the Berlusconian era and from the two Hollywood icons Leonardo DiCaprio and Claire Danes" (101). In terms of my argument here, I want to underline that TV repeatedly appears in the film in the form of news commentary, and that it is not only in tune with the more generalized racism that pervades Palermo, even when it overtly speaks *for* integration and *against* racial hatred,[21] but it is also instrumental in bringing it into being. This is the case with the episode of the death by heart attack of Uncle Vincenzo, when the rumor that his death is linked to the fact that he has spent the night with Romea becomes a televisual truth that directly leads to the expulsion of the Nigerian community from Palermo

It is precisely in order to contrast the world of the two lovers with the vociferousness of the media—and TV in particular—that Torre decides to present the balcony scene as one in which Toni and Romea do not exchange words. They communicate with gestures, facial expressions and other parts of the body. We see Toni leaning on the railings of the balcony, stretching out his hand and his whole body, touching his heart and throwing passionate kisses at Romea; we see Romea reciprocating with movements of her body, with the light glinting off her golden earring,[22] and by repeatedly holding up the palm of her hand, as if to reference the "palm to palm" of another famous scene of Shakespeare's play (1.5.99). The language of the body repeatedly *tends* toward the spoken word and yet continuously stops on the brink of vocalization, so that what we have is mostly a suspended paradox,

Figure 4.1   The balcony scene.

a *simulation* of a scene from a silent movie that, furthermore, appears to develop in slow motion. In a sense, Shakespeare's language is conspicuous by its absence. This may have to do with Torre's attempt to combine a critique of the vociferousness of the media with a skeptical re-marking of the endless self-parodic global reproducibility of the language that accompanies the balcony scene (cf. Anderegg 56–58). But, if Shakespeare's language is absent as such, it also re-presents itself in a remediated and irremediably spectral form precisely as the *archaism* of the conventions of the silent movie, which are further emphasized by the ubiquitous melodramatic musical score in the background. The scene thus draws attention to the singular chance encounter between two "migrants." It is in fact a *tableaux vivant* that explores *tenderness* as a tending toward/attending to the "other," and even, allegorically, as a tending toward/attending to "Shakespeare" as "other" in non-Anglophone films.[23] This modality of approach toward, and response to, the "other" is not a form of appropriation, grasping or possession. It differs from, and defers, merging. In fact there is no contact at all between the two lovers in this scene. One may go as far as to argue that the scene shows the extent to which the relationship between Toni and Romea approximates what Emmanuel Levinas calls a "relation without relation," a relation that keeps the distance of infinite separation "without this distance destroying this relation and without this relation destroying this distance" (*Totality* 41).[24] Distance/difference *and* relation: this also points toward an undermining of the "conventional" notion of hospitality, which operates by "folding the foreign other into the internal law of the host" (Derrida, "Hostipitality" 7); by turning, that is, the "other" into the *host/self's* "other," an "entity" that the host/self produces, possesses and incorporates without remainder. Toni and Romea act in a liminal space outside the boundaries of "home," and they are completely oblivious to their surroundings. Subjected to an "asynchronous" temporality that rephrases the linear unfolding of time (e.g. their gestures in slow motion) and repeatedly threatens to come to a standstill, each of these two "migrants" plays host/guest to the other. As far as Toni and Romea are concerned, the fixity of the roles of "host" and "guest," which is synonymous with hos(ti)pitality, does not obtain. Neither does the rigidity of gender roles. In fact, both Toni and Romea appear to reinvent themselves beyond traditional gender roles, and this is most noticeable with Romea, who is undoubtedly more active than the Shakespearean Juliet or the "Victorian Juliet" in Luhrmann's film (Anderegg 62), while Toni shifts from a relative passivity to a more active position after the banishment of the Nigerian community. The malleability and permutation of roles facilitates the hospitality of love. The film ultimately bears out Derrida's assertion that the hospitality that takes place beyond conditional hospitality "can only last an instant" ("Hostipitality" 8), and that it remains to come from a future that does not present itself in the form of presence. Yet the French philosopher would probably be reluctant to associate unconditional hospitality with the hospitality of love. But I want to argue that the terms he uses to envisage this—im/possible—"beyond" are reminiscent of aspects of the *silent* affirmation of hospitality the two lovers enact in the balcony scene. For Derrida, "hospitality awaits [*attend*] its chance,...it holds itself out to [*se tend vers*] its chance beyond what it is, namely, the paralysis on the threshold which it is" (14).[25]

There is of course no home for this love that feeds on displacement. Neither is there "clos[ing]" of "hands with holy words" (2.5.6), not even in the form of a mock marriage before shop mannequins, as is the case with *West Side Story*. As pointed out earlier, for Toni there is a continuous migration *from* identity, an almost interminable and mobile process of identification that repeatedly raises specters of "home" that are problematic. As to Romea, given her doubly "unhousèd...condition" (*Oth.* 1.2.26) after her meeting with Toni, she metaphorically strives toward a Palermitan "home" to share with Toni, and it is in this context, as we have seen, that "Shakespeare-in-translation" emerges as an improbable sign of the "local." Significantly, this "Shakespeare" is also forced to cohabit with other paraphernalia of the "local" that turn out to be equally uninhabitable. Not only, that is, does Romea (mis)quote Shakespeare; she also starts listening to local popular music on the radio, which, once again, drives her friends Mercutia and Baldassarra crazy.[26] Ironically, the truly local Palermitan music is *Neapolitan* music—the "music that makes you dream," as Giuseppona puts it in voice-over. Speaking of so-called traditional Neapolitan music to make a more general point about music as a site of potential transit and translation through which the Mediterranean can be re-imagined beyond the homogeneous narration of the Nation, Anglo-Neapolitan critic and philosopher Iain Chambers points out that "the melisma and micro-tones so crucial to the lamenting tonalities of Neapolitan voice perhaps owe much more to the musical scales of the Arabic *maqám* (modal mood) than to the disciplined parameters of European harmony." Neapolitan songs, he adds, are "musical cousin to the flamenco of Seville and the *fado* of Lisbon, as well as to...the improvised music of *ughniyna* in Cairo...and, more recently, Algerian *raï*" (*Mediterranean* 45). The specific "traditional" song Romea listens to, Carmelo Zappulla's *Siempe* (*Forever*), extends the re-routing of musical roots that Chambers underlines. Its lyrics in Neapolitan dialect fit in with Romea's predicament as a woman in love. But they are also lyrics that are sung to the rhythm of Argentinean tango, itself a hybrid tradition, and thus the song frustrates any sense of a clearly identifiable "home."[27] But of course it is not only in the context of Romea's fraught search for a new home that music undermines, to refer to Chambers again, "any obvious anchorage in a timeless localism that claims universal validity through its assumed uniqueness" (*Mediterranean* 47). Throughout the film music and dance symptomatize the lack of cultural homogeneity. They often become paradigmatic of the wider process of "translation," which blurs the boundaries between the local and the global and produces some kind of uncanny overlapping between a number of cultural constructs that are supposedly rooted and idiosyncratic, from culinary practices to magic/religion, from body fashioning to crime. Moreover, the language of music and dance re-presents itself, as we shall see, as an uncanny supplement to the Shakespearean textual constraints that inexorably lead the film to its tragic ending.

These constraints make themselves increasingly felt as the film draws to a close. After the banishment of Romea, Toni steals the money Giuseppona has accumulated for the celebration of Saint Rosalia, presumably to run away from Palermo and join his beloved. With nobody else to rely on, he visits the tavern *Da Zu Pippo* once again. Like any good confessor/superego, *Zu Pippo* already knows about Toni's crime but offers to help. He supplies him with a "magic sleeping potion" (a *pozione* made of peppers) so that he can fake his own death and leave Palermo for good. At this point Toni performs a song whose lyrics indiscriminately appropriate and recycle Juliet's doubts about the Friar's motives in 4.3 as well as Romeo's "strange dream" (5.1.7) at the beginning of act five of Shakespeare's play: "Are you sure I'll fall asleep?...I'm having an ominous premonition...I sleep very little, I sleep very badly...A recurring dream torments me." In the end he decides to drink the "potion." His body in the "borrowed likeness of shrunk death" (4.1.104) will later be discovered by his aunties, who have brought a cake to his room probably to mend his broken heart. While in Africa, an Africa that is strongly reminiscent of Palermo, except for a few notes of local color, Romea reads about Toni's death. She jumps on a train directed to Palermo (in the film Africa is just as close to Palermo as Mantua is to Verona in Shakespeare's play) and urges it to go faster with the song *Corri treno corri* (*Run, Train, Run*). Back in *Vicolo Anello*, she finds Toni's body lying on his heart-shaped bed and surrounded by cardboard cutouts of his pop idols. After sobbing and blaming him for not having waited for her, she kills herself with a dagger she has stolen from her Nigerian pimp. (Like the Juliet in Luhrmann's film, Toni wakes up just as she is about to take her life but cannot avoid the catastrophe). Significantly, lights with the colors of the Italian flag (i.e., the *tricolore*, made of white, red, and green) cover both her arms and the dagger as she performs some kind of hara-kiri. In the meanwhile Toni's aunties, in extreme close-up and in a Brechtian fashion, tell the camera: "She killed herself for him"; "What an odd story"; "What a trag-edy." At this point everything goes "live," broadcasted in black and white as "breaking news," and we witness Toni's murder by two old men who are members of Giuseppona's entourage. As the film switches back to color, we see the bodies of the two lovers lying on the floor next to one another, ironi-cally draped with the lights of the national *tricolore*, which shows that in Berlusconi's Italy, racist hostility toward the miscegenation of bodies is not merely a local Palermitan matter.

The film does not end with the journalist delivering the concluding speech of Shakespeare's play in Italian, a speech to which I referred earlier. First of all, we hear Giuseppona's voice from beyond the grave repeating the last three lines, which confers an even more spectral quality to a speech whose origin has already been put under erasure by processes of surroga-tion and remediation, both locally (i.e., previous news report) and globally (i.e., Luhrmann's film). Second, as the end credits begin to roll, they are suddenly interrupted by Saint Rosalia who tells us that she has forgotten to tell us that she has finally agreed to share her place in heaven (i.e., in the picture frame) with Saint Benedict the Moor. She also asserts that things in "heaven" are much easier than "down below," but she reminds us that not even in "heaven" they "are all the same" (and she repeats "all the same" an indefinite number of times). Indeed, a close-up of the picture frame clarifies what she means: we see her reclining on a crocodile in a Cleopatra-like pose with a black servant—presumably the newly integrated Saint Benedict—fanning her, which ironically shows once again the "unconscious" of the "liberal" notion of hospitality and integration and, more specifically, its

Figure 4.2 Romea's suicide.

disquieting contiguity with Orientalist fantasies of the "other." The last word, however, is left to the music, with the soundtrack *Sud Side Stori*, which is an incredible, and incredibly effective, mélange of global, national, and local languages and music styles. The soundtrack's lyrics speak of the "other" as an exotic body to be explored, "dis-covered" and possessed: "Sud Side Stori . . . Come here from six' clock at night onwards and you'll find the darkest Africa . . . your black woman . . . your woman in a shop window." But the "thirty thousand *lire*" needed for this journey into the unknown additionally become the spectral "thirty thousand feet" that incessantly "move and dance." They "move and dance" *a sud del mondo*, exceeding the bounds of this local performance and enacting a *rapprochement* between two of the Souths of the world. In fact, as the soundtrack plays on over the end credits, we cannot fail to recall what is perhaps the film's extensive transfiguration of the play's "love-performing night" (3.2.5): the visually excessive collective central scene when the Nigerian prostitutes sing and dance in the streets of Palermo, selling their bodies but also "carnivalizing" and appropriating the body of the city. This performance, in which the rhythmic movements of the body combine with a music whose "local accents . . . are crossed by transnational modalities" (Chambers, *Mediterranean* 46), exposes the neurosis of homogeneity that obstinately permeates the Palermitan cultural landscape. But I want to retrace my steps a little and return to the "feet" that "move and dance." These "feet," according to the song's lyrics, are caught in a vertiginous movement and seem to acquire a force of their own, as if they were on a "merry-go-round" (*come fosse un girotondo*). The whirling movement of these feet makes them uncannily resemble the "feet" of Shakespearean verse. These are "feet" that unceasingly "dance" and circulate in a spectral and unpredictable way on the world stage, continuously crossing national boundaries and enacting rearticulations of the "global" through the "local" and vice versa, without ever finding a fixed point of anchorage.

Ramona Wray has recently pointed out that there is "a wealth of . . . Shakespearean filmic initiatives that unfold in languages other than English" (279) that "have slipped under the radar of mainstream criticism" (280). *Sud Side Stori* is one such film. Yet the film deserves airing not only because it is not often included in the "canon" of non-Anglophone Shakespearean films, but also because it trenchantly interrogates the politics of cultural homogeneity and attitudes of racial hostility toward the migrant (even when the latter present themselves under the guise of "liberal" multiculturalism), which extend far beyond the film's fictional location in Southern Italy. *Sud Side Stori* often pursues this interrogation by insisting on the "foreignness" of Shakespeare and associating it with the "foreignness" of the migrant(s). This is a "foreignness" that *remains* foreign as the film develops, and it is made even more so when the language of Shakespeare-in-translation is remediated through the language of music and dance, or the conventions of silent movies Roberta Torre discreetly reinvents. But then, one may ask, just how "native"—how much "at home"—is the Shakespeare of *Anglophone* films?

CHAPTER 5

"Shakespeare in the Extreme": Ghosts and Remediation in Alexander Fodor's *Hamlet*

My body's gone / But my eyes remain / Hovering, witnessing / Cold as a ghost.

— Marillion, *The Invisible Man*

Shot entirely in high-definition digital, premièred at the Cannes film festival and subsequently released in DVD format with a 12-page booklet and extra material, Alexander Fodor's experimental low-budget adaptation of *Hamlet* (2006) blatantly presents itself as some kind of "Shakespeare in the extreme."[1] And, indeed, Fodor's film contains many elements that could be classified as "extreme" when compared to Shakespeare's *Hamlet*: Polonius becomes Polonia (Lydia Piechowiak), a scheming femme fatale who would not be out of place in a film *noir*, and goes as far as to seduce a Reynaldo-turned-Reynalda with luscious cherries and red wine; Ophelia (Tallulah Sheffield) is a drug addict who relies on her elder sister Polonia for her drug supply; Horatio (Katie Reddin-Clancy) switches gender; Laertes (Jason Wing) is a vicious Cockney thug; the Ghost (James Frail) is omnipresent. Yet, if by "extreme" one means a drastic distance from Shakespeare's language, Fodor's version can hardly be said to be so radical: it does not alter the lines from the play it keeps, except when it needs to meet the changes it introduces in terms of gender and kinship. (For instance, Polonia is referred to by Ophelia and Laertes as "sister.") This chapter explores the double-edged notion of "Shakespeare in the extreme" in Fodor's film. It argues that this is a strategy of remediation that predominantly insists on the "out-of-jointedness" of time and space, and that it articulates itself as a process that frequently evokes ghosts, including, as the film performs a series of self-allegorizing moves, the ghost of the "original" and, more generally, the ghost of a (Shakespearean) textual *corpus* that refuses to stay put.

Not unlike other recent Shakespeare films, the paradigmatic example of which being perhaps Baz Luhrmann's *William Shakespeare's Romeo + Juliet* (1996), Fodor's *Hamlet* attempts to grab the viewer's attention from its very outset. The initial scene, which takes place before the opening credits, borrows the cinematic style of supernatural thrillers to introduce us to one of the film's most striking revisions of the "original": Ophelia's addiction. We see Ophelia rummaging through a closet in the dark, presumably looking for drugs; we hear an enigmatic offscreen voice that leads her through a corridor that vaguely recalls the terrifying interiors of *The Shining* into a brightly-lit room (i.e., the "ghost room," as the director calls it in the DVD commentary); we see her picking up a hypodermic needle lying on a table and shooting up a dose of heroin; we then witness her violent untimely death while the Ghost, clad in a retro, long black leather coat, crosses the room and watches impassively. It is worth adding that after injecting heroin and experiencing a supreme moment of bliss, Ophelia turns her head around more than once, and begins to act as if she could hear, along with the viewer, the crying of seagulls. Combined with the extra-diegetic splashing of waves that obsessively reverberates in the background, this aspect of the scene invites a rereading of her predicament within the sequence. It suggests, that is, that Ophelia is simultaneously in the ghost room *and* elsewhere, perhaps under water in the throes of death while dreaming of one last fix as a means of escape.

This scene re-presents itself in its "proper" place later on in the film. (This time it is not an uninterrupted sequence but is part of a montage; it alternates with the dialogue between Claudius and Laertes in 4.7 in which they finalize their "cunnings" against Hamlet [4.7.128]).[2] It ends with a final shot of the dead body of Ophelia lying on a beach, a body whose pose is strikingly similar to the one she adopts in the ghost room. Yet the repetition of the Ophelia sequence is far from signifying the reassertion of the truth of the "original": Ophelia's death is in fact a "muddy death" (4.7.155), a death by water. Reiteration is a process of transformation. What we witness is a compressed visual remediation of Ophelia's fate, almost a photographic still frozen in time, which is superimposed upon the previous radical re-imagining of the last moments of Ophelia's life. Neither of these instances of death erase the other. They uncannily coexist. To adopt the theoretical considerations on performance developed by W. B. Worthen in relation to

Baz Luhrmann's *William Shakespeare's Romeo+Juliet*, this is an example of how Fodor's adaptation is not "a performance *of* the [original] text." It is not, to clarify Worthen's argument, an unproblematic reiteration of a fixed and stable entity called *Hamlet*, an entity that somehow pre-exists—and authorizes—performance or adaptation. It is not "a translation of the work but...an iteration of the work, an iteration that...invokes and displaces a textual 'origin'" ("Performativity" 1104). Put differently, in Fodor's version the "original" is (retrospectively) *produced* as one of the film's intertexts, and is forced to enter into dialogue with other intertexts and/or inhabit a number of "citational environment[s]" (1104).[3] This is a process that blurs the boundaries between a "before" and an "after," between the "first time" of the "original" and the "second time" of repetition and remediation, as is clearly the case with the Ophelia sequences. In the film, the "ghost room" often becomes an emblem of this blurring. Whatever happens in this "room" is itself *and* something else. This room is an unconscious-like place where the logic of contradiction and the linearity of time do not apply. It is a place where "out-of-jointedness" rules with its specters.[4]

One of the most prominent citational environments established by the film is undoubtedly that of contemporary youth drug culture, and it is the insertion of the "original" play-text within this citational environment that allows the film to update and recycle the system of gender constraints to which Ophelia is subjected. Gender oppression becomes synonymous with bodily addiction. This is nowhere more explicit than in the scene in which Polonia rebukes Ophelia for being a credulous "green girl" (1.3.101), and warns her against Hamlet's "tenders of...affection" (99–100) while helping her to shoot up heroine. Polonia's words of advice (and implied threats) are an antidote against the "poison" of desire, the burning of "blood" (116)—in Laertes's previous words, "the shot and danger of desire" (35) that is "most imminent" in "the morn and liquid dew of youth" (42, 41). But they are supplemented by an antidote (i.e., the addictive substance) that is itself a poison, a kind of Derridean *pharmakon* (cf. *Dissemination* 95–172), in that its incorporation turns Ophelia into a pawn in Polonia's scheming and traps her in a circle without future that potentially inscribes not only the death of *sexual* desire but death itself.[5] The repetition compulsion of the "toxic drive" to which Ophelia is subjected also functions ironically, in that it shows how *un*safe is the "safety" (1.3.43) that the system of constraints regulating behavior—in this case, gender behavior—supposedly ensures for its "weak" subjects.[6] A "green girl" such as Ophelia is, from the point of view of the dominant, never quite safe (hence the "un/safe" injection), no matter how much she keeps her own self "in the rear of [her] affection" (34). (The confined space in which Polonia and Ophelia find themselves after the party celebrating Claudius's takeover, a narrow room with blinds pulled down, makes the whole scene claustrophobic, and this enhances the sense of unsafe safety.) Moreover, the need to supplement words uttered from a position of authority with the injection of an "artificial" substance should give one pause. It symptomatizes the extent to which Ophelia's subjection is subjection "in the extreme." Yet it also implicitly underlines the fragility of ideological interpellation, Ophelia's unwillingness to spontaneously subscribe with her whole self to the "organicist" metaphors of the body politic that permeate both Laertes and Polonia's speeches, and in particular to the role of the younger sister who is *naturally* in need of guidance. The final shot of the scene emblematizes the tension between her supposedly "natural" subjection and the incorporation of an "artificial" substance that perhaps reproduces subjection differently. We are shown a close-up of Ophelia absorbedly looking at the prominent needle in the foreground and uttering the following words, perhaps ironically, while Polonia is entirely out of sight: "I shall obey my sister" (136; "my sister" instead of "my lord").

"Addicted" (2.1.19), in the mildly negative connotation of being inclined toward something, occurs only once in Shakespeare's *Hamlet*, in the context of the dialogue between Polonius and Reynaldo in 2.1. It is one of those "forgeries" (20) and "slight sullies" (40) Reynaldo is asked to "put on" (19) Laertes (along with gaming, drinking, fencing, swearing, and so on), one of the "indirections" (66) in Polonius's strategy of surveillance by means of which he intends to find out the "truth" (63) about Laertes's behavior. In Fodor's film, as mentioned earlier, the dialogue that corresponds to 2.1 is between two female characters, and the scene provides a striking example of how an accurate reproduction of Shakespeare's lines functions, through performance, as a displacement of the "truth" of the "original." Displacement, that is, is not confined to scenes that dispense with Shakespeare's lines altogether, as is the case with the initial Ophelia scene. In short, to borrow from Cartelli and Rowe's study of Shakespeare on film, the scene shows that Fodor's adaptation is one of those experimental "camp" films, as opposed to films that operate in the mode of "revival," that "maintain a measured distance from their source-texts—even when they launch most fully into them" (24).[7]

Through a number of close-ups slowly following upon one another, the viewer is invited to enter Polonia's *boudoir*. Or, perhaps, s/he is forced to occupy the position of the voyeur peeping into it. The highly theatrical and stylized mise-en-scène, with its various tonalities of red (i.e., from the cherries to the wine, from the fabric of the furniture to Polonia's silk dressing gown), provides a radical decontextualization and recontextualization of Shakespeare's lines. It implicitly inserts them in the citational environment of a film *noir*, an environment in which Polonia qua femme fatale moves with incredible ease. Indeed, the lines themselves become elaborate "items" in a game of (lesbian) seduction. Through the actresses' performance, they are invested with an unusual erotic charge. They are not so much *about* the "dis-covery" of the truth of Laertes's behavior as an exploration of the extent to which talking about transgression is itself a form of transgression that affects the position of the subject of enunciation as well as that of the acquiescent listener. Even Polonius's "comic" forgetfulness—"what was I about to say? By the mass, I was about to say something" (50–51)—is "translated" as awkward hesitation that is imputable to the *crescendo* of sexual tension. In a sense, "unreclaimèd blood"—one of Laertes's hypothetical attributes—claims central place, with all its "savageness" (35). Its "fiery" (34) redness colors and permeates everything, from the mise-en-scène to the logic of the signifier. It is, indeed, "of general assault" (36). One could go as far as to argue, from a Lacanian perspective, that some kind of *jouis-sense*—the enjoyment of the signifier "impregnated" with *jouissance*; the enjoyment of what is left over from the signifier's ability to signify—infiltrates and undermines the circuit of communication and meaning (cf. Zizek, *Looking* 39, 129).

The scene is indisputably "extreme": one may want to argue that it does not make sense at all as a Shakespearean scene. It concludes with Polonia moving behind Reynalda's back and sliding the belt of her dressing gown across her throat while saying, with accurate infidelity, "God b'wi' ye. Fare ye well" (69), which points to yet another erotic game or, more probably, to the femme fatale's inexplicable murderous will. (At this point Ophelia enters the room and interrupts whatever it is that is going on.) However, no matter what one thinks of this scene, it illustrates what happens when the "logic-and-deduction" quasi-detective model of "dis-covery" (a model so often embodied by Polonius in the "original" text) evokes *jouissance* but fails to contain it as a mere and temporary diversion on the way to truth. It reminds the viewer, that is, of what *exceeds* this model, and postulates a relationship between this excess and the *noir* universe. The repeated appearance of the ghost throughout the scene, who seems to embody some kind of mysterious force acting through the characters and malevolently guiding them, points in the same direction.

To raise the question of the kinship between *Hamlet* and the realm of the *noir*, as the film implicitly and explicitly does, is not as far fetched as it might at first appear. It is a question that has been at the center of recent reinterpretations of the complex cultural phenomenon called *Hamlet*, and especially of the vexed liaison between Old Hamlet and his son. As Linda Charnes succinctly puts it, *Hamlet* is "the first fully *noir* text in western literature, and prince Hamlet the first *noir* detective. Or rather, the first *noir* revenger" (31). For Courtney Lehmann, Shakespeare's text inscribes the memory of its future transpositions into another medium, the cinematic medium, the memory of what "passeth [theatrical] show" (1.2.85). It articulates "the desire-called-cinema," which is more specifically a desire for the *film noir* (*Shakespeare Remains* 90, 109–10). Crucial to both critics is Slavoj Zizek's Lacanian reinterpretation of the distinction between the "classical" logic-and-deduction detective novel (and film) and the "anti-logic" (in terms of space, time, and causality) of the so-called hard-boiled novel (and film *noir*). For Zizek, "the logic-and-deduction novel...relies on the consistent big Other" (*Enjoy* 171), the Symbolic Father, the Father who is always-already dead and thus facilitates one's entry and integration into the Symbolic framework (i.e., the realm of the Law) as well as the possibility of narration. The realm of the *noir* symptomatizes, instead, a disturbance in the field of the Big Other, which is also a disturbance in terms of identification and narration: "the *noir* universe is characterized by a radical split, a kind of structural imbalance, as to the possibility of narrativization" (171). Underneath the Father as the (apparently) neutral placeholder of the Law, there lurks another Father, according to Zizek, a *Père-Jouissance*, a Father who enjoys too much. This is "the obscene, uncanny shadowy double of the Name of the Father,...an excessively *present* father, who, as such, cannot be reduced to the bearer of a symbolic function" (180). By aligning *Hamlet* with the *noir* universe, both Linda Charnes and Courtney Lehmann underline the "obscene" aspect of Hamlet *senior*, a Father who is *un*dead and whose symbolic function uneasily combines with the intermittent but vivid evocation of his "enjoyment," his being "cut off even in the blossom of [his] sins" (1.5.76), "full of bread, / With all his crimes broad blown" (3.3.80–81). It is because of this "enjoyment" that he is "confined to fast in fires / Till the foul crimes done in [his] days of nature / Are burnt and purged away" (1.5.11–13). As Charnes argues,

> At once delivering the injunction to "revenge his foul and unnatural murder" and revealing his own sinister "double," the ghost commands Hamlet to "Remember me" even as he makes the task impossible, delivering the mandate from a corrupted and compromised position that can scarcely lay claim to moral authority.

"The ghost's disclosure," she adds, "reveals a figure hopelessly at odds with the 'Hyperion' Hamlet wishes to champion" (32).

Fodor's film accentuates the ghost's distance from Hamlet's idealized picture of his father. In the film the ghost is very much unlike "Hyperion," and

Figure 5.1 Meeting the ghost.

more similar to a "satyr" (1.2.140). For instance, after the Ophelia scene, and as the initial credits roll, we are offered a framed close-up of each of the main characters. In the case of the ghost (James Frail) we are shown a "picture" (3.4.52) of him lasciviously and threateningly licking his lips, as if to announce that what we are about to see is "the thing" (2.2.606)—*his* thing—wherein he'll catch the conscience of all the characters. He is undoubtedly the incarnation of an uncanny "ob-scene" force, as he repeatedly seems to be pulling the strings from behind the scenes. I have already mentioned his role as impassive witness of Ophelia's death as well as his intrusive presence in the background during the dialogue between Polonia and Reynalda. His first meeting with Hamlet in the "ghost room," a place over which he presides with the help of little children, who are perhaps simulacra of Hamlet himself, confirms his viciousness.[8] He is not content with uttering the words "Mark me" (1.5.2); he thumps Hamlet twice, perhaps to make sure, by means of a tangible sign, that his "commandment all alone shall live" (102) in the memory of his son. Moreover, he implicitly and/or explicitly chastises him through the use of a "re-markable" cavernous voice that is made even more disturbing by being amplified and distorted.

In a sense, Hamlet gets what he deserves because in Fodor's version he is an estranged and wayward son. He first appears at the party in honor of the dead king, and most certainly does *not* "with [his] vailèd lids / Seek for [his] noble father in the dust" (1.2.70–71).[9] He seems to enjoy the anonymity the party provides. Leaning on a wall, he observes what is going on with narcissistic detachment and a brazen face, while periodically exchanging glances

with Ophelia. When Horatio, Marcellus, and Barnardo take him aside to
reveal the apparition of the ghost, he reacts with extreme skepticism. He
continues to eat grapes as he speaks to them, as if to underline his incredulity. Moreover, the battery of questions about the ghost's countenance
("Armed, say you?"; "From top to toe?"; "Then saw you not his face?"; "What
looked he, Frowningly?"; "Pale or red?", and so on [1.2.226–42]) is far from
articulating a sense of growing anxiety on his part. These questions become,
instead, a way of mocking what he sees as his interlocutors' belief in the
supernatural. If he agrees to meet them "upon the platform" (251), which
is a beach in Southend-on-sea, it is only in the hope of proving how wrong
they are.[10] In short, he adopts the same incredulous pose as Horatio's at the
beginning of the first scene of the original text (1.1.21–28).

This is not to exclude that Hamlet may be putting on a "show" (1.2.85)
at the party, with a white shirt rather than an "inky cloak" (77). In any
case, the film underlines the traumatic effect of Hamlet's meeting with his
father's spirit, which is simultaneously a "real" meeting and an unconscious
experience with nightmarish overtones triggered by the shrieking voice of a
perhaps not-so-innocent child who may be Hamlet himself. Once Hamlet
realizes that he is back on the "platform"/beach, he starts behaving in a
disturbed and disconcerting manner, as if indeed "he had been loosèd out
of hell" (2.1.84). For instance, he shouts the lines that mostly emblematize the uncanniness of his experience in the "ghost room" as well as his
newly acquired openness to the alterity of the apparition. When Horatio
says: "It is wondrous strange," he lashes out: "And therefore as a stranger
give it welcome. / There are more things in heaven and earth, Horatio, /
Than are dreamt of in our philosophy" (1.5. 166–69). However, the lines
that conclude the first act of the play ("The time is out of joint. O cursèd
spite / That ever I was born to set it right!," 189–90) do not appear in the
film. What we have instead, just before the scene with Polonia and Reynalda,
is yet another example of the "original" text emerging in a displaced form
through processes of surrogation and remediation. The "dis-jointedness" of
time becomes a fragmented narrative in which flashbacks, flash-forward,
and "real" diegetic time disquietingly overlap. Moreover, this narrative is
told visually in a different way in each of the three sections that split the
screen.

The discontinuity of narrative combines with the "de-centering" of the
viewer's perspective effected by the split screens to suggest a radical revision of categories of space, time, and causality. In a sense, throughout this
montage the time of the ghost—what Nicholas Royle calls *Hamlet*'s "ghost
tense" (*In Memory* 29–34)—reigns supreme. Meanwhile, the "recycling"
of the concluding lines of 1.5. is also pursued through the audio track,

Figure 5.2 "The time is out of joint."

"Invisible Man" by Marillion. Its lyrics speak of a "world" that has "gone mad." They express a sense of mourning for a self that has "evaporated." They also appear to "translate" the play's "cursèd spite" into the invisible man's inability to intervene in the series of events he scrutinizes: "My body's gone / But my eyes remain / Hovering, witnessing / Cold as a ghost." There is, perhaps, no hope to "set it right" (1.5.190). In other words, what one witnesses—and the accumulation of memories this entails—fails to provide a cue for action, which is also a way of addressing through the medium of music one of the vexed questions that *Hamlet* raises: how does one reconcile memory and revenge?[11]

* * *

In Shakespeare's play, Hamlet notoriously responds to the ghost's injunction "Remember me" (1.5.91) by promising that "from the table of [his] memory / [He]'ll wipe away all trivial fond records, / All saws of books, all forms, all pressures past / That youth and observation copied there," and by enacting it somehow through the act of writing: "'Adieu, adieu, remember me'" (98–101, 112). This has led critics such as Linda Charnes to argue that the play articulates the patriarchal fantasy of cloning (53–72). As a clone, Hamlet's only history is that of his donor ("Remember *me*," emphasis

added), a history that is "unmixed with baser [female] matter" (1.5.104).[12]
In Fodor's film the ghost's "commandment" (102) lives on especially in the
form of Hamlet's obsessive, reiterated visualization of a scene that shows
the half-naked dead body of his father lying on a slab in what looks like
a morgue, while each of the main characters (including Hamlet), dressed
in black, kisses him on the lips. It is a traumatic memory, and whenever it
surfaces, Hamlet is projected back into the "ghost room," his dead father's
realm. This may be symptomatic of the fact that Hamlet's memory is the
(downloaded) memory of the other/ghost (cf. Charnes 66–69), a memory
that incorporates the trace of the other to an extreme. To pursue this line of
argument, it is worth pointing out that within the economy of the film this
is a scene that, by presenting Hamlet's father in a passive posture, diverts
attention from the active, malevolent role he consistently plays. It disguises
the fact that the donor (i.e., the ghost) acts through his replica (i.e., Hamlet)
to seek revenge. What is also striking about this scene is that it offers a
simulacrum of a funerary rite; or rather, it presents a funerary rite and its
"dark" underside, its *envers*. It is a funerary rite that does not "properly"
take place, not least because it does not take place in its "proper" place—a
cinematic emblem of the "maimèd rites" (5.1.214) that Shakespeare's play
continually evokes. It centers around an excessively present body that is *neither* alive *nor* dead and buried, a body that seems to exert a magnetic pull on
the characters in mourning, turning formal obsequies into a rite of morbid
eroticism. In Lacanian terms this is a body that situates itself in the realm
of the "in-between-two-deaths," a body that is still infused with *jouissance*
and thus cannot be properly symbolized and/or find its suitable place in the
symbolic "text" of tradition (cf. Zizek, *Looking* esp. 23).[13] This is undoubtedly a "Shakespeareccentric" scene. And yet, paradoxically, it can be seen as
an allegory of the functioning of the Shakespearean *corpus*, a *corpus* that is
similarly *un*dead, an irreducible and indeterminate ensemble of marks that
lends itself to a multiplicity of adaptations in a variety of media, and refuses
to be integrated into any definite symbolic framework.

Significantly, the morgue scene re-presents itself in a condensed form
both at the beginning and at the end of what is perhaps the quintessential
Shakespearean speech, the "To be or not to be" speech. It also reappears
more than once while Hamlet is delivering it. The soliloquy thus seems to be
an attempt to "archive" the traumatic haunting memory of a father who has
only apparently just been laid to rest. But Hamlet's speech is also, I want to
suggest, a way of coming to terms with the "extreme" version of Shakespeare
within which it is included, an "extreme" version that finds in the morgue
scene one of its most emblematic moments. This coming to terms goes hand
in hand with the attempt to play one medium against another.

Peter Donaldson has often emphasized that a number of Shakespearean films, especially recent ones, display a "sustained thematic attention to media regimes and practices," and that in these films "media themes rise to the level of subject matter, vying for attention with and sometimes supplanting the story line of the source play" ("Bottom" 23). Fodor's *Hamlet* by no means draws attention to the cinematic medium it utilizes, or the other media it includes, in a sustained and coherent manner. It does not become, that is, a self-conscious media allegory in the way Luhrmann's *William Shakespeare's Romeo + Juliet* or Almereyda's *Hamlet 2000* arguably are. Nonetheless, the "To be or not to be" scene shows a high degree of cross-media self-reflexiveness, since it introduces a "new" medium that is meant to counter-act Hamlet's traumatic memory as well as the (cinematic) medium in which this memory finds expression: we see Hamlet in the same room as the one used for the ghost-room scenes; he picks up an "archaic" piece of equipment, a Ferguson reel-to-reel tape recorder and moves it to the center of the room; after a few poignant pauses, he starts recording/delivering the speech.

The "ideological" fantasy articulated by this scene is that recording on an old-fashioned tape recorder is a form of remediation that is closer to the "original" than other processes of surrogation. When Hamlet starts the tape recorder, the film implies, he does not erase or destroy, but simply adds something to what has already been recorded or transcribed. (An adaptation of *Hamlet* is, in this sense, an unproblematic, and ultimately unnecessary, supplement to the text of tradition). The assumption is also that recording may magically prompt the emergence of a benign ghost; or, alternatively, that recording may trigger the appearance of a (ghostly) "original" that is end-lessly reproducible in an accurate and uncomplicated way. Yet the end of the scene shows that there is hardly any solution to the trauma; and, by implica-tion, that recording as a technique of archiving *can* and *does* work against itself. The morgue scene that is beginning to take shape after Hamlet's lines "And lose the name of action" (3.1.90) *does* fade out, as if to signify that the undead body of Hamlet's father has been dispelled. But what we find in its stead is *Hamlet*'s body, a body that is lying in the same horizontal position as his father's in the morgue, and then we see Ophelia bending over to kiss his lips. Repetition reasserts itself, as well as the threat of the *ad infinitum* prolif-eration of clones, which is the uncanny, reverse side of recording as exact and faithful reproduction. Allegorically, the Shakespearean *corpus* re-presents itself as a spectral "Thing" that insists and persists (Derrida, *Specters* 22).

The "To be or not to be" scene thus shows that "Shakespeare in the extreme" is not incompatible with what Richard Burt calls "Shakespearecentric" con-cerns ("Introduction" 5). The self-deconstructive dynamic in which the scene is involved does not erase, that is, the desire for something that approximates the "original," some kind of "archive fever."[14] In fact the film continually shifts from "Shakespeareccentric" to "Shakespearecentric" concerns and back again. Fodor uses experimental (i.e., "Shakespeareccentric") cinematic techniques such as split screens, jerky camera movements, freeze frames, CCTV-like sequences (the latter especially in the scene between Hamlet and Gertrude in the closet). He also introduces a "grainy" black-and-white silent film within the film, which replaces the play within the play, and draws attention to the meta-cinematic aspects of the film by using one-sided mirrors as opaque screens behind which the characters/spectators hide or even get what they (supposedly) deserve. (Examples are the "To be or not to be" scene, the "nunnery scene," and the scene between mother and son in Gertrude's closet, in which Polonia, hiding behind the one-sided mirror, is shot dead.) Yet these "extreme" interventions do not fail to recall forms of mediatization employed in previous *Shakespearean* films, and thus somehow reestablish the film's "Shakespearecentricity," what counts as Shakespeare at the beginning of the third millennium. (For instance, CCTV-style flickerings and the film within the film implicitly or explicitly function as intertextual references to Almereyda's *Hamlet*. The one-sided mirror recalls both Branagh's and Almereyda's *Hamlet*). Fodor's experimental techniques are juxtaposed to more "naturalistic" cinematic strategies that attempt to convey, especially when combined with an emphasis on the natural delivery of lines, the impression of reality, a reality effect. This is especially the case with the scenes with Rosencrantz, Guildenstern, and Hamlet. In these scenes, which have the feel of an improvisational workshop, each of the characters in turn speaks directly to the camera, and the camera itself becomes a character. They are meant to have an antielitist edge and bring the audience closer to the Bard.[15] Yet, this "naturalism" is also a move away from "Shakespeare," in that it evokes "Shakespeareccentric" cinematic genres such as documentary film or even *cinema-verité*. Both "Shakespearecentric" and "Shakespeareccentric" concerns show that there is no unmediated access to "Shakespeare": the film cannot adapt Shakespeare without repeatedly conjuring up the processes of remediation through which "Shakespeare" is consumed, reprocessed, and recycled.

Fodor's version of "Shakespeare in the extreme" does not exclude the theatrical medium from the processes of remediation it evokes and to which it contributes. It incorporates a theatrical performance by a "travelling troupe" of three classically trained, fierce-looking, German-speaking actors. Shakespearean critics have often commented on the screening of the stage in Shakespeare films, the inclusion of a medium within the cinematic medium that allegedly supersedes it, and have reached different conclusions. For instance, referring to a group of films that include stage performances, Mark

Thornton Burnett argues that in these metadramatic films Shakespeare is coded as "a repository of enduring values that can be accessed through performance" (*Filming* 28). In his "Introduction" to the section on spin-offs in *Shakespeares after Shakespeare* Douglas Lanier summarizes the main features of a wide range of metadramatic Shakespearean films by arguing as follows:

> Metadramatic films register the extraordinary cultural authority of Shakespearean language and performance,...while at the same time they demonize specifically theatrical performances of his work, suggesting that on the stage Shakespeare's power can enter real life in ways that are uncontrollable, poignant, (self-)destructive, and even prone to violence. ("Virtues of Illegitimacy" 135)[16]

The inclusion of the German actors' theatrical performance in Fodor's film (a performance that is all in German) has multiple meanings, and can be read by using both Burnett's and Lanier's approach. It has to do with what remains the film's irrepressible, compulsive desire to get to the roots of the "Shakespearean," which it paradoxically, and in a self-annihilating gesture, identifies with the "raw force" of a rival medium. (In this sense, as Burnett argues, the "true Shakespeare" can only be "accessed through performance.") The theatrical performance, the film implies, subjects the audience to some kind of shock treatment with the hope of setting them free from their "addiction" to standardized versions of Shakespeare. "Shakespeare in the extreme" then also means the desire to retrieve the "true spirit" of Shakespeare. In this sense, it provides a cure. It injects new life into the moribund *corpus* of Shakespeare. To Hamlet, the character who witnesses the performance with Horatio, and plays the part of the audience, the performance is a cure, in the sense that it makes him realize that "the play's the thing / Wherein [he]'ll catch the conscience of the king" (2.2.606–7). But it is also as lethal as a poison. In Lanier's words, this is a performance that enters the "real life" of the fictive character "in ways that are uncontrollable [and] (self-)destructive" (135). It implicitly functions as an analogue of the ghost's blow ("Mark me," 1.5.2) and a repetition of the ghost's injunction to remember. During the German actors' performance Hamlet increasingly looks as if under a spell. We hear him breathing heavily and then we witness the emergence of the morgue scene in its unabridged form, a scene, as suggested earlier, that is nothing but an induced traumatic memory, and that allegorizes *not* the "true meaning" of Shakespeare but the inexorably mediated, inassimilable character of the ghostly Shakespearean "original." It can also be argued that this theatrical performance furtively introduces a couple of intriguing ideas. It suggests, first of all, that "foreign Shakespeare" may be more powerful and spellbinding than the "original," more "original" than the "original"; second, that the language of the "original" may be the language of the other, and even of the (M)other: Gertrude intermittently speaks German, and she speaks English with a German accent. In short, the scene intimates that there may some kind of prosthesis at the origin.[17]

To conclude, Fodor's *Hamlet* is simultaneously iconoclastic and reverential. It presents a version of "Shakespeare in the extreme" but also pays homage to a "Shakespeare" that *is* "extreme," always-already implicated in a process of remediation and yet irreducible, an aporetic construct that whets the appetite for what cannot but be acknowledged as always-already lost.[18] The beginning of the film plays with the notions of reverence and iconoclasm. After the initial Ophelia scene, and as the credits roll, we are shown a close-up of the Ferguson reel-to-reel tape recorder that we will encounter again in the "To be or not to be" scene. We then see a hand pushing the PLAY lever, which conveys the impression that what we are about to see is a straightforward reproduction of something that precedes the reproduction. I have already commented on how the tape recorder as technological prosthesis, archaic as it may be, is incompatible with notions of re-presentation as mere reproduction. I want to point out now that as the tape recorder starts playing, we hear the very first words of the film, and they are the lines Hamlet addresses to Polonius/Polonia after murdering him/her: "Thou wretched, rash, intruding fool . . . / I took thee for thy better" (3.4.30–31). These lines, which are of course taken out of their original context, half-jokingly suggest that if what we are about to see is a repetition, it is, as Linda Hutcheon points out in her more general study of adaptation, a "repetition without replication" (7). They brazenly exhibit the status of this adaptation as something different from what is "better." They boldly apologize in advance for frustrating the viewer's expectations ("I took thee for thy better"). It is perhaps a lucky coincidence that these lines have to do with a violent act, and thus they also point to the radicality of the act of repetition without replication. But pushing the PLAY lever does not just start the film. It also marks the beginning of the audio track "You Love Me To Death" by Hooverphonic, whose lyrics suggest that love and death are inextricably entwined, just as reverence and iconoclasm. At the beginning of the twenty-first century "Shakespeare" often remains what Lacan would call the "subject supposed to know" (*sujet supposé savoir*) (*Four* 225), some kind of analyst/Other to whom most mainstream adaptations, in much the same way as in the process of transference, offer unconditional love. An adaptation of "Shakespeare in the extreme" such as Fodor's endeavors to break away from the vicious circle of transference, from what Lacan calls the essential deception of love (254), but with ambiguous and sometimes unconvincing results. It is an adaptation that seems to be saying, as if it was an analysand frustratingly addressing his/her analyst: "I love you, but, because inexplicably I love in you something more than you, . . . I mutilate you" (268).

CHAPTER 6

"Restless Ecstasy": Addiction, Reiteration, and Mediality in Klaus Knoesel's *Rave Macbeth*

> A phantom's return is, each time, another, different return, on a different stage.
>
> —Jacques Derrida, "Artifactualities"

> Ghosts, a.k.a. media, cannot die at all. Where one stops, another somewhere begins.
>
> —Friedrich A. Kittler, *Gramophone, Film, Typewriter*

Like Fodor's *Hamlet*, Klaus Knoesel's *Rave Macbeth* (2001), the very first feature-length film to be shot on a Sony's 24P-1080 digital camera, resituates Shakespeare in the context of contemporary urban youth culture.[1] It makes Shakespeare's *Macbeth* inhabit the realm of rave culture, a nocturnal culture that finds its expression in a nameless rave club, and that re-marks the play as essentially a tragedy of the "thick night" (1.5.49). In the film the obsessive reiteration of music and the incessant bodily movements of 14,000 dance ravers combine with the repeated ingestion of hallucinogenic and addictive substances such as ecstasy—the film's transposition of the "insane root / That takes the reason prisoner" (1.3.82–83) and/or its update of the "vap'rous drop...distilled by magic sleights" (3.5. 24; 26).[2] Thus, as Douglas Lanier more generally argues in relation to products of popular culture he dubs "Shakespop," the film selects aspects of *Macbeth* that resonate with pop culture—in particular the play's rich array of "metaphysical" (1.5.28) substances—and re-activates and extends their meanings

(*Shakespeare* 97).[3] Moreover, *Rave Macbeth* is a highly self-reflexive film, drawing attention to multiple forms of (bodily) reiterations that often allegorize the film's own status as a multifaceted reiteration and remediation of a Shakespearean story in mass media culture. Part of its self-reflexivity has to do with a male character named Hecate, chief drug dealer and media savvy who, unlike many other filmic versions of *Macbeth*, plays a prominent role and can indeed be seen as "the close contriver of all harms" (3.5.7).[4]

Rave Macbeth tells the story of Marcus (Michael Rosenbaum), an ambitious young raver who becomes Dean's "second" with his best friend Troy (Jamie Elman), as the witches, renamed the Petry girls, had predicted ("A great turn of events...All hail Marcus and Troy...From sheep to shepherds"). Yet his movement up the rigidly hierarchical drug organization that operates in the rave club is only a "prologue...to the swelling act / Of the imperial theme" (1.3. 127–28); for Marcus, in a way that recalls Macbeth when he is hailed "Thane of Cawdor," the "greatest [title] is behind" (114–15), which in the film means to be "crowned King of the Rave." Marcus's "dearest partner of greatness" (1.5.10), his girlfriend Lidia (Nicki Aycox), fundamentally contributes to the (re)activation of his "black and deep desires" (1.4.51): she arouses his jealousy by making him believe that Troy has made a pass at her, and by insinuating that Dean (Kirk Baltz) and Troy are conducting business behind his back. Under the influence of ecstasy and the Petry girls, he thinks he can see Troy making love to Lidia in the bathroom of the dance club when they are just exchanging a friendly hug, and in a bout of rage kills him. He then murders Dean with the knife the latter had given him as a token of trust and loyalty. Meanwhile, Lidia eliminates a potential witness to Troy's murder, his naïve girlfriend Helena (Marguerite Moreau), by force-feeding ecstasy pills to her, which causes her to die of a drug overdose. Lulled into a false sense of security by the Petry girls' assurance that "the day is lost only when blood rains from heaven," Marcus and Lidia triumphantly walk across the dance floor to reach a raised platform where they are welcomed by the DJ and acclaimed by the crowd. Yet their joint leadership as King and Queen of the Rave is short-lived. Confronted by MacDuff, the leader of the security guards who has discovered Dean's dead body, Marcus shoots him dead but one of the bullets hits the network of pipes that runs across the ceiling of the building. Thus blood does indeed start "rain[ing] from heaven," which is presumably the result of Troy's blood seeping into the plumbing system from the toilet where he has been murdered. This marks the end of Marcus and Lidia's journey, which is in many ways a drug-induced bad trip. Another security guard called Lennox shoots Lidia and then Marcus, who continues to reassure her up to the point in which they both exhale their last breath. At the end of the film Lidia and Marcus rise up to occupy a central position on a stagelike platform where they are soon joined by the other "mortal" characters who have also met a premature death. They stand still as if about to bow to an absent audience while the closing titles begin to roll.

Speaking to Marcus and Troy after "the motherload... Hecate's new shit" (i.e., a plastic box with a huge quantity of ecstasy) has been tossed from a high speed train, Dean shares with his newly appointed "seconds" his pearls of wisdom on the logic of drug dealing: "it is no secret that the scene is getting bigger and therefore the masses... they are looking for something a little bit stronger... I'm guaranteed that the stuff in this box is going to take people to new heights." The "scene" Dean refers to is of course the drug scene, a scene in which his rave club fiercely competes with others. But the drug scene is also, and only slightly more obliquely, the *Shakespearean* "scene." As Avital Ronell puts it in a different but theoretically related context, "drugs resist conceptual arrest... Everywhere dispensed, their strength lies *in their virtual and fugitive patterns*" (51, emphasis added). Knoesel's film, I want to argue, is not only a spin on *Macbeth* that surrogates the "original" through the styles of behaviors, bodily codes and music of a specific subculture. It also reflects upon its own status as a product offered for consumption—a kind of "Shakespeare-on-drugs" for the "masses"—in an increasingly eager and competitive global market in which postfidelity "Shakespeare" contin- ues to circulate at high speed and in a variety of media formats. Through Dean's words, the film articulates itself as a Shakespearean product that is "a little bit stronger" than usual and can thus be said to belong to the realm of what I referred to in chapter 5 as "Shakespeare in the extreme." As such, it tests boundaries and raises a number of metadramatic questions: how far can one "push" Shakespeare? What "new heights" can Shakespeare reach? Can the audience, consumer, or critic take it?

Being a shrewd entrepreneur in a highly competitive world, Dean hopes that customers will be satisfied so that they come back for more. As he explains to Marcus and Troy: "Your customers are still looking for six hours of happy and we don't want to give them six hours of hell." He knows that Hecate's "new shit" is stronger when compared to previous supplies but does not know by how much. He thus asks Troy, who, like Marcus, is under the effect of the sample batch of pills as he speaks. (Contravening one of Dean's rules, they have "eaten the product" themselves instead of distributing it to potential customers). Troy replies that Hecate's updated version of ecstasy is "kind of fierce," and gives Dean the following piece of advice: "You might want to take it down a notch."[5] However, Dean disagrees: "I don't think so." He miscalculates the potency and/or side effects of Hecate's new drug as well as the more general unpredictability of consumption as an essentially reiterative act. This will eventually lead to his being knifed to death by Marcus. Therefore bad trips—the "six hours of hell" to which Marcus succumbs—are a real possibility, perhaps a near certainty when reiteration is involved. This equally applies to ecstasy and "ecstasy Shakespeare": the two products—one synthetic, the other mediatized but both designed for the "masses" and sharing to a large extent, as the film suggests, a *modus operandi*—may induce good vibes or cause consumers, audiences, or critics to totally "freak out" (Dean's words).

The exchanges between Dean and his "seconds" intimate that the film engages with the question of the (pharmacological) supplement (cf. Derrida, *Dissemination* esp. 95–171). They show how "artificial" chemical substances replace one another within the rave circuit, continuously providing customers with what Dean calls "a little more kick," which does not guard against the possibility that things may turn awry. They also suggest that the film engages with the question of *itself* as a supplement: *Rave Macbeth* willingly inscribes itself within a chain of *Macbeth*-like stories governed by the law of iterability that is also a principle of replaceability. It sees itself as an addition to a series of adaptations of *Macbeth*, and especially to those set in a criminal underworld and/or that associate the witches' "metaphysical aid" (1.5.28) with the power of addictive substances, from Ken Hughes's *Joe Macbeth* to Roman Polanski's *Macbeth*, from Vishal Bhardwaj's *Maqbool* to Geoffrey Wright's *Macbeth*, from Greg Salman's *Mad Dawg* to Elyse Lewin's *Borough of Kings*.[6] And indeed, as we shall see, the logic of the supplement extends well beyond these exchanges to permeate the film as a whole, including the latter's articulation of issues of transmediality. For the moment, it is worth pointing out that even the betrayal of Dean by a character called TC (an avatar of the disloyal Thane of Cawdor), Dean's right hand whom he "trusted like a brother," is construed in terms of (pharmacological) supplementarity. According to Dean, who not only nominates *two* new "seconds" after the murder of TC but also has another "right hand" to watch his back, chief security guard MacDuff (i.e., his "eyes and ears"), TC "created a bogus product, put my name on it and then introduced his own to make mine look like shit." Yet of course Dean's own "product"—the product TC fraudulently supplements—is not quite his own but Hecate's. In other words, if this play of *différance* of brands points to an origin, this is a *spectral*, "inhuman," and supernatural origin. The irony is compounded by the fact that Hecate, who portrays himself as the originator of what he calls the "odyssey" of ambitious figures such as Macbeth or Marcus, borrows his name from a Shakespearean character—"the mistress of [the witches'] charms" (3.5.6)—who is not quite Shakespearean herself but, rather, given the attribution of 3.5 and parts of 4.1 to Middleton, a hybrid textual creature.

*   *   *

In her groundbreaking *Shakespeare's Ghost Writers*, Marjorie Garber underlines the proliferation of the uncanny in *Macbeth* as well as the uncanniness of *Macbeth* itself. According to Garber, Shakespeare's play "presents us with what is in effect a test case of the limits of representation." She adds that "the boundary between what is inside the play and what is outside it...is continually transgressed, and marked by a series of taboo border crossings: sleep/waking, male/female, life/death, fair/foul, heaven/hell, night/morning" (91). Among the most prominent examples of this "transgression" (a word, one may add, that perhaps inadvertently reinscribes the idea of a pre-existing clear-cut division between an "inside" and an "outside") are the stage history of *Macbeth*, a history that often replicates the most uncanny aspects of the play and is thus not merely "extrinsic or anecdotal" (94); or the sleepwalking Lady Macbeth of 5.1 who marks in advance the play's afterlife by compulsively performing a compressed and fragmentary "adaptation" of *Macbeth* before two characters, the Gentlewoman and the Doctor, who also double as audience. One could slightly rephrase Garber's argument by claiming that *Macbeth* is the name for an irreducible, iterative, uncanny structure with *inde*terminate spatial and temporal boundaries. It is a play that does not *properly* end. As Garber points out, the play "begins with the (offstage) head of a rebel fixed upon the battlements" (i.e., Macdonwald); it ends "with another rebellion, another battle, and the 'usurper's cursed head' [i.e., Macbeth] held aloft by Macduff," a doubling that supplements the less than reassuring forms of doubling permeating the whole play (104). One may add, with Alan Sinfield, that this mirroring has unsettling implications for the politics of the play: "Macduff at the end stands in the same relation to Malcom as Macbeth did to Duncan in the beginning. He is now the kingmaker on whom the legitimate monarch depends, and the *recurrence* of the whole sequence may be anticipated" (102, emphasis added). In other words, no matter how hard the ostensible political project of the play attempts to create, or re-create, a distinction between legitimate and illegitimate violence, this uncanny doubling obliquely announces, to refer to Giorgio Agamben's work, that the "state of exception," an "unbound" state in which "everybody is bare life and a *homo sacer* for everybody else" (*Homo Sacer* 106), is not "absolutely without relation to the rule" (17); that this "state" is not just the prerogative or the idiosyncratic mark of the reign of terror instigated by the "butcher" (5.11.35) Macbeth. Furthermore, *Macbeth* is also a play that does not *properly* begin.

According to Mallarmé's "uncanny" essay on *Macbeth*, "*La fausse entrée des sorcières dans Macbeth*," the play begins "*extra-scéniquement*" (349), with some kind of supplement that does not fit in with the rest of the play.[7] It begins with the spectral apparition—not an entrance—of creatures who reign over the threshold.[8] The first scene is not quite a scene; "it is something else, not a scene" ("*quelque chose d'autre, non une scène*," 349). This indeterminate "something else" marks the violation of temporal boundaries. It inscribes a temporality that does not unfold in a linear way.[9] For Mallarmé, it is as if "the curtain had simply risen a minute too soon, betraying fateful goings-on"; it is as if "that canvas that separates us from mystery has somehow . . . prematurely given way, before the moment established for it" (qtd. in Garber 92, translation modified). The time of the weird sisters is thus the time of the untimely, of the lack of coincidence of the present with itself. The furtive instant of their spectral apparition is not docile to time: they appear to disappear; they meet to "meet again" (1.1.1). In retrospect, as Mallarmé emphasizes, one could say that this "prodigy . . . did not take place, at least not in an ordinary way and in relation to the play as a whole."[10] Nonetheless, it is an event. In fact, it is precisely because the spectral apparition of the witches is "extraordinary," bearing the mark of the "out-of-jointedness" of time, that it can be called an event. It is a singular event that affects. It forces the audience into the uncomfortable position of the witness.[11] The witches are surprised and exposed by the premature lifting of the curtain, but they also surprise and expose *us*. This "fortuitous violation" proliferates anxiety. It shows the audience "the very thing that seemed to have to remain hidden," the "thing" that is "knotted up from behind and effectively to the invisible." It allows "everyone [to] examine . . . and disturb . . . the kitchen in which the deed is cooking," the place in which the heinous crime is being arranged (qtd in Garber 92). Yet, as Mallarmé repeatedly observes, this is an improper, even indecent, "dis-covery." It does not provide the audience with a sense of visual mastery over the offstage "non-scene" of the spectral apparition. For the audience, it is a disconcerting form of implication.

The beginning of *Rave Macbeth* makes us privy to "the kitchen in which the deed is cooking," and this is a similarly ambiguous disclosure. As the opening titles run, taking shape as if they were a visual representation of static electricity against a vaguely futuristic background, we hear the voice of chief drug-dealer Hecate who tells us the following:

At the time when people didn't dare to doubt the power of wizards and witches, Shakespeare immortalized the story of Macbeth, a man who let himself be seduced by such forces into a dangerous game of madness, power, greed and love.

These "forces" are nothing but "the Petry girls and [himself]," their "master." To Hecate, both the story of Macbeth and the story that we are about to watch are part of a series with no beginning or end. Reiteration rules: "Stories repeat themselves."[12] If there is change, it concerns the "medium" through which these evil forces act on humans—what Hecate calls "the tools of our trade": "Gone are the potions and poisons of yesterday, the herbal infusions and elixirs. Presently we use chemicals instead, which are far more potent and effective, such as 'E'...ecstasy." He pronounces these words as he sits in front of a gigantic TV/computer screen with his back to us, which surreptitiously establishes a connection between the new chemical "medium" through which he and the Petry girls operate (i.e., ecstasy), and the more general issue of the practices of mediation and remediation of *Macbeth*-like stories. More specifically, Hecate's power as a wizard and drug dealer turns out to be contiguous with his power to play and replay, by means of a remote control, video clips of events that have taken place just before the start of the film, and that run parallel to each other in separate windows, most notably the violent disposal of Dean's "right hand" TC after his Macdonwald-like treachery. Furthermore, as Hecate's "Prologue" progresses, we realize that this spectral resurrection of the past is uncannily interspersed with the mediatized evocation of the present: we see Dean on this TV/computer screen deeply engaged in a phone conversion with Hecate himself about suitable "replacements" for TC; we watch what in temporal terms follows Hecate's "Prologue" and is in many respects the first scene of the film as one of the screen windows expands to show Marcus, Troy, Linda, and Helena sharing a joint in a car and commenting on the "bloody deeds" of the previous night before entering the rave club; we are brought back to the conversation between Dean and Hecate with the latter showing again his overarching power by predicting the names of the prospective trustworthy "seconds" the former has in mind: "Marcus and Troy." To Hecate, drug users "live and die" at his "command." The self-reflexive initial sequence of the film suggests that the characters of *Rave Macbeth* also "live and die" at the "command"—the switch—of Hecate's remote control. In a sense, the film is over even before it begins. Its "present" is itself a replay, a potentially endless replay that brings back to life characters on a screen. To paraphrase Mallarmé's argument, the screen that appears before us for most of the film is "knotted up from behind and effectively" to Hecate's "invisible" and supplementary screen. (Of course, if one attends to the omnipresent supplementary logic of the film, the "main" screen facing us is also a "secondary" screen, nothing but one of the "windows" of Hecate's screen). Like the first "non-scene" of *Macbeth* in Mallarmé's interpretation, Hecate's "Prologue" breaks the frame of representation *before* it has been established. It forces the viewer to witness what happens behind the scenes; to occupy the position of a voyeur vis-à-vis the "very thing" that should have remained hidden. As if to emphasize that this is an awkward and anxiety-ridden position, we are confronted with the intermittent appearance of a huge eye that emits rays toward us. The viewer is not the master of the visible: the screen looks back as we watch.

Rave Macbeth's self-reflexivity thus strengthens Peter Donaldson's argument that in Shakespearean films, and especially contemporary films (at least since media-saturated Baz Luhrmann's *William Shakespeare's Romeo and Juliet*), attention to media themes and practices is pervasive, and to such an extent that it often displaces "the story line of the source play." Donaldson usefully adds that "not all of these films imply a narrative exclusively concerned with *cinema*." In fact, they "often suggest journeys *across* media" ("Bottom" 23). Like the films to which Donaldson refers in this and other essays,[13] *Rave Macbeth* is keenly aware of media themes and practices but this awareness is not confined to the cinematic. It includes journeys across the languages and rhythms of rave music and dance. One of the reviewers goes as far as to argue that the film "can work without dialogue, like a music video" (Wisehart n. pag.). Moreover, as Carolyn Jess-Cooke points out in her study of twenty-first-century "McShakespeare" films, these journeys across music and dance also engage with "the escalating commercialism of the rave scene" as well as with the "nostalgic urge to recapture the rave's glory days as a counter-culture community founded on 'peace, love, unity and respect'—the rave rules that Marcus and Lidia break" ("McShakespeare" 170). Knoesel's film thus presents a "Shakespeareccentric" exploration that surrogates "the story line of the source play" in a variety of ways. Yet, I want to suggest, this "Shakespeareccentric" journey across media is also, at one and the same time, a movement *back* to Shakespeare. It also creatively responds to the indeterminate, uncanny, reiterative structure of *Macbeth* and, in particular, to the play's metadramatic emphasis on theatre as a self-consuming medium whose temporality is irremediably spectral, as most radically embodied in Macbeth's "Tomorrow, and tomorrow, and tomorrow" speech (5.5.18–27). It imaginatively responds to *Macbeth*, that is, by repeatedly drawing attention to the *essentially* reiterative, self-destroying "nature" of the media languages of rave culture; by identifying them as performances that are compulsive and addictive and thus also contiguous with the repeated ingestion of drugs: "Life" in the geographically undefined environment of the rave club—a life made of pill-popping, hypnotic pounding beats and trancelike movements—is nothing but "a poor player / That struts and frets his hour upon the stage [or the dance floor], / And then is heard no more" (5.5.23–25). This life is, indeed, "full of sound and fury" (26). We hear Macbeth's "Tomorrow, and tomorrow, and tomorrow" speech, spoken by the Petry girls twice, when Marcus and Lidia walk amid a still and silent crowd to reach the DJ on a raised platform and occupy their newly acquired position as leaders of the rave process who dictate the beat. As Douglas Lanier points out in his *Shakespeares after Shakespeare* entry on the film, the Petry girls' lines suggest "the emptiness of [Marcus and Lidia's] achievement" (Lanier, "Spin-Offs" 215). Indeed, the two lovers' rule is short-lived, even shorter than in the "original": it will not be long before they find their way to "dusty death" (5.5.22). But the lines also offer a more general ironic comment on the senselessness of the reiterative languages of rave music and dance. The final part of the film hones in on this point when it shows that the E-driven rave participants carry on dancing to the beat of techno in spite of the shootings in their midst, and in spite of the "blood" that "rains from heaven"—the beginning of the end of Marcus and Lidia's "kingdom," as the Petry girls had predicted. It is worth adding that while the reiterations *within* the film are associated with self-consumption and senselessness, the film itself obeys the logic of iterability. As pointed out earlier, *Rave Macbeth* is an addition to a series, and an addition that transforms what it adds itself to as it responds to it by means of reiteration. To recall Hecate's words, stories *do* "repeat themselves." Yet there is no repetition without difference, which concerns what repeats, in that it can be repeated again and thus displaced and/or replaced, *and* what is being repeated. On the one hand, the logic of iterability (retrospectively) guarantees the identity of the same. On the other, it spells "catastrophe" for identity,[14] but a catastrophe that may also mark the emergence, or re-emergence, of a singular (spectral) event.[15] As Derrida puts it, "a certain iterability (difference in repetition) ensures that what comes back"—in our case, the spectral return of *Macbeth* as *Rave Macbeth*—"nevertheless remains a wholly other event" (Derrida and Stiegler 24).[16]

Hecate's "Prologue," delivered for the most part as he sits in front of a giant screen with a remote control, introduces the idea that the reiterative self-consuming "life" of the characters of the film is a "walking shadow" (5.5.23), a spectral life whose first time on screen, to borrow from Derrida's more general description of the temporality of specters in *Specters of Marx* (10), is indistinguishable from the second time of repetition, coming back and replay. In a sense, this is a "life" that emblematizes the uncanny "phantom structure" of cinema (*Ghost Dance*), its hauntological "nature" as a medium that does not provide life *or* death, a medium, according to Derrida, that is essentially a form of *survivance* and thus by no means a reproduction of reality and/or the presence of the present.[17] What is also most intriguing about Hecate's "Prologue" is that it shows the relation of

Figure 6.1 Hecate's screens.

mutual implication between the cinematic and the post-cinematic; or, to be more precise, the extent to which the cinematic includes and is haunted by what it announces as its future, and perhaps its future erasure. It is almost as if the film's emphasis on a reiterated, self-consuming life—life as theatre, music, dance, and addiction—extended to the life of the cinematic medium itself. As argued earlier, the "main" cinematic screen we are watching doubles as Hecate's giant supplementary screen, a screen that emulates a computer or TV screen and splits into other screens/windows.[18] By means of his remote, "master" Hecate selects scenes; he cuts from one scene to the next and then cuts back again, "jumping o'er times" (*H5* "Prologue" 29) and thus simulating the fast-forward and rewind mode of a DVD player; he zooms in and out of a scene and then plays events in the modality "live"; just before Dean's murder, he rewinds the action back to the beginning and then even pauses it so that he can reappear on the "main" cinematic screen—a ghostlike figure who has crossed over to the "other side"—and have a tête-à-tête with Dean about the development of events. This is and is not cinema. It is, perhaps, cinema's apotheosis *and* its erasure.[19] To return to my previous argument, if *Rave Macbeth* offers itself as a product—"ecstasy Shakespeare"—to be consumed, it does not offer itself as an exclusively cinematic product. The film is itself *and* a version of itself in DVD format with menus and scene selections to be operated at will; it is itself *and* a music video without dialogue and even a video game. As to the elements of videogames it incorporates, one only needs to consider that at the very beginning of the film we are presented with the five main characters rotating on some kind of carousel, as if they were part of the initial menu of an interactive fantasy role-playing game awaiting selection; and that at the end of the film, they come back from the dead onto a stagelike platform, standing with the same expressionless faces they wear at the beginning, as if waiting to be brought back into action, and deployed in yet another rerun of a *Macbeth*-like story. Furthermore, Hecate wakes up the Petry girls with the words: "Let the battle begin"; later on, he incites them to "lead them [i.e., Marcus and Troy] into to the arena and let the game begin." As to the Petry girls, they continually give the players/characters (misleading) instructions on how to overcome obstacles, instructions such as "You must separate your friends from your foes," so that they can reach the final aim of the game: to be "crowned King of the Rave."

Richard Grusin points out that in a digital age film is no longer "confined to the form of its theatrical exhibition but is distributed across other media as well." This "remediation" indicates "a fundamental change in the aesthetic status of the cinematic artifact" (212). This is true of a digital film such as *Rave Macbeth* and other Shakespearean and non-Shakespearean contemporary films.[20] Yet what is most significant about Knoesel's film is that it includes within its narrative its (potential) distribution and diffusion across multiple media platforms. In particular, Hecate's supplementary screen repeatedly simulates a scenario of what may be called, after Henry Jenkins, media convergence.[21] It is a screen that foregrounds a co-simultaneous, paratactic delivery of a variety of multimedia "contents" (including the life of the characters), and that appears to mark, within the specificity of the cinematic medium, the erasure of the specificity of each individual medium: the film is a video game; is a DVD version of itself; is a music video; is a dance performance.[22] In short, *Rave Macbeth* articulates itself as a multilayered site of inscription of media traces, a transmedia product that simulates and anticipates its circulation and consumption (e.g., its being played and replayed, fast-forwarded and rewound) on a variety of screens and media platforms.

*   *   *

When the main characters return from the dead, showing their willingness, or resignation, to play a role in yet another permutation of a *Macbeth*-like "story of greed, love, atonement," Hecate is nowhere to be seen. His absence forcefully suggests that he has vacated his position of mastery. This points to a silent transmission of power to the viewer, a power to be exercised over the field of the visible, and which the film consistently construes as largely indistinguishable from one's ability to interact with, and manipulate, a field of mediality. Of course, the power "master" Hecate spectrally bequeaths concerns the future (and future reruns of *Macbeth*). Yet the assumption of an all-controlling "supernatural" position on the part of the viewer is marked in advance as problematic. As with many other reconfigurations of temporality in the film, this is a future that takes the form of what can be called a "pro-re-gression." One may be tempted to gloss this legacy with Derrida's description of temporality as affected by the comings and goings of specters: "what seems to be out front, the future, comes back in advance: from the past, from the back" (*Specters* 10).[23] The periodic re-emergence of a gigantic eye looking back at the viewer—an ironic reminder of the uncanny overlapping of powerfulness and powerlessness—can be reinterpreted as a warning that also extends to the future, a future that "comes back...from the past, from the back."[24] Moreover, as the film develops, the exposure of the viewer to this eye is increasingly identified with an exposure to the gaze of the screen that makes his/her position largely unsafe.[25] In turn, the unsafe position of the viewer becomes more and more associated with that of a drug-addled Marcus confronted by mirrors turning into opaque screens.

The last appearance of Hecate in the film underlines the unsafe implications of being a viewer and reasserts the association between Marcus and (present and future) spectating subjects. Sitting in front of his giant screen for the last time, Hecate uses the words with which the "original" Hecate predicts Macbeth's misguided reaction to the illusory "artificial sprites" magically concocted out of a "vap'rous drop" (3.5.27, 24), thus implicitly transferring to the film the interdependence of a false sense of security, vision, and "metaphysical" substances: "He shall spurn fate, scorn death, and bear / his hopes 'bove wisdom, grace, and fear; / And you all know security / Is mortals' chiefest enemy (30–34). Except for the "Tomorrow, and tomorrow, and tomorrow" speech, these are the only lines from the "original" included in the film, which is in itself significant. What is also noteworthy is that these lines are delivered *after* Marcus and Lidia are shot by Lennox, the security guard, and as they are in the throes of death. They are thus an anachronistic form of "pre-diction." In a sense, they contain a literal ironic comment on the shooting: a *security* guard is, indeed, Marcus's most immediate "enemy." Perhaps more interestingly, especially when considering that they are delivered as Hecate sits in front of a screen showing the Petry girls, these lines look *back*, on the one hand, to Marcus's confusion when faced with "th' equivocation of the fiend" (5.5.41); on the other, they look *ahead* to the future to include all "mortal" overreachers—and all potential viewers when faced with the contemporary media equivalents of the "artificial sprites"—in a Macbeth-like *hubris* that is also a form of *hubris* connected with vision.[26]

Nicholas Royle argues that "safe" is one of *Macbeth*'s keywords, a point of entry into a play that continuously blurs clear-cut distinctions between seemingly opposed terms. To Royle, "safe" (along with related words such as "safer," "safely," and "safety") is a word that repeatedly transgresses its boundaries, as when Lady Macbeth asserts that "'Tis safer to be that which we destroy, / Than by destruction dwell in doubtful joy" (3.2.8–9), which Royle glosses as: "it's better to be dead than in a state of doubt, or a murderee than a murderer" (93); or when Banquo is said to be "safe [i.e., dead] in a ditch" (3.4. 25). (Of course, in the latter example irony adds to irony because the ghost of Banquo will soon appear, showing that he is not safely dead but, rather, *un*dead). In short, "safe" seems to be "a ghostly word, a word of ghostly meaning," "troubled, ironic, *unsafe*" (94, emphasis added). Royle also comments on Hecate's "security / Is mortals' chiefest enemy," which he paraphrases as follows: "the best way of being safe is never to suppose you are secure. There is no security in thinking you are safe" (94). In the film the complexity of the question of safety is enhanced by the fact that it is inextricably bound with the question of the media, and in particular with the question of one's position vis-à-vis mirrors/screens that function as ambiguous projections and prostheses of one's desire. Marcus is lulled into a false sense of security when the Petry girls appear on the mirror of the bathroom where he has killed Troy, and announce that "the day is lost only when blood rains from heaven." (The smug looks he exchanges with Lidia bear witness to the fact that he feels safe, as does the ensuing impromptu dance to what, in the context of the film, is an unusually mellow tune, Alex McGowan's "Guru Flute.") Yet, one does not need to wait until the end of *Rave Macbeth* to realize that Marcus's reaction to the Petry girls' words is part of the unsafe security that Royle describes in relation to *Macbeth*. After the murder of Troy, in the course of a scene in which he is forced to have a drink with an increasingly suspicious Dean, Marcus hallucinates drops of blood falling "from heaven" into his glass, which are presumably his best friend's. (Once again, the "future...comes back in advance...from the past.") One can therefore argue that if Marcus falls prey to "th'equivocation of the fiend" (5.5.41), this not only has to do with the "content" of the Petry girls' prediction but also with its "form"; it not only has to do with what they say but also with the "medium" of the message. As he stands before a mirror that quickly turns into a screen, Marcus misconstrues this screen as a "window" into the future ("Can I see the future as clearly as I can see you?"), a transparent surface that unproblematically supplements the mirror, as if it continued to reflect his "imaginary" position as master of vision (in a Lacanian sense).[27] The appearance of Hecate in this scene consolidates and seals Marcus's *méconnaisance*. When the Petry girls tell Marcus that they "do not have the answers [he] seeks," and that "it's him [he] must see," this "him" materializes on the screen as soon as Marcus pronounces the word: "Hecate." But Hecate refuses to answer Marcus's questions: "It's all in your mind. The puzzle is up to you to put together. I have given you the picture, now finish the puzzle." After the Petry girls deliver their "riddle," Hecate reappears: "Does this clarify things for you?"[28] What is crucial is the "formal" arrangement of the conversation between the two, namely the fact that in this scene Hecate shifts from the position of the powerful observer, which he keeps for most of the film, to that of the observed. This allows Marcus to relocate himself in the supposedly omnipotent "imaginary" position "from which perspective is [fully] grasped" (Lacan, *Four* 96), a position from which the alternation of images on the screen appear as the subject's *own* images, an adequate and satisfactory representation of his self and his desires. Yet, to adopt Lacan's discussion of the dialectic between the eye and the gaze in *The Four Fundamental Concepts of Psycho-Analysis*, the readability of the "picture" that Hecate offers, like the readability of the ana-morphotic skull floating in the background of Holbein's *The Ambassadors* to which Lacan refers, is not a function of the imaginary positioning, or re-positioning, of the subject. It is, instead, a function of its annihilation. In other words, Marcus's "imaginary" sense of security is an avoidance of the fact that in the field of the visible "something slips, passes, is transmitted, from stage to stage, and is always to some degree eluded in it," a "something" that is irreducibly opaque, much like a screen, and that Lacan calls "the gaze" (73). It is a defense against the elusiveness of the gaze, an "instrument" through which the "I" is "*photo-graphed*" and becomes, indeed, "a picture" (106, Lacan's emphasis).[29]

To feel safe—no matter what degree of *méconnaisance* is involved therein, visual or other—is not synonymous with inaction. To recall Royle's approach to *Macbeth*, one is never safe enough. In spite of being told that "none of woman born / Shall harm Macbeth" (4.1.96–97), the Scottish king declares that he will "make assurance double sure" (99). Neither this prediction nor other "sweet bodements" (112) will do. In *Rave Macbeth*, at the end of the scene in which they consult the mirror turned into a screen, Marcus and Lidia, already steeped in blood, seal a demonic pact as they dance: "Even if we have to kill every fucking person in this place, we'll get through this." Therefore, to be lulled into a false sense of security does not put an end to aggressivity or violence. In fact, in both Shakespeare's play and Knoesel's revision, it acts as a trigger.[30] This is not just aggressiv-ity and violence toward the other but also toward one's self, both "external" and "internal."[31] Immunity inescapably turns into autoimmunity, which Derrida defines as "the strange illogical logic" (*Rogues* 123) whereby "a

living being, in quasi-*suicidal* fashion, 'itself' works to destroy its own pro-
tection, to immunize itself *against* its 'own' immunity" (Borradori 94). As
Derrida's scare quotes suggest, there is no sovereign self present to itself—no
living being or any other entity founded on the values of the "proper"—
that precedes and/or is able to function as an active relay of this process.
According to the French philosopher, "autoimmunity is always...cruelty
itself, the autoinfection of all autoaffection. It is not some particular thing
that is affected in autoimmunity but the self, the *ipse*, the *autos* that finds
itself infected" (*Rogues* 109), a self that cannot therefore pose as the origin or
author of the "illogical logic" of autoimmunity. It is worth adding that, for
Derrida, life is not exclusively on the side of immunity, just as death is not
entirely on the side of autoimmunity. As he clarifies, "between the immune
and that which threatens it or runs counter to it...the relation is neither
one of exteriority nor one of simple opposition or contradiction" (*Rogues*
112).[32] In a sense, therefore, autoimmunity is an extension of the logic of
immunity. It explores what in the logic of immunity is always-already—and
constitutively—hyperbolic, namely the fact that this logic implies an "excess
above and beyond the living," a life that "has absolute value by being worth
more than life, more than itself" (emphasis added). Therefore, this is a life
that, in an apparently spontaneous but in fact irrepressibly compulsive and
machinelike fashion, "opens the space of death that is linked to the automaton...to technics, the machine, the prosthesis: in a word, to the dimension
of auto-immune...supplementarity [and]...[the] death-drive" ("Faith and
Knowledge" 51).[33]

It is this life "more than life, more than itself" to which the Macbeths
aspire in 3.2., echoing each other, a life that is devoid of "doubtful joy"
(3.2.9) (Lady Macbeth) or "restless ecstasy" (24) (Macbeth), a *safe* life that
should be brought closer by murder and "destruction" (9) but is endlessly
deferred, a life that uncannily coincides with death, as emblematized by
the enviably safe status of a Duncan whom "nothing / Can touch...fur-
ther" (3.2.27–28). (Of course death itself, as articulated in the play, does
not fail to be immune to the restlessness of living on, or the "doubtful
joy" of compulsive spectral returns.) In *Rave Macbeth*, the quasi-suicidal
logic of autoimmunity is first of all intimately related to the experience of
drug-taking. This is not just to point out that Hecate's "new shit," which
is supposed "to take people to new heights"—to guarantee a kind of life
that is "more than life"—turns out to be, indeed, merely "shit," a lethal
batch of pills that causes bad trips and ultimately leads to death as well as
to the destruction of the values of friendship and community connected
with rave culture. (Speaking from beyond the grave in voice-over, Marcus
admits: "Lidia and I have broken all the rules, the only rules: peace, love,

unity, and respect. Somehow we replaced everything with hate.") It is also to underline the more general "illogical logic" of drug-taking presented in the film, a logic that somehow reshapes the relationship between life and its other(s). The ingestion of ecstasy is undoubtedly an expansion of life, a "life more than life." As the four friends test the sample batch of pills, Marcus informs us in voice-over that there is "happiness in a pill," and that "E[cstasy] melts your inhibitions away." Thus, an "artificial" chemical substance such as ecstasy turns the body into a "body natural," or returns the body to a kind of prelapsarian state: it induces freedom from external social and psychic constraints so that the body can finally, or once again, be at one with itself and its desires (cf. Derrida, "Rhetoric of Drugs" 244). And yet ecstasy is part of a process of autoimmune supplementarity whereby life becomes "more than life, more than itself." According to Marcus, "E[cstasy] slows down and speeds up everything all at the same time." As a type of *pharmakon* (i.e., simultaneously life-enhancing *and* deleterious stuff), this product inscribes "another time"—the time of what Derrida calls "the automaton . . . technics, the machine, the prosthesis" ("Faith and Knowledge" 51)—in the supposedly natural life and rhythms of a body that is already in itself "natural" only in so far as it finds itself in a chemically induced altered state. It activates an "artificial" process whose time is clearly not the time of the living present but, rather, the dislocated, out-of-joint time of acceleration and deceleration that divides and "spectralizes" the present in much the same way as the iterative processes of what Derrida calls "teletechnologies" (*Ecographies* 35–39). In other words, the addicted body of *Rave Macbeth*, a body, as shown earlier, that is also subjected to the law of iterability of music and dance, inhabits a spectral configuration of temporality that is analogous to the one inhering in the "phantom structure" of "teletechnologies" and, more generally, the trace structure of archival technologies.[34] According to Derrida, the *modus operandi* of these media technologies involve an uncanny mixture of (temporal and spatial) distance and proximity, retention and protention, speed and deceleration. These are technologies that offer "a maximum of life (the most life [*le plus de vie*]), but of life that already yields to death ('no more life' [*'plus de vie'*]" (Derrida and Stiegler 39), and thus interrogate definite boundaries between the living or organic and the mechanical or technical, the "human" and the "non-human" (cf. *Beast II* 130–31).

As part of its self-reflexivity, *Rave Macbeth* juxtaposes the question of mediality to the (pharmacological) logic of the life-enhancing/life-threatening (autoimmune) experience of drugs. Like ecstasy, media technologies inscribe themselves on the body and "slow [. . .] down and speed [. . .] up everything all at the same time." It is not by chance that, as Marcus utters these words on ecstasy, we are shown a slow-motion sequence of black-and-white images of the four friends—the "spectral" time of teletechnologies—and then, by means of a rotating overhead shot, we are quickly transported to the accelerated rhythms of the dance floor, which reinforces the sense of the interimplication of the experience of drugs and the experience of mediality. This interimplication is crucial in a film that goes as far as to allegorize itself, and interchangeably, as drug for "the masses" *and* a multi-faceted media product for the global market, and that could also be read, in more general terms and perhaps a little simplistically, as an ironic reflection on how the "culture industry" (in Adorno and Horkheimer's sense) is in fact a drug industry ruled by the evil genius Hecate. The scene also explicitly restates the complexity of consumption as an act that does not fail to affect the consumer. Although less obviously so, this equally applies to the consumption of media images. As argued earlier, the film repeatedly turns Marcus's position into an emblem of the fraught position of present and future spectating subjects/consumers, and consistently associates this position with the *hubris* of vision. In the scene in question, there is no "security" in vision, to use Hecate's word, if by vision one means a form of consumption of media images; there is no subject present to himself/herself who is able to inspect and consume images from a safe distance: the viewer is forced to share the drug-induced, out-of-joint, hallucinatory perspective of Marcus, and can thus hardly be said to be in control of the field of the visible. In this and many other scenes, especially those in which Marcus meets the witches, the logic of hallucinations and dreams prevails, a logic whereby "nothing is / But what is not" (1.3.140–41). Like Macbeth, Marcus repeatedly experiences a loss of stable boundaries; he finds himself in a displaced position that recalls the position of the subject of the dream, a "position," to refer to Lacan, that is "profoundly that of someone who does not see": "the subject does not see where it is leading, he follows" (*Four* 75). In some of these scenes, Marcus literally "follows," as in the crucial moment when the Petry girls take him by the hand and silently point in the direction of the bathroom where Troy and Lidia are heading; he "follows," and is not aware of what is going to happen, of "where [this] is leading"—a drug-induced fit of jealousy resulting in the murder of his best friend Troy.

By insisting on the displacement of the subject as master of the visible, the film interrogates what may be called "the core fantasy of humanism's trope of vision," the idea that "the perceptual space is organized around and for the looking subject," and that "the pure point of the eye...exhausts the field of the visible" (Wolfe 132).[35] To paraphrase Derrida, there is no "*ego* certain of itself"—no "I"/eye of either the film's protagonist or the film's spectator/consumer—that is able to "ensure [its] own technical mastery over the totality of what is" ("The Principle of Reason" 139 qtd. in Wolfe 133). Something escapes, but what escapes is not "another visible," "something that does not yet appear or has already disappeared" (*Memoirs of the Blind* 51–52); it is not, strictly speaking, something invisible, at least not in the sense of something that "has not yet been seen by a subject who is, in principle, capable of seeing all" (Wolfe 132).[36] What radically eludes the viewing subject's supposed mastery over the visible—the subject as subject *of* representation—is "something visible...but of the invisible visible," a something that is "visible only insofar as it is not visible in flesh and blood" (Derrida and Stiegler 115). This is what Derrida calls spectrality, a spectrality that "regularly exceeds all the oppositions between visible and invisible, sensible and insensible." For Derrida, who is here speaking of media technologies, "a specter is both visible and invisible, both phenomenal and nonphenomenal: a trace that marks the present with its absence in advance" (117). This spectrality introduces a visibility that is "a night visibility" (115) beyond any living present, in that it is inextricably bound with technics, iterability and reproducibility.[37] Put differently, what exceeds and haunts the ocularcentrism of the viewing subject posing as the origin and end of vision and representation is the inherently spectral "technological condition" ("Rhetoric of Drugs" 244): there is no subject placed and positioned *before* an object that can circumvent, in its very constitution as a subject of vision, the technological supplement "'originarily' at work and in place...at the heart of the heart" of the subject (244–45).[38] This dangerous spectral supplement marks the imbrication of vision in the "artificiality" of technics and, more generally, the irremediable prostheticity and mediality of being—what a leading media theorist such as Bernard Stiegler, deeply influenced by Derrida's work, calls "technicity as constitutive of life as ex-sistence" ("Memory" 72), a life that is thus " fundamentally exteriorized...by means other than life" (71).[39]

*　*　*

When Marcus and Lidia join the DJ on a raised platform to be acclaimed by the crowd of rave dancers and dictate the beat, the "real time" of jubilation intersects with the "spectral time" of dejection: at the very moment of triumph, the "night visibility" asserts itself in the form of repeated black-and-white shots of the King and Queen of the Rave experiencing intense anguish and pain. On the one hand, therefore, this "coronation scene" brings to a climax the sense of security that most forcefully emerges when Marcus and Lidia face a mirror/screen predicting immunity. On the other, it announces what they are about to go through as they are shot by a security guard.

Figure 6.2 Coming back from the dead.

Moreover, given the powerful impact of the black-and-white shots in terms of affect, one is tempted to suggest, by looking back at the prediction scene, that immunity was always-already the hyperbole of itself, exceeding itself and tipping over into the "life more than life" of autoimmunity, the auto-immunity of "technics, the machine, the prosthesis" (Derrida, "Faith and Knowledge" 51) that is just another name for the death drive. In any case, while thematically referring to the immediate future, these black-and-white shots in slow motion re-mark the extent to which one is "spectralized by the shot, captured or possessed by spectrality in advance" (Derrida and Stiegler 117); the extent to which, that is, from a more general and "formal" point of view, the spectrality of media technology does not wait for death to inscribe death.

This may appear to be a bleak account of the spectrality of media as allegorized by a film that repeatedly pulls in a "Shakespeareccentric" direction to reflect on its own status as media/drug product as well as on the more general problematics of mediality. Yet, from a Derridean perspective, if media technology "brings our death," "our disappearance," this "disappearance... promises and conceals in advance another magic 'apparition,' a ghostly 're-apparition'" (Derrida and Stiegler 117). It is worth recalling in this context one of the most cogent interpretations of Derrida's thoughts on mediality, Cary Wolfe's. He underlines the spectrality "produced by *any* media, any archival technology whose iterability and repeatability anticipate and in some sense forecast our eventual absence, our death." Yet he also points out that it is precisely "on the basis of that fact that the possibility of the future depends, a 'living on' or 'to come'...that can only happen because...'the time is out of joint'" (xxxiv). It is this "living on" that Marcus addresses at the end of the film when he concludes his frank summary of events with the words: "I just hope that sometime...somewhere...Lidia and I get the chance to dance again...forever." And of course he addresses this living on by *enacting* it, since he *is* by now a spectral surviving voice speaking from beyond the grave. After Marcus's words, as pointed out earlier, all the main characters, with the exception of the "supernatural" characters, rise from the dead and line up in the foreground of the screen, while techno music obsessively keeps on playing to punctuate this "re-apparition."[40] However, the film does not just show yet another spectral embodiment of survival; the pose of the characters also suggests that they anticipate another rerun, or even multiple reruns, of the story. What kind of living on this is likely to be, the film leaves undecided. Marcus's final words point to a reiteration that alters and displaces, perhaps a rerun of the story in which he and Lidia "get the chance to dance again...forever" without entertaining murderous thoughts. The position of the by now invisible but no less powerful "master" Hecate suggests otherwise. From his perspective, the character's expectations are nothing but an instance of self-deception. This is not least because anticipation may be what "neutralizes" the future, what "reduces, presentifies, transforms into memory [*en mémoire*], into the future anterior and, therefore into a memory [*en souvenir*], that which [is] still to come" (Derrida and Stiegler 106–7). In terms closer to the film, and to cite Hecate's words from the beginning of *Rave Macbeth*, "stories repeat themselves" and thus always-already belong to the modality of a "future anterior" that deactivates the irruption of the event and the production of the new. To Hecate, change has to do with change in "the tools of [the] trade" of wizards and warlocks such as himself. A shift in terms of the "medium" through which he operates (i.e., the shift from yesterday's magical "potions" to today's "chemicals") does not affect the logic of reiteration, which remains a reiteration of the same. Yet the film shows that the shift of "medium"—the emphasis on "restless ecstasy" (3.2.24)—becomes entangled with the more general problematics of the "out-of-jointedness" of media technology, its radical untimeliness and anachrony. In particular, it is mostly through this shift that the film articulates a trenchant critique of disembodied visuality, and raises questions about the cinematic medium as an exclusively visual medium to be solely and safely "consumed" visually. Thus, stories *do* "repeat themselves." Yet, there is no repetition without difference. To quote Derrida one last time, the logic of iterability ensures that "a phantom's return is, each time, another, different return, on a different stage" (Derrida and Stiegler 24). That the characters tread a bare and empty stage that evokes or simulates the "original" medium of Shakespearean performance adds a further spectral dimension to the possibility of a return that is "each time, another, different return," a return as event and singular form of living on. If the pose of the characters, suspended between eagerness and resignation mixed with exhaustion, is a call for further remediations that are structurally almost devoid of content, it is a call for remediations in which no medium supersedes and absorbs another. Through ghostly silhouettes inscribing and anticipating iterability, the film extends to the future a scenario of multimodal forms of mediality that it often articulates in all its complexity, especially by drawing attention to Hecate's "supplementary" screen. This is a scenario of spectral coexistence of media, a scenario in which each medium (including the simulation of the "archaic" theatrical medium) haunts the other, a scenario that is thus one of *uncanny* media convergence, not one of absolute translatability across media.[41] Therefore, the end of the film implies that it is through the spatial and temporal "out-of-jointedness" of media and forms of reciprocal haunting—what Richard Burt may call the "dialectic of reanimation and de-animation" (*Film and Media* 29) through which old and new media uncannily relate to one another—that "Shakespeare" survives as a perpetually vanishing "Thing."

CHAPTER 7

"He Speaks…Or Rather…He Tweets": The Specter of the "Original," Media, and "Media-Crossed" Love in *Such Tweet Sorrow*

This chapter focuses on *Such Tweet Sorrow*, a modern-day performance of *Romeo and Juliet* on the social networking platform Twitter that took place over a period of almost five weeks in 2010, produced by the UK-based multimedia company Mudlark in collaboration with the Royal Shakespeare Company, digital media company Screen WM, and Channel Four's now-defunct digital investment fund 4iP.[1] Unlike previous experiments with Twitter-based Shakespeare,[2] *Such Tweet Sorrow* stands out as the first professional Twitter adaptation of a Shakespearean play, and still the only one to date, in which actors associated with the Royal Shakespeare Company interacted with one another as well as with the audience of Twitter followers in "real time," improvising on the "missions" they received each day from Mudlark's writing team (Tim Wright and Bethan Marlow),[3] and reacting to events taking place at the time, such as the 2010 political elections in Britain, the London Marathon and Champions League matches. It was the first adaptation, therefore, that attempted to explore the dramatic potential of Twitter as an online interactive social platform, and add entertainment to its "traditional" uses as a microblogging platform, source of information and general-purpose networking.[4] What also differentiates *Such Tweet Sorrow* from other forms of Twitter Shakespeare is that it continually drew attention to itself as a Twitter adaptation, as indicated, for instance, by Mercutio's tweet to Romeo that gives the title to this chapter ("Oh he speaks…or rather…he tweets," 24 Apr., 10:12 a.m.), a playful citation and transformation, with homoerotic overtones, of Romeo's reaction to Juliet's initial words in the balcony scene ("She speaks," 2.1.67).[5] Additionally, and relatedly, this Twitter version of *Romeo and Juliet* consistently engaged with, and incorporated, the whole gamut of Web 2.0 social networking platforms, including YouTube, AudioBoo, Yfrog, Twitpics, Tumblr, Spotify, Facebook, and even Skype, thus articulating itself as a dramatic example of the "flow of content across multiple media platforms" typical of what Henry Jenkins may call "convergence culture" (2).[6]

As it charts its innovative aspects, the chapter shows that *Such Tweet Sorrow* repeatedly oscillates between "Shakespeareccentric" and "Shakespearecentric" concerns (Burt, "Introduction" 5–6): it often uncannily combines a self-reflexive orientation toward its medium (and the media it incorporates) with a "spectral" movement toward the language of the "original," a language that is always-already remediated through the "aphoristic" 140-characters constraints of Twitter, and that can be said to obey, more generally, the "cut/copy and paste" logic of contemporary practices of remix.[7] The chapter adds that, from the perspective of Shakespeare studies at least, the interaction of Shakespeare and social media inevitably raises questions about the role of Shakespeare in contemporary media culture: What is Shakespeare doing on Twitter? What is Twitter doing *to* Shakespeare?[8] Is the appeal to Shakespeare, initially signaled in the title of the performance, a rewriting of a line from the balcony scene, merely an empty and opportunistic gesture that is meant to confer cultural prestige to emerging media practices alien to the Bard?[9] Moreover, is this appeal a function of product placement within the increasingly global constituency of social media? (*Such Tweet Sorrow* was sponsored by two phone companies, one of which provided free mobile phones to selected customers to follow the performance).[10] To what extent, if at all, is this example of Twitter Shakespeare a *Shakespearean* adaptation in the first place?

In *Such Tweet Sorrow* the *dramatis personae* of *Romeo and Juliet* is drastically reduced to a cast of six characters, each with their own Twitter account and pseudonym: Juliet Capulet (juletcap16, played by Charlotte Wakefield), a Twilight-obsessed, overprotected and somewhat naïve girl who is just about to turn 16; Tybalt, her brother (Tybalt_Cap, played by Mark Holgate), a simultaneously introspective and aggressive 17-year-old boy who is expelled from boarding school when he is found in possession of drugs; Jesse, Juliet's and Tybalt's eldest sister (Jess_nurse, played by Lu Corfield), nicknamed "Nurse" because she took care of her siblings after their mother Susan was killed in a car crash; Romeo Montague (romeo_mo, played by James Barrett), a vain handsome boy stuck in a dead-end job who compulsively plays videogames, especially *Call of Duty* on Xbox; Mercutio (mercuteio, played by Ben Ashton), a serial womanizer and Romeo's flamboyant best friend; and Larry (LaurenceFriar, played by Geoffrey Newland), a hippyish, ambiguous character with a dodgy past who runs the alternative, Amsterdam-style Electric Kool-Aid Café, and secretly supplies soft drugs to the town's kids, including Tybalt, Romeo, and Mercutio.[11] The characters' initial tweets "lay [the] scene" ("Prologue" 2) in a small town near Manchester in contemporary Britain, ten years after the death of Susan Capulet. Little by little we learn that the "ancient grudge" (3) between Capulets—or "Crapulets," as Mercutio irreverently calls them—and Montagues has to do with the affair between Susan Capulet and painter Charles Montague that indirectly led to the former's death. (They were in the car together, and Charles was driving, when Susan died). Like in *Romeo and Juliet*, this "ancient grudge" is mostly perpetuated by the younger generation, but this time through the use of media platforms, which includes the creation of rival Twitter groups (e.g., *#TeamCapulet*, which also supports the Blues, Manchester City soccer team, and *#TeamMontague*, which supports the Reds, Manchester United soccer team), the exchange of unpleasant tweets, and the uploading of offensive YouTube videos.[12] Or at least this is so until these media "frays" (1.1.114) are replaced by "real" violence: Tybalt kills Mercutio with a machete during a pitch invasion at the end of the derby Manchester City versus Manchester United, and is in turn killed by Romeo in self-defense, who is then forced into exile in a Dutch town while the police are looking for him. As the love story between Romeo and Juliet develops, it is inferred that its future may be nothing but a spectral reiteration of the doomed affair between Susan Capulet and Charles Montague, a "prequel" that supplements, and is eventually supplemented by, the Shakespearean "prequel." Put differently, the story moves forward just as much as it moves backwards, and doubly so, each "prequel" competing with the other until the Shakespearean "prequel" prevails, claiming the death of *both* lovers. In this sense, and from the point of view of this Twitter play, *Romeo and Juliet* not only inscribes fate as one of its themes; it is *itself* the spectrality of fate. What further complicates the structure of this Twitter performance is the addition of an odd extra character, Jago (played by one of the writers, Tim Wright), sometimes called Jago Mosca, a 15-year-old boy who incorporates, as his name indicates, aspects of the Shakespearean character such as malignity, resentment, and the ability to manipulate as well as features of the Jonsonian parasite such as the penchant for social commentary and critique.[13] Continuously blurring the boundaries between "fiction" and "reality," this is also a character whose Tumblr pages mainly function as a kind of metadramatic multimedia blog/ chorus that intermittently provides a partial and ironic commentary on

the (fictional) events as they take place or soon afterwards.[14] He is simultaneously inside and outside the performance. He is mostly invisible to the
other characters ("Nobody sees me in this town . . . I see everything, but they
don't see me"), including Juliet, one of his classmates ("She's in my class
at school. not that she ever looks at me," *TW* 11 Apr., 3:56 p.m.), and it
is this invisibility that allows him to interfere with the action, as when he
hacks into Mercutio's mobile phone and starts sending death-threatening
tweets to Tybalt.[15] However, he is by no means invisible to the audience.
Not only does he clarify in the "Who I Am & What I'm About" section of
his Tumblr blog that this is the right place to "tune in to the gossip, catch
a whiff of that stench coming up from the Capulet drains or fall down the
gaps between the Montague tweets"; he also strongly encourages interaction. Taking advantage of the specificities of Tumblr as a medium, he invites
the online audience to "Ask [him] anything."[16] His enigmatic, disingenuous,
and sometimes impertinent answers complement his activity as a twitterer
who is exceedingly aware that interaction, and retweeting in particular, are
the *conditio sine qua non* for the performance to become a "trending event"
on Twitter, as shown by one of his first tweets, a message launched in the
Twittersphere before the performance "properly" starts: "U peeple need to rt
[i.e., retweet] more and talk to strangers" (*TW* 8 Apr., 4:05 a.m.). Yet, this
is only one side of this multifaceted small-town Iago-like character. Even
as he attempts to trigger participation by the audience to ensure his and
the performance's popularity, he does not forget that he is himself part of
the audience, a self-defined cynical "spectator" (*TM* 16 Apr., 12:41 a.m.)
who relishes his role as an "outsider." [17] In fact, as the performance develops, he arguably becomes a stand-in for the audience's skepticism towards
the story characters: Mercutio is a "spoilt bastard" (*TM* 11 Apr., 5:21 p.m.),
Laurence Friar a "community jerk"(*TM* 12 Apr., 11:59 a.m.), Romeo a "poor
little dumb blonde" (*TM* 17 Apr., 12:49 p.m.), "not exactly bright" (16 Apr.,
12:46 a.m.), Tybalt a "walking soap opera" (*TM* 14 Apr., 10:59 p.m.), and so
on.[18] This skepticism also concerns Twitter as a "social" medium that tends
to replace "real life" ("You guys tweet too much like u don't have a life or
sumthing," *TW* 7 Apr. 4:03 a.m.), and significantly extends to the effectiveness of crucial dramatic moments of the Twitter performance itself.[19] As the
show comes to a close, he looks back at the tragic events and sarcastically
comments: "This ended up being not the floorshow I imagined in my head
but never mind" (*TM* 13 May, 11: 15 a.m.). Specifically reacting to Romeo's
final tweets ("Our first kiss set me free, with our last I'll lie with thee," 12
May, 2:22 a.m.), which he duly retweets, he lashes out: "*boring, no? where's
the f***ing drama? where's the poetry? why didn't we see the BLOOD?! f***ing
killjoys*" (*TM* 13 May, 11: 15 a.m.). One may be tempted to sum up the

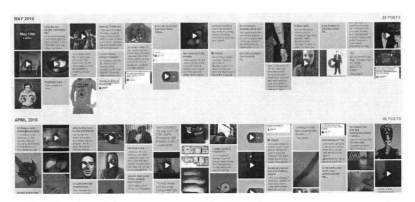

Figure 7.1   Jago's Tumblr blog.

complexity of this character by referring to the words he uses to define himself at the beginning of the show, which are of course words he appropriates from one of his literary predecessors: "I am not what I am" (*TM* 9 Apr., 12:06 p.m.).[20]

*   *   *

"*Where's the f***ing drama? Where's the poetry? Why didn't we see the BLOOD?*" Like his Shakespearean antecedent, and in a postmodern fashion, Jago is "nothing if not critical" (*Oth.* 2.1.122) vis-à-vis a performance in which he is himself ambivalently involved as a character. Moreover, whatever opacity he may be said to possess, his tongue-in-cheek questions lucidly identify issues—the dramatic and poetic possibilities of Twitter or lack thereof; the aesthetic conventions of a Twitter performance—that are also part of the critical debate on *Such Tweet Sorrow*. This debate begins to take shape on the web, and in particular in the blogosphere, before the production actually comes to an end. John Wyver's *Illuminations* blog is probably the first to offer an in-depth, articulated response to this radical digital experiment, only a couple of days after it starts, with an update a few days later that includes a long string of thought-provoking comments and links to other blog posts and web reviews. John Wyver is intrigued by "what the aesthetics of a Twitter performance might be" and concedes that *Such Tweet Sorrow* is a significant experiment in form, "a smart application of social media." Yet he is all in all "troubled" by it. As he explains:

> Bringing new audiences and new readers to Shakespeare is a great and
> glorious thing, but not if the plays and the language and the ideas are

trivialized... There's precious little of the play's language left in the [Twitter] project—and textually-focused throwback that I am, somehow that seems crucial to what 'Shakespeare' is and should be. *Romeo and Juliet* is *not* just a plot, even if the plot is unquestionably available, just as it was to Shakespeare, for any and all uses you may wish to put it to. (13 Apr. 2010)[21]

To refer to Jago's (tongue-in-cheek) critique, where is the poetry, indeed, without Shakespeare's language?[22] This does not mean that "there is not room for all sorts of Shakespeare," including this Twitter experiment. Yet this "Shakespeare ultra-lite" should not be mistaken "for the real thing." *Such Tweet Sorrow* is thus *not* Shakespeare, in much the same way that *West Side Story* is not Shakespeare:[23] the essential and authentic "Shakespeare" resides in the language of the plays. And yet it is a kind of "Shakespeare," an "ultra-lite" travesty of "the real thing."

A number of comments on John Wyver's original post challenge this "Shakespearecentric" approach to the Twitter treatment of *Romeo and Juliet*. In two separate posts, Barbara Henley insists on the medium speci-ficity of adaptations of Shakespeare, and contests Wyver's reliance on the language of the original as the sole criterion for the evaluation of *Such Tweet Sorrow*:

First of all, who is saying that it IS Shakespeare? You seem to be strug-gling with whether this is strictly Shakespeare or not. Well, you're right, it's not. But no-one is saying that it is. It's a modern re-working of the story... My point is that I don't think that John can use the fact that it's not Shakespeare, or not like Shakespeare, to criticise *Such Tweet Sorrow*... It's like saying that Prokofiev's *Romeo & Juliet* ballet isn't great because it's not Shakespeare or it's lost a lot of the textual/ poetical intri-cacy. It's a whole different medium. As is Twitter. If Mudlark/the RSC wanted to make it more 'like Shakespeare' then they'd put it on stage, using Elizabethan language. Which would be doing nothing creative, interesting or new with it at all. (13 Apr., 11:31 a.m.; 3:30 p.m.)

Specifically referring to Barbara Henley's first post, Holly Gramazio dis-agrees with her interpretation but maintains that *Such Tweet Sorrow* needs to be judged on its own terms as a critical response to Shakespeare's play, and not on the basis of its faithfulness to the language of the "original":

I think it's perhaps a little disingenuous to say that it isn't meant to be Shakespeare... This is a project from (among others) the RSC, retaining many character names from the Shakespeare version. Its title is a direct allusion to the play. I can't imagine it would have been made by these people, in this way, if it wasn't meant to be considered explicitly as a response to or retelling of Shakespeare. So, no, it's not meant to be Shakespeare as such; but when trying to judge how well it works, it seems fair to consider it as an interpretation of, or response to Shakespeare. (13 Apr., 2:54 p.m.)

Alan Turner argues along the same lines as Barbara Henley but a little more sarcastically, and similarly applauds the RSC's aesthetic decision to explore the language of social media:

> There must be at least four or five other Twitter users who share John's reservations about the language in which RSC have chosen to stage *Such Tweet Sorrow*. Perhaps they should get together and tweet a copy of Shakespeare's 'original.' Tone problem solved. I personally can understand why RSC may have decided to abandon any half-way position, and to commit instead to the vernacular of contemporary social media. This being Twitter and all. (13 Apr., 4:22 p.m.)

Yet for some commentators the trouble is precisely with "this being Twitter": the "vernacular of contemporary social media" tends to reduce the complexity of Shakespeare's language, and of English more generally, to "text speak." As Helen argues,

> The problem is not that it's a different version of "Romeo and Juliet." It's that it's Twitter's version of "Romeo and Juliet." I find little value in the one-sentence, off-the-cuff comments that populate Twitter. I believe this form of communication devalues the English language and discourages users from developing well-thought-out commentary. (13 Apr., 3:18 p.m.)[24]

Where is the poetry, indeed, on Twitter?

I have cited extensively from John Wyver's *Illuminations* blog first of all because it includes representative samples of the responses to *Such Tweet Sorrow* in the blogosphere and on the web more generally;[25] secondly, because it shows that in the debate on Twitter Shakespeare, in much the same way as in the discussions about appropriations of the Bard in popular culture studied by Douglas Lanier, the question remains how far one is "willing to extend the name of 'Shakespeare,'" a question that is inextricably bound with "assumptions about what constitutes the essential or authentic

Shakespeare." Lanier further explains, and in a way that can be usefully applied to Twitter Shakespeare:

> Popular appropriations are controversial because they often extend what counts as "Shakespeare" beyond the limits of where many are willing to go. The "Shakespeare" of popular culture is relatively unburdened with worries about historical accuracy, interpretive precision, or faithfulness to the letter of Shakespeare's scripts. Because of this, for those invested in "proper" Shakespeare, Shakespop is at best an amusing form of kitsch and at worst a travesty that threatens to displace the real thing. (*Shakespeare* 9)

It must be added that to willingly embrace *Such Tweet Sorrow* as *not* "the real thing" raises a number of questions of its own. It may inadvertently—and by contrast—reproduce a "Shakespeare" that survives in a separate aesthetic realm, and is wholly unaffected by processes of remediation. It may suggest, that is, to refer to Barbara Henley's post again, which insists on the positive aspects of it *not* being "Shakespeare," that staging something "more 'like Shakespeare,'... using Elizabethan language"—some kind of more straightforward "Shakespeare"—is an entirely unproblematic option. Moreover, as Lanier also observes, "delighting in the ways that Shakespop flies in the face of received authority" may underestimate the fact that "the act of transgression paradoxically depends upon preserving—at least initially—some conception of an authentic, original, or proper Shakespeare" (19).

*   *   *

Whether *Such Tweet Sorrow* is Shakespeare or not, and to what extent, are questions to which this chapter will return. The "precious little of the play's language" that is "left in the [Twitter] project" (Wyver)—what may be called the spectral remainder of the language of *Romeo and Juliet*—will also be further explored.[26] For the moment, it is worth pointing out that members of the production team, or people variously associated with this Twitter project, repeatedly appeal to "Shakespeare" to promote it as a legitimate and viable form of adaptation. To be more precise, they invoke a low-brow "populist" Shakespeare, a "Shakespeare" that embodies antiauthoritarian and democratizing impulses, "freed from the shackles of highbrows and professionals and returned to the 'people'" (Lanier, *Shakespeare* 18), the kind of "Shakespeare," that is, as Douglas Lanier has demonstrated, that often circulates, and with ambivalent ideological valences, in popular culture. In an interview with *The Stage*, Roxana Silbert, director of *Such Tweet Sorrow* but also associate director for the Royal Shakespeare Company, speaks of the project in the following terms: "I am hoping that it will allow a lot of people to follow a really brilliant story in a way that's accessible and very populist and, of course, Shakespeare was a very accessible, very populist playwright" (qtd. in Woolman n. pag.). This "accessible" and "populist" Shakespeare is also the Shakespeare of the potentially expandable realm of a online participatory culture: "a lot of people" stands for both younger audiences who are frequent users of social networking and microblogging websites—who are, in short, already "tweeple"—*and* prospective new users who are intrigued by this Shakespearean adaptation on Twitter. [27] In another interview Roxana Silbert describes *Such Tweet Sorrow* as "not very reverential." Yet when asked what Shakespeare would make of it, she replies, rather predictably: "I think he would've loved it," and continues as follows: "All you've got on Twitter is the actor, the story and the audience. I've directed at the Globe where there aren't lights, sound effects or much staging so in fact there's something rather pure about this" (qtd. in Kennedy n. pag.).[28] Paradoxically, given Twitter's potential as a cross-media platform, which will be fully exploited in the course of the performance of *Such Tweet Sorrow*, she chooses to emphasize the latter's relatively "un-mediated" characteristics ("there is something rather pure about this"), which supposedly recall the "naked" style of productions of Shakespeare at the reconstructed Globe (and, by implication, the "original" unadorned staging of Shakespeare's plays in Elizabethan and Jacobean times).[29] To adopt Bolter and Grusin's terms, in the interviews with Roxana Silbert hypermediacy becomes immediacy (5), or at least an almost total erasure of traces of mediation. By the same token, Twitter emerges as not merely a new medium but, rather, as an *old* new medium, which is arguably a way of negotiating the oxymoronic qualities of a "Twitter Shakespeare." As to Jason Hall, one of the coinvestors in the project through Screen WM, he decides to stress the highly interactive nature of the Twitter performance, but in a way that also highlights the uncanny mixing of temporalities: what appears to be a brand new phenomenon, connected with the emergence of new media, and social media in particular, is in fact, and to a considerable extent, a spectral return of the past: "And as much as it's tempting to say this is a 21st Century version of Shakespeare, there's so much about it that harks back to the way Shakespeare would have been performed in his day to the cheers and jeers from the balconies and groundlings" (n. pag.). The first time of Shakespeare on Twitter, or at least of this Twitter Shakespeare, is thus the second time of repetition(s). Put differently, in these general descriptions of the project the appeal to a "populist" Shakespeare alternates with considerations about a medium that turns out to be not entirely, or not at all, "Shakespeareccentric": it is an "anachronistic" old new medium that embodies a multilayered temporality, or even the "countertime" of anachrony.[30]

As mentioned earlier, *Such Tweet Sorrow* continuously draws attention to itself as a Twitter adaptation. This self-reflexivity takes many different forms. At the beginning of the performance, as the characters tweet to establish themselves as credible "tweeple" with their own peculiar traits (and as characters worth following), the emphasis is mostly on the position of each character vis-à-vis Twitter as a medium. Moreover, this position arguably replicates, or simulates, the predicament of members of the audience itself, an audience that, like the characters, is made of both experienced users and potential users who are initially reluctant to join the world of social media. For example, Juliet's first tweets are all about her being new to Twitter, and her astonishment at the possibilities and flexibility of the new medium. She struggles with it at first ("Hello Twitter!…OK so…how does this work? As you can probably tell I am totally new to this! I've only just joined!", 11 Apr., 5:03 a.m.), and thus asks her more experienced sister Jesse for help. She then introduces herself: "Totally haven't introduced myself yet! My name is Juliet. I'm 15 and SO proud to be a Capulet! I turn 16 in 12 days and I am sooo excited! x" (5:47 a.m.). She soon realizes that she can follow "celebs," including her idol, Robert Pattinson, playing Edward Cullen in *The Twilight Saga* film series. (She keeps a life-size cutout of the actor in her room.) She expresses bewilderment at the number of *her* followers—in fact, only 80 as she speaks but she will become the most popular character at the height of the performance with 5,778 followers.[31] While welcoming the discovery of Twitter by her "little sister" ("I never thought this day would come! Finally, you've stepped into the technical generation! Get tweeting little one!", 5:08 a.m.), Jess is also slightly ironic about her use of the medium: "This place [i.e. Twitter] is your idea of heaven: a place to share gossip without having to step out of your flea pit" (5:32 a.m.). She thus embodies the relatively more detached attitude of some experienced users. Moreover, her tongue-in-cheek remarks also function as more general sardonic comments about a medium—a virtual "place"—that allows "tweeple" to interact without "properly" interacting. In a sense, this is the very definition of being "social" in the world of what Geert Lovink calls "living-apart-together [social] media" (45). Yet, as a new user, Juliet is clearly enthusiastic, and quickly picks up the possibilities Twitter offers. In her own words: "I am getting pretty Twitter sussed" (7:29 a.m.). It is worth adding that, like in Shakespeare's play, Juliet is "a stranger in the world" (1.2.8), a secluded and overprotected young woman who is never allowed out after school and detests the healthy-food fanatic her father married after the death of her beloved mother Susan. If Twitter rapidly becomes a means of escape and her "idea of heaven," it is because of the claustrophobic atmosphere of her father's house, which is a reworking of the patriarchal constraints to which the "original" Juliet is subjected in "fair Verona" ("Prologue" 2): "I feel sooo trapped in this house!!! I feel caged in! I am so thankful for my Netbook :)" (12 Apr., 12:49 p.m.). Although they are mostly oriented toward the new medium, Juliet's initial tweets are therefore not entirely "Shakespeareccentric," in that they also offer a creative response to elements of the characterization of Juliet in the "original" play. A little predictably, her increasing mastery of the medium parallels her coming of age, and is further enhanced by her "sexual awakening" that occurs when she meets Romeo at the birthday party, or "twarty," organized for her by her sister. In a way, her penchant for the medium is just as "rash…unadvised…sudden" (2.2.160) as her love for "fair Montague" (140). Her expertise soon extends to other social networking platforms: she creates a Facebook page for the party, uses TwitPic to upload pictures of the masks that will be the main "props" for the event, and contributes to the party's Spotify list. She goes as far as to upload lonely girl15-like YouTube videos, including one in which she frankly talks about her post-party sexual experiences with Romeo. This resonates with, and intensifies, the boldness that the "original" Juliet exhibits in the balcony scene under "the mask of night" (127), and can be usefully contrasted with versions of Juliet as a relatively desexualized "Victorian" character popularized in filmic adaptations of the play such as Baz Luhrmann's *William Shakespeare's Romeo + Juliet* (cf. Anderegg 62). Yet this "re-vision" also raises a number of more general questions about the aesthetic conventions of a Twitter performance. For instance, what happens to the dialectic between public and private, between what must be kept secret and what can be disclosed, a dialectic that is so crucial to *Romeo and Juliet*, when we are faced with an online performance in which everything is by definition available and on display?[32] Does this Twitter play invite us to reconsider what being online means, rearticulating it as a phenomenon of intermittent access and/or distracted perception? As we shall see, as the performance develops, this type of questions will become more and more central.

Laurence Friar, nicknamed Larry, the 38-year-old owner of a local internet café and alternative bookshop, starts tweeting while attending a three-day conference on "Building Communities in Britain." He is at first as hesitant as Juliet vis-à-vis the medium, and he is equally keen on learning more: "Oh gosh I see! People can actually reply to what I'm 'tweeting'. Amazing! I think we cover that tomorrow on the course" (12 Apr., 10:07 a.m.). However, unlike Juliet, his main interest is in how social media facilitate young people's involvement in their communities, and in particular how they may help overcome antisocial behavior—the contemporary equivalent of the "civil brawls"

(1.1.86) of Shakespeare's play. And indeed, the main "problem" in his community is the feud between Capulets and Montagues ("In my small town the big problem is family feuding. montagues & capulets. Would love 2 talk 2 others about how to deal with *that* problem," 4:01 a.m.), which he, with the same zeal as the "original" Friar Laurence, duly endeavors to stop by offering (often unsolicited) advice to the other characters, organizing table tennis tournaments to allow youngsters of opposed factions to socialize, and acting as "assistant" (2.2.90) to the love between Romeo and Juliet. Needless to say, as in *Romeo and Juliet*, this only produces disastrous results.[33] His ambition to play a role in the community through social media does not make him forget the other opportunities offered by new technologies: "course over, coach home:-(learned so much re Twitter? intend to use it from now on to give my cafe a much bigger presence in cyberspace" (14 Apr., 7:45 a.m.). Once back home, he uploads and regularly updates a webpage to promote his Electric Kool-Aid Café, a webpage that also plays an essential role in terms of plot development. (It is on this webpage, and in the form of an acrostic, that Juliet is given instructions on where to find the "remedy" [4.1.76]—a "vial" [93] of Propofol, a general anesthetic also called "the milk of amnesia"—and thus "undertake / A thing like death . . . / That cop'st with death himself to scape from it," 73–75).[34] But, as one soon learns, and as it can be inferred from the motto that appears on his Twitter profile ("Some things best kept private. Come in to cafe and ask me if you want to know"), Laurence Friar is also involved in another kind of "business": selling soft drugs to the town's kids so as to prevent them from being hooked on hard drugs. Or so he says, almost as if responding to, and taking to the extreme, the paradoxical logic of the "original" Friar's argument that "virtue itself turns vice being misapplied, / and vice sometime's by action dignified" (2.3.21–22). This makes his character an odd combination of naïveté, self-deception and hypocrisy and in this, too, he is not unlike Shakespeare's Friar. Of course, the fact that he still smokes dope, in spite of posing as a reformed character who has been clean for ten years, and that he sells drugs to youngsters, throws an ironic light on his project of reaching out to young people through social media. It can be argued that this irony also functions in a more extended metadramatic way. In other words, it is through the ambiguous characterization of Laurence Friar that we are invited *not* to take too seriously *Such Tweet Sorrow*'s own ambitious project of bringing *Shakespeare* into the lives of young people through social networking media. It is not by chance, one may add, that this playful self-reflexive process develops in relation to Laurence Friar, as he is the character, as we shall see, who cites Shakespeare's language more than any other.

The pre-Juliet Romeo of *Such Tweet Sorrow* is a character who "private in his chamber pens himself, / Shuts up his windows, locks fair daylight out"

(1.1.135–36) in order to play *Call of Duty* on Xbox, and it is by doing so that he meets an online game player called Rosaline, with whom he becomes infatuated. He is thus by no means as "bookish" as the pre-Juliet Romeo of Shakespeare's play. Still, he is the character who offers a temporary resistance to Twitter as a medium and thus also allegorizes the position of potential members of the audience who are intrigued by the performance but reluctant to "follow" it. As his best friend Mercutio reports: "Ooh ladies & gentleman of twitter romeo is calling all twitter users twatters—what do you say to that?" (11 Apr., 1:16 p.m.). A few days later, he adds: "'Twitter is for twats' according to Romeo" (15 Apr., 8:02 a.m.). This causes Laurence Friar's reaction, applauded by Mercutio, who gently rebukes Romeo with the words of Shakespeare's Friar, thus combining "Shakespeareccentricity" and "Shakespearecentricity." He is probably smoking dope as he tweets: "Twitter is for twats!?—be plain, good son, and homely in thy drift! Ha, Romeo needs an open mind; puff puff give" (8:06 a.m., cf. *Rom.* 2.2.55). Romeo's unwillingness to play the Twitter game also triggers the creation of hashtag groupings to get Romeo on Twitter such as #getromeontwitter. It is only on the fifth day of the performance that he decides to sign up to Twitter: "I've seen all the tweets from the people that merc stalks…I mean follows!. so ok here I am. gota give the fans what they want" (15 Apr., 8:30 a.m.). He chooses, that is, in terms closer to Shakespeare's play, to be "sociable" and to be the "Romeo" of social media (cf. *Rom.* 2.3.82), although we already know his voice and physical appearance through Mercutio's YouTube videos and TwitPic pictures.[35] As to Mercutio, Jess Nurse and Tybalt, they stand in for more experienced Twitter users. Mercutio, in particular, is a raucous, boisterous, and larger-than-life character whose Twitter style is unique. As Romeo acknowledges once he starts using Twitter, comparing himself unfavorably to his friend: "merc has his computer brain and nimble typing fingers. I, on the other hand, have typing fingers of lead" (15 Apr., 9:12 a.m.).[36] He repeatedly, and from the very beginning, engages with his followers, retweeting their tweets and thus continuously blurring the boundaries between characters and audience. He is usually as inventive in his punning as the "original" Mercutio, and perhaps as bursting with misogynistic jokes. In particular, he outrageously flirts with the female audience, and goes as far as to upload pictures and videos of women's cleavages illegally captured with his mobile phone, creating the controversial #uploadthatload site, to which Romeo also occasionally contributes.[37] He is tremendously at ease with the whole gamut of social media, and he shows this in a condensed form after he is hurt by Tybalt's machete and in the throes of death. First of all, he tweets in an introspective style that is quite unusual for him ("Who wants to bring me flowers or something? Don't like being on my own," 3

May, 2:09 p.m.); he then reacquires a "laddish" persona through the upload of a "Hello Nurse" YouTube video; he retweets a tweet by a female gym instructor who has finally accepted to go out with him and comments on the irony of this; he provides his #mercutiogroupies with a link to his online "testament," Jack Hylton's YouTube version of the bitter sweet "Life Is Just a Bowl of Cherries," and this just after delivering his final Twitter lines, which are arguably an effective, medium-oriented rewriting of "A plague o' both your houses" (3.1.91): "@romeo_mo @Tybalt_Cap May both your families rot in hell! Fuck #teammontague from now on its only #teammercutio" (3:24 p.m.). In short, if *Such Tweet Sorrow* in any way recaptures the spirit of Elizabethan and Jacobean performances, as people associated with the production often claim (see Hall), it is mostly because of Mercutio, who is not only a character but an emblem of the highly interactive and cross-media nature of the performance. He is a character, moreover, whose "life" extends well beyond the bounds of the performance, as shown, for instance, by the Facebook memorial page that a group of followers put together to celebrate their hero after his death.

* * *

The characters' persistent awareness of the medium, which is part of the production's extensive self-reflexivity, shows that *Such Tweet Sorrow* not only dramatizes a story of tragic love between two "tweeple" in the universe of Twitter; it also tells a story about its medium and the other social media it incorporates, making them an essential part of its "message." To borrow from Peter Donaldson's groundbreaking investigation of a wide range of Shakespeare-related filmic material that implicitly and/or explicitly allegorizes its "cross-media self-consciousness" ("Media" 61), in this transmedia Twitter experiment "media themes rise to the level of subject matter, vying for attention with and sometimes supplanting the story line of the source play" ("Bottom" 23).[38] In other words, not unlike the Shakespearean adaptations Donaldson analyzes, the "theme" of *Such Tweet Sorrow* is also the "ferment in communications technologies" ("Media" 61). Yet of course since the publication of Donaldson's articles the "rapidly shifting mediascape" to which he refers (61), in connection with films such as Baz Luhrmann's *William Shakespeare's Romeo + Juliet*, has itself rapidly shifted. In a recent article on "New Media," Mark B. N. Hansen underlines that

> the explosion of user-generated digital "content" (blogs, discussion forums, photo-sharing, video animation, and so on) has refocused the function of computational media from storage to production, from the

archiving of individual experience to the generation of collective presence and connectivity itself. (180)

The appearance of a number of social networking platforms such as MySpace, Flickr, Facebook, and YouTube shows that "what is mediated by Web 2.0 is less the content that users upload than *the sheer connectivity*" (180, emphasis added). In other words, "connectivity emerges as an end in itself, distinct from the actual sharing of... (traditional) media content" (181). According to Hansen, this symptomatizes "a widespread mediatic regime change...a change in the vocation of media and mediation themselves" (180–81).[39] In an article published in *Critical Inquiry*, media theorist Lev Manovich similarly underlines "the explosion of user-created media content on the web (dating from, say, 2005)," and argues that this "has unleashed a new media universe" that is not simply "a scaled-up version of twentieth-century media culture." Building on the work of social media designer Adrian Chan, he boldly states that "we have moved from *media* to *social media*" (319).[40] He goes as far as to argue that crucial terms such as "*content, cultural object, cultural production*, and *cultural consumption*" (Manovich's emphasis) are being redefined by Web 2.0 practices, and to such an extent that, as terms, they run the risk of becoming obsolete. To Manovich, we witness "new kinds of communications where factual content, opinion, and conversation often can't be clearly separated." He continues by suggesting that "often *content, news*, or *media* become tokens used to initiate or maintain a conversation. Their original meaning is less important than their functions as tokens" (326)—in Hansen's terms, what matters is connectivity itself, and this over and above any "content" that is being exchanged and/or the media through which this exchange is taking place. Manovich's examples of these "conversations" are blogs whose entries are made up of "comments about an item copied from another source"; uploading pictures on each other's pages on MySpace or commenting on YouTube videos, either in the form of written comments or in the form of video responses or both, and so on. In all these examples the "original"—the original post, video, picture, or any other media item— may "generate a long discussion that goes into new original directions, with the original item long forgotten" (326).[41] He adds that although one could find historical precedents and/or contemporary analogues for these Web 2.0 conversations, what is particularly striking about them is how they "become distributed in space and time"; the fact, that is, that "people can respond to each other regardless of their location," and that "the conversation can in theory go forever" (327).

Much of Manovich's argument could be extended to Twitter—a social networking platform he does not take into account—and, in particular, to a Twitter performance such as *Such Tweet Sorrow*. In *Such Tweet Sorrow*, one could surmise, the "Shakespearean" tweet is just as significant—or just as insignificant—as the vernacular tweet, or a picture on Twitpics, or a video on YouTube, or an audio file on Audioboo. They all function as post-hermeneutic "tokens" in a conversation—a *dramatic* conversation, in this case—that takes place not only among characters but also between each character and his/her followers as well as among the followers themselves. This is a conversation that continually crosses the boundaries between "fiction" and "real life": a character's tweets mix with a follower's "real" daily feeds; a follower who tweets a character becomes to an extent himself/herself a character; a character who retweets a follower's tweet is simultaneously a character and a member of the audience.[42] Moreover, it is a conversation that does not have any limits, at least potentially, neither in terms of space—followers can respond to the characters as well as to other followers "regardless of their location"—nor in terms of time. It is true that *Such Tweet Sorrow* only lasted five weeks. Yet the performance is made of "conversations" that are potentially endless: followers who have become friends (i.e., who started following each other) as a result of the performance may continue to tweet each other—and they do as I write; as mentioned earlier, the #mercutiogroupies dedicated a memorial page to Mercutio; the most enthusiastic followers organized an online *Midsummer Night's Tweetmare Virtual Party*, a spin-off of the performance that took place on 18 June 2010, over a month after the end of the show.[43] What is also worth pointing out is that all *Such Tweet Sorrow* characters are still on Twitter, and thus one may still follow them, or respond to the YouTube videos or pictures or audio files uploaded by them; and that the vast majority of followers have not taken the time of "unfollowing" the characters, nor have the characters unfollowed those they followed, including celebrities and their own followers. Indeed, to return to Manovich, "the conversation can in theory go forever" (327).[44]

Yet, is Shakespeare's language in *Such Tweet Sorrow* a mere "token" in what may be called, after the "original" play, the "silk thread" (2.1.225) of global and asynchronous conversations? And what about Twitter as a medium? Is an exchange of tweets the same as, say, the exchange of gifts on Facebook? While mostly in agreement with interpretations of the transformation of contemporary media culture such as Manovich's, I now want to underline aspects of *Such Tweet Sorrow* that respond in a singular way, and often creatively, to this (new) media configuration, a configuration in which this Twitter play participates, and which it can even be said to allegorize. If the "Shakespeareccentric" theme of *Such Tweet Sorrow* is the "ferment in communications technologies" (Donaldson, "Media" 61), and, more specifically, the exchange of tokens and/or connectivity itself, this does not exclude a "Shakespearecentric" movement toward the language of the "original." In fact, one could argue that the performance is at its most effective when it inscribes a double-edged movement toward *and* away from Shakespeare, as when Laurence Friar, as mentioned earlier, juxtaposes a medium-oriented remark with the language of the "original" ("Twitter is for twats!?—he plain, good son, and homely in thy drift! Ha, Romeo needs an open mind," 15 Apr., 8:06 a.m.); or when a character-spectator such as Jago intriguingly weaves Shakespeare's language into the language of Twitter, announcing on his Tumblr page that "If I end up following you [i.e., on Twitter], it's because I only really follow myself" (9 Apr., 12:06 p.m.) (cf. *Oth.* 1.1.42). Of course, and as these examples already show, the "original" does not re-present itself as such, not even when the tweets exchanged by the characters incorporate, and read like, the "original." Put differently, in this online performance, and in much the same way as in contemporary media adaptations of Shakespeare that simultaneously evoke and displace "Shakespeare" (and its authority) through processes of "surrogation," the language of the "original" does not so much appear as *re*-appear.[45] Moreover, it re-appears, as we shall see, in very idiosyncratic and specific ways, often in the form of parodic citing and re-citing but not exclusively so. It re-emerges as the spectral effect of a process of adaptation that irremediably supplements the source and thus puts under erasure any clear-cut distinction between the "first time" of the source and its repetition. Subject to the "aphoristic" 140-characters constraints of Twitter, the "original" is a ghostly trace that is forced to cohabit with other languages, including media languages, and is thus recontextualized and repurposed, as when Laurence Friar inserts the language of *Romeo and Juliet* in the "citational environment" (Worthen, "Performativity" 1104) of youth football culture: "Tackles like that are horrific. Could have been career threatening. Violent delights have violent ends" (3 May, 8:35 a.m.) (cf. 2.5.9), a tweet that, in this context, is a premonition of Tybalt's and Mercutio's deaths. However, that the language of *Romeo and Juliet* re-presents itself in the form of spectral remainders does not diminish its power. If these Shakespearean remains are transformed through their interaction with the other languages incorporated by the performance, and especially media languages, they also in turn implicitly and/or explicitly interrogate the *modus operandi* and conventions of these languages. For instance, and to stay with an example already cited, Jago's disquisition on following ("If I end up following you, it's because I only really follow myself," 9 Apr., 12:06 p.m.) is a condensed reflection on the labile distinction between self and other on Twitter. It draws attention to, and perhaps even exposes, the obsessive rites of self-management, self-promotion, and self-inflation permeating the world of social networking media (cf. Lovink 38–49). This is a world, according to media theorist Geert Lovink, made of "walled gardens" that "seal off the aggressive Other" (17). From Jago's perspective at least, the other is the *self's* other; following is not an interaction but feeds back upon a self that is eager to be followed, and perhaps "mentioned" or "favorited."[46]

To further consider the question of Shakespeare's language in *Such Tweet Sorrow*, it is worth underlining its *absence* at the beginning of the performance, except for the word "ladybird" (cf. 1.3.3), frequently used by Jesse to address her younger sister. This absence is even more remarkable because the characters profusely cite from other literary sources, from Chaucer to Yeats, from Bukowski to Larkin, from Tolstoj to Keats. This is not a casual absence, I want to suggest, but a resounding silence, perhaps the symptom of the production team's uncertainty as to what to do with the language of *Romeo and Juliet*: it may be linked to a sense of reverence toward the language of the Bard or, alternatively, to doubts about its relevance to the world of Twitter. Whatever the reasons for the initial absence of the language of Shakespeare, this silence reads like a strategy of avoidance that does not fail to bear the mark of that which it excludes. It implicitly rearticulates Shakespearean textuality as "spectro-textuality," a ghostly absent force that keeps on haunting.[47] As we are three days into the performance, this strategy of avoidance breaks down, which does not dispel spectrality but, rather, re-marks it. Put differently, the language of *Romeo and Juliet* does not so much appear as *re*-appear. In terms of the stylistic conventions of Twitter, it literally materializes in the form of what "tweeple" abbreviate as "RT"; it emerges for the first time as a retweet of a tweet sent to Laurence Friar by one of the followers whose Twitter persona is—rather appropriately—Daisy B.: "RT @dovof: @LaurenceFriar Within the infant rind of this sweet flower Poison hath residence, and medicine power!" (13 Apr., 4:21 p.m.).[48]

One needs to point out that at this stage of the performance this is the only "Shakespearean" tweet by a follower that is being retweeted by a character and is thus the only one that acquires visibility in the timeline of the production's official website. Yet this tweet is one among the many "Shakespearean" tweets through which some of the followers interact, or attempt to interact, with the characters: at the beginning of the performance, that is, members of the audience repeatedly remind the characters—and will continue to do so at crucial turning points of this Twitter play—that they are *Shakespearean* characters, thus implicitly acting as relays of the "spectro-textuality" haunting the production from its margins. This always-already remediated "Shakespearecentricity" interestingly coexists with a simultaneous movement away from Shakespeare, one of whose most captivating examples is undoubtedly the attempt by a considerable number of followers such as the #savemercutio group and the #mercutiogroupies to alter (what they perceive as) the *excessively* "Shakespearecentric" storyline of *Such Tweet Sorrow* and thus save Mercutio. The main site of resistance to the faithful reproduction of a plot development that inexorably condemns Mercutio to death is a transmedia blog coordinated by the #mercutiogroupies ("Berries").[49] Packed with mock posters aimed at enrolling "tweeple" in the "Save Mercutio" campaign, and including repurposed film stills and YouTube videos as well as poems, artworks and even an advert for a language kit to "learn how to speak Mercutian" (2 May, 10:33 p.m.), the blog insists that "not even Shakespeare wants [Mercutio] to die." One of the most creative followers elaborates on this idea, and decides to contribute to the campaign by uploading a fake update of the online page of *The Guardian* (4:21 p.m.). This hoax webpage reports the discovery of a lost version of *Romeo and Juliet* in which Mercutio does not die but falls in love with the Nurse, which shows how "Shakespeareccentric" concerns articulate themselves through an appeal to a notion of the "original," however parodic this may be.[50]

To return to the reappearance of the language of the "original," it is worth adding that Laurence Friar not only retweets but also comments on the Shakespearean lines from 2.2. immediately afterwards, and this in a separate cheeky tweet: "thanks @dovof I know the very flower you speak of!" (13 Apr., 4:22 p.m.), a tweet in which he presumably associates the Shakespearean "flower" with cannabis. In spite of the fact that he presents himself as a "reformed character,"[51] we find him enjoying the party that takes place at the end of the conference on social media, and especially the "most

Figure 7.2 Tweeting Shakespeare on drugs.

mellow Merlot" (2:55 p.m.), but missing other intoxicating substances: "I know what I want but it ain't on the menu" (2:47 p.m.). Getting away from the party and sitting outside the conference building, he finally manages to smoke weed, as one can infer from the following "poetic" tweet: "Dip in the night, but the Friar is getting higher" (5:42 p.m.). As he is about to smoke, he cannot refrain from offering pearls of wisdom on the contemplative aspects of rolling a joint *and* tweeting: "There's something meditative about skinning up" (4:39 p.m.); "Come to think of it, there's something meditative about tweeting" (4:45 p.m.). Back home, and still recovering from the excesses of the night before, he returns to the language of his Shakespearean ancestor, juxtaposing the latter's metaphysical reflections on the sublunar world with the words from a postcard from India he has just received. Once again under the effect of cannabis, he almost compulsively concludes by shifting into a parodic mode: "Ah, from Manali with love; the powerful grace that lies in plants, herbs . . . & stoners?" (14 Apr., 6:22 p.m.). ("Stoners" replaces Friar Laurence's "stones," 2.2.15–16.)

In much the same way as in the samples of Shakespop analyzed by Douglas Lanier, the parodic transformations of Shakespeare's language in this Twitter adaptation display a mixture of "reverent recognition and playful revisionism" (*Shakespeare* 55) vis-à-vis a "Shakespeare" that is simultaneously and ambivalently perceived as "high-brow," an icon of high culture, and "one of us," a property of "the people"—in Roxana Silbert's words, a "populist Shakespeare"(qtd. in Woolman n. pag.).[52] The "Shakespearean" tweets sent by Laurence Friar, the character who most consistently cites and re-cites Shakespeare, and often when he is high, are an essential part of these complex cultural dynamics. They are by no means belligerent appropriations. Still, they implicitly engage, in a typically opportunistic and unsystematic way, with "the network of practices, connotations, and hierarchies of taste that dominant cultural institutions attach to Shakespeare's name" (Lanier, *Shakespeare* 106).[53] They do so by repeatedly bringing Shakespeare's language into the gravitational orbit of drug culture, a culture that is supposedly closer to the younger "tweeple" who are the main target audience of *Such Tweet Sorrow*.

*   *   *

"Be plain, good son, and homely in thy drift! . . . puff puff give" (15 Apr., 11:06 a.m.): Tweeting Shakespeare and smoking weed appear to be mutually reinforcing activities, and they are both inextricably bound with metadramatic emphases on Twitter as a medium.[54] Laurence Friar's Shakespeare is thus more often than not a "Shakespeare-on-drugs," whatever the "content" of the Shakesperean lines he tweets. One can go as far as to argue that just as he supplies the town's kids with light drugs within the safe environment of the Electric-Kool Aid Café in order to prevent them from using hard drugs, so does he circulate a light version of Shakespeare within the protected "walled gardens" of social media platforms (cf. Lovink 16) as a kind of defense against the presumably "hard stuff" of "high-brow" Shakespeare. Yet, as pointed out earlier, Laurence Friar's distinction between light drugs and hard drugs is ethically dubious, and is not borne out by either his behavior or the kids', as they all appear to be willing to do anything to get high.[55] Moreover, as *Romeo and Juliet* teaches us, when drugs (or letters) are at stake, one can hardly draw a clear-cut dividing line between remedy and poison: what is beneficial has the uncanny ability of swapping places with, and merging into, what is detrimental. The use of drugs (or letters)—both prosthetic technologies—irremediably shifts into abuse or misuse: by definition, they exceed any volition on the part of the user. To paraphrase a line from Shakespeare's play duly repeated by Laurence Friar (12 May, 5:45 a.m.), they possess a "power" that "thwart[s]...intent" (5.3.153–54). Put differently, Larry does not merely select drugs as a theme from the Shakespearean source in order to explore it further. Together with the Shakespearean "flower," he extracts from the "original" the logic of the *pharmakon* (i.e., drugs as "poison"; drugs as "medicine," 2.2.24), an ambivalent logic that defines whatever he does and whatever he tweets, from his often unsolicited advice to the town's kids, or to Jess, to his fundamental role as a go-between connecting Juliet and Romeo. This is also a logic that re-emerges at critical dramatic points in the performance and permeates its denouement, as when Juliet drinks a "vial" (4.1.93) of Propofol, following Larry's veiled instructions on the Electric-Kool Aid Café website. Moreover, I want to suggest, the reactivation of this logic is coterminus with *Such Tweet Sorrow*'s intensification of the allegorization of its own medium. Responding to, and countersigning, the singular Shakespearean logic of the *pharmakon* in its own idiosyncratic way, this Twitter performance raises the stakes of self-reflexivity by drawing attention to the ways in which the "recreational" use of Twitter irresistibly morphs into addiction. (*Pace* Laurence Friar, tweeting turns out to be addictive rather than meditative.) Of course, from the point of view of the performance, the addictive nature of the medium is the *conditio sine qua non* for its success as a *Twitter* performance: what would *Such Tweet Sorrow* be without the characters' (simulated) addiction to the medium, or the audience's obsessive following—what is often referred to as "stalking"?[56] From a more general theoretical point of view, the production's emphasis on addiction indirectly prompts questions about aforementioned approaches to social media such as Manovich's, which highlight conversation, exchange or interaction as defining features of social networking platforms: even when "form" is said to prevail over "matter" (i.e., the exchange of tokens over and above what is being exchanged through these tokens), conversations, exchanges, or interactions are all terms that are implicitly predicated upon the notion of an addiction-free subject fully present to himself/herself. As to this Twitter play, the stress on addiction also raises questions: Is addiction the be-all and end-all of the performance? For instance, how does addiction to the medium, which typically manifests itself through a series of acts of communication or phatic events that crowd the public sphere, relate to *Such Tweet Sorrow*'s recycling of the problematics of the secret that is so central to the original play?

Before the performance properly starts, Jago sets the tone by underlining the addictive nature of tweeting: "You guys tweet too much like u don't have a life or sumthing" (*TW* 7 Apr., 4:03 a.m.), which can be seen, if one considers his role in the production, as a blend of sarcasm and hope. Yet, paradoxically, given his initial resistance to the medium, it is Romeo who often elaborates on the addiction to the medium: "I've just woken up and my first thought was twitter! 'Trainspotting' was about heroin addiction, maybe we cud do a Tweetspotting?" (17 Apr., 5.53 a.m.). After he falls in love with Juliet, he cannot resist tweeting her, and Juliet reciprocates. The addiction to love feeds upon the addiction to Twitter and vice versa. In fact, the two Twitter lovers stretch the conventions of the medium by mixing tweeting with sex while Juliet's sister Jess is running the London marathon, with Romeo playing upon the word "twexting," and reinventing its meaning: "Making love and tweeting combine in the word 'twexting.' So, is this what you'd call twexting?" (25 Apr., 10:51 a.m.).[57] Moreover, "twexting" (with) Juliet goes hand in hand with Romeo's movement away from his exclusive bond with Mercutio, a bond that reaches its homoerotic climax when Mercutio uploads a video on YouTube in which he sings and dedicates Eric Carmen's "All by Myself" to his friend, adopting the pose of the dejected lover. Indeed, Romeo grows increasingly tired of what he now perceives as Mercutio's infantile misogynistic games such as #uploadthatload, a game, as pointed out earlier, that consists of taking pictures of women's cleavages and posting them on Twitpic: "Why would I play upload that load. Its like looking at a photos of Las Vegas when you could move to Paris. Not interested, sorry @mercuteio" (24 Apr., 4:09 p.m.). At the height of his relationship with Juliet, and as Mercutio keeps on sending ironic messages such as a short tweet containing only two words—"Sonnet 129" (24 Apr., 4:58 p.m.)[58]—as a warning against what the original play identifies as being "effeminate" (3.1.114), Romeo goes so far as to "block" his friend, a capital offense in the land of Twitter. Mercutio is at first incredulous: "What does it

mean if I can't see someones feeds that I'm following?" (27 Apr., 4:41 p.m.).
Yet he is soon forced to admit to himself the painful truth: "@romeo_mo
So you've blocked me now? To forget a friend is sad; not everyone has had a
real friend" (5:10 p. m.).

The reverse side of feverish addictive tweeting is to metaphorically block
oneself: to tweet one's unwillingness to tweet; or, alternatively, not to tweet
at all and/or to go offline. Juliet experiments with these alternatives after a
"Shakespearean" tweet by Jesse Nurse in which she reveals the identity of her
younger sister's lover: "@julietcap16 Hmm...now who could I mean? Oh
yes. You know the one whose name is Romeo? And a Montague? The only
son of your great enemy?" (26 Apr., 9:33 a.m.) (cf. 1.5.135–36). Shocked by
the news, and torn between her loyalty toward her family and her love for
Romeo, Juliet announces: "Not really in the mood to Tweet" (27 Apr., 9:19
a.m.). She refuses any contact with her lover, to the latter's rising frustration,
and carries on being offline for at least 24 hours. But Juliet's temporary
withdrawal from the world of Twitter is only a minor example of *Such Tweet
Sorrow*'s exploration of a breakdown in communication. In actual fact, its
most dramatically effective scenes depend on this exploration, as when Jesse
Nurse desperately tries to get in touch with Tybalt after hearing on the radio
of the eruption of violence following the football match between the Reds
(supported by the Montagues) and the Blues (supported by the Capulets);
or when Mercutio goes silent for hours after the same events, with the followers, and the #mercutiogroupies in particular, eagerly waiting for a sign
of life. (Of course, Tybalt cannot tweet back because he lies dead on the
pitch; as to Mercutio, he has been rushed to hospital). The final phases of
the performance exploit to the full the dramatic possibilities of the inability
and/or unwillingness to access Twitter: the characters switch to an offline
mode that alternates with a being online as intermittent access and/or distracted perception. While on the run, after killing Tybalt in self-defense,
Romeo switches off his mobile phone for two days because he is afraid the
police might be able to track his movements ("@julietcap16 I need to turn
my phone off, apparently the cops might be able to track me. I love you with
all my heart, we'll be together soonxxx Romeo," 10 May, 12:12 p.m.), and
provides a link to a news website discussing this issue. He is thus unable
to receive tweets. When he decides to turn his mobile phone back on, he
quickly goes through the rambling tweets Juliet keeps on sending under the
effect of Propofol, the "milk of amnesia," but ignores Laurence Friar's previous tweets in which he drops hints about his plan to reunite the two lovers,
suggesting that they meet up. As to Larry, early in the morning of the fatal
day, and still suffering from yet another hangover, he tweets his surprise
about Romeo not turning up: "romeo_mo benedicite, where art thou?" (12

May, 5:11 a.m.). He soon realizes that Romeo has not read his messages
and thus sends another worried tweet: "@romeo_mo O, Pale! You've had no
notice of these accidents!? ANSWER YOUR PHONE! Thy Love is asleep,
only ASLEEP!!!" (5:21 a.m.). But it is all in vain. Discovering Juliet's apparently inanimate body in Larry's flat ("I am too late and too early. The light
of Juliet's beauty has not yet set but death has carried her to the west," 12
May, 1:29 a.m.), which replaces the Capulets' tomb, Romeo is so devastated
that he kills himself: "Our first kiss set me free and with our last I'll lie
with thee" (2:21 a.m.). As to Juliet, she wakes up and finds Romeo lying
dead next to her. She does not pick up the phone and fails to pay attention
to Larry's and her sister's tweets, including a message in which the former
warns her by using Friar Laurence's language: "@julietcap16 Come from
that nest of death & unnatural sleep" (5:44 a.m.) (cf. 5.3.151–52). She kills
herself with words slightly tinged with archaism: "My sweet, sweet Romeo,
my love, my life…Upon Rapier's point, I give all of myself to thee" (3:15
a.m.). In the meantime, both Laurence Friar and Jess Capulet are unable to
physically reach the flat because they are stuck in traffic, which symptomatizes an interruption of circulation at all levels. These contemporary avatars
of Romeo and Juliet on Twitter are thus, indeed, not only "star-crossed lovers" ("Prologue" 6) but also "media-crossed lovers"; the "passage of their
death-marked love" (9) is also an exhilarating and tragic journey across the
world of social media, at once inscribing privation and supplementation.

In an aphoristic reading of *Romeo and Juliet* that contests interpretations
of the play exclusively focusing on chance (or, to be more precise, on the
fortuitous character of chance as *mere* chance),[59] Jacques Derrida argues as
follows:

> The desire of Romeo and Juliet did not encounter the poison, the con-
> tretemps or the detour of the letter by chance. In order for this encoun-
> ter to take place, there must *already* have been instituted a system of
> marks (names, hours, maps of places, dates and supposedly "objective"
> place-names) to thwart, as it were, the dispersion of interior and het-
> erogeneous durations, to frame, organize, put in order, render possible
> a rendezvous: in other words to deny, while taking note of it, non-coin-
> cidence, the separation of monads, infinite distance, the disconnection
> of experiences, the multiplicity of worlds, everything that renders pos-
> sible a contretemps or the irremediable detour of the letter. ("Aphorism
> Countertime" 420)

And yet, Derrida adds, "the desire of Romeo and Juliet is born in the heart of
this possibility. There would be no love…without discordance." Thus, "the

accidental contretemps comes to *remark* the essential contretemps. Which is as much as to say it is not accidental" (420).

It is tempting to associate Derrida's "system of marks"—what he calls in another section of the essay "the codes that we cast like nets over time and space...in order to reduce or master differences, to arrest them, determine them" (419)—with a social media networking platform such as Twitter that similarly attempts to reduce "the separation of monads, infinite distance, the disconnection of experiences, the multiplicity of worlds" (420) by making entities of various kind (from tweeple to media) proximate one another through sheer connectivity. It is also tempting to see this platform as that which also, and simultaneously, proliferates the disjunctions, dislocations and separations that it is supposed to preempt—in short, the "contretemps-traps" (419) that do nothing but re-mark, as preeminently shown by the final phases of *Such Tweet Sorrow*, the essential impossibility of any absolute "real-time" synchronization or convergence between tweeple or media.[60] Bearing in mind Derrida's argument, it is worth underlining once again, from a more theoretical point of view, the paradox of a performance that often draws attention to the tweet that does not necessarily arrive at its destination; a performance that emphasizes the Janus-faced "nature" of Twitter as a medium that is at once "medicine"—it intensifies Romeo and Juliet's love; in fact, it literally feeds it in the form of "feeds"—*and* "poison" (2.3.24), and a "poison," moreover, even when it presents itself as "medicine," as when Romeo blocks himself and goes offline to safeguard his love for Juliet. Needless to say, this paradox has little to do with the law of the Twittersphere, or at least with its official rhetoric, in that this law decrees that to be is to be online at all times, follow and retweet, a making contact "by distributing (traces) of [oneself] on many-to-many computational networks" (Hansen "New Media," 181). The paradox, I want to suggest, is a *Shakespearean* paradox, or, to be more precise, a Shakespeare-induced paradox, the mark of Shakespearean spectrality. It is a paradox that verges on aporia. In other words, once the language of *Romeo and Juliet* (a language, as pointed out earlier, that never appears as such), the constraints of its (endlessly recyclable) plot, and, more generally, the logic of the *pharmakon* informing the play, are brought to bear upon *Such Tweet Sorrow*, this Twitter play responds in an idiosyncratic and often imaginative way. It experiments with its own medium's erasure. It plays with the death of its own medium in order to be dramatically effective, and ultimately with its own disappearance as a performance.[61] It implicitly rewrites Twitter as a fully asynchronous medium, a medium that does not disregard the death that structurally and irremediably haunts "live" communication and transmission (cf. Derrida and Stiegler 39). Hence the emphasis on an offline mode, or the insistence on random and/or inattentive access as its online spectral equivalent, a being online, one may argue, in the "borrowed likeness of shrunk death" (4.1.104). In short, *Such Tweet Sorrow* can be said to respond to the spectral effect of that extended aporia which is *Romeo and Juliet*—the oxymoronic entanglement of love and death, cure and poison, friend and foe, fate and chance—by creating a self-reflexive, medium-oriented aporia of its own: a hybrid remediation that takes place at the crossroad of a variety of social media feeding upon each other without necessarily converging, a remediation that includes within itself the possibility of remediation's silence and effacement.

I want to conclude by referring to a short emblematic example of the aporetic construction of remediation within *Such Tweet Sorrow*, the tweet that Romeo, on the point of death, sends to his dead friend Mercutio after desperately appealing to him[62]: "@mercuteio @mercuteio @mercutio @ merctueio @mercuteo @mercuteio @mercuteio @mercuteio @emrcuteio @ mecuteio @mercuteo@mercteio@mercuteio@meru" (12 May, 12:02 a.m.). In this tweet, the medium has indeed become the message but the message, from an addressor who is about to die to an addressee who is already dead, only speaks, and confusedly, of interference, noise and self-erasure.[63] It thus foregrounds a logic that is other than the logic of conversation and interaction allegedly inhering in the world of social media, or at least indicates the possibilities of its aesthetic re-articulation; it points to a logic that is other than the logic of being always "on" (i.e., "I tweet therefore I am"), and that is not necessarily opposed to the latter. This "other" logic is not a logic whereby the Shakespearean tweet circulates as mere token of exchange, without spectral force, in a potentially infinite series of conversations distributed and redistributed across time and space. "Within the infant rind" of *Such Tweet Sorrow*, one may argue, "poison hath residence" (2.2.23–24), "poison" as the silencing of the medium as well as of the performance itself. But the drive toward self-erasure does not necessarily signify a lack of impact or effectiveness. In fact, it may be its "medicine" (24), its distinctive feature as a social media performance. It may be its "power" (24) as a Twitter adaptation of Shakespeare that not only exposes the rhetoric of "sheer connectivity" (Hansen, "New Media," 180) and rephrases its meanings, including the all-too-easy identification of online activity with self-possession, but also draws attention to the threat and chance of living a tweetless life.

Notes

Introduction: Shakespeare, Spectro-Textuality, Spectro-Mediality

1. "Inhabiting," as distinct from "residing," suggests haunting; it is an uncanny form of "residing." See also, for instance, Derrida's musings about the verb "to inhabit" in *Monolingualism* (58). For reflections on this, see especially chapter 4 in this book.

2. Questions of survival are of course central to Derrida's work. Derrida's "classical" formulation of the relationship between the living-on of a text and (un)translatability is in *Parages* (147–48). See also "Des Tours" on "the necessary and impossible task of translation" (171) and its relation with the surviving dimension of the work (182), a reading of Walter Benjamin's "The Task of the Translator." In one of his posthumously published seminars, he stresses that survival—or, as he prefers to call it, "survivance"—is "neither life nor death pure and simple," and that it is "not thinkable on the basis of the opposition between life and death" (*Beast II* 130). "Survivance" is a trace structure of iterability, a "living dead machine" (131). To Derrida, what is commonly called "human life" may be seen as one of the outputs of this structure that exceeds the "human." For a cogent "posthumanist" understanding of Derrida's work, and the notion of the trace in particular, see Wolfe.

3. There are of course significant exceptions, and this book is indebted to these studies. Examples are Wilson; Lehmann, *Shakespeare Remains*; Joughin, "Shakespeare's Genius" and "Philosophical Shakespeares"; and Fernie, "Introduction." Richard Burt's work is often informed by Derrida's writings. See especially *Film and Media* and his recent "Hauntographology." See also Nicholas Royle's work, which often makes Derrida and Shakespeare interact in interesting ways, especially *How To Read* and *In Memory* (1–37).

4. For Derrida, "to set it right" is in the play a "movement of *correction*, reparation, restitution, vengeance" (20), and this is arguably inseparable from a teleologically driven trajectory of reappropriation of meaning. Yet these economies of calculation cannot suppress an "an-economic ex-position to others" (21). For

Derrida, "dis-adjustment" is also "the very possibility of the other" (20). While mostly adopting a Derridean framework to read contemporary media adaptations of Shakespeare, this book also hopes to practice an "ex-position to others" and other readings.

5. The Shakespeare-on-film boom of the 1990s is not the subject of this book, but I am aware that I am running the risk of reproducing an Anglo-centric narrative here. According to Mark Thornton Burnett, if one attends to "alternative systems of production and distribution, a more nuanced picture emerges" ("Applying" 114). For a questioning of Anglo-centric narratives in the area of Shakespeare-on-film studies, see also Huang (1–18).

6. Burt adds that "Shakespeare has always been 'Shakespeares,' mediatized and subject to dislocation, decontextualization and fragmentation" (3). The theoretical implications of *Spectral Shakespeares* undoubtedly point in this direction.

7. Richard Burt points out that "Shakespeare's popularization on DVD has involved the transformation of film itself" as well as "a shift in reception from historical to posthistorical time": "the horizon of reception…is composed of multiple viewing possibilities that reframe the initial theatrical viewing…in media that are often old and new (DVDs textualize film, for example by dividing scenes up into chapters)" (Burt and Boose, "Editors' Cut" 1, 4).

8. For a short but thoughtful account of the position of "Shakespeare" in our current mediascape, see Cimitile and Rowe, "Shakespeare Mediascapes." For an excellent special issue on digital Shakespeare, containing articles ranging from discussions of online scholarly editions to issues of performance, pedagogy, and the use of multimedia tools for research, see Galey and Siemens. See also Rowe, *New Media*. On dslan's *HyperMacbeth*, see Lessard; on Fritsch's *Hamlet X*, see Wiens. Among the number of articles addressing the Shakespeare on YouTube phenomenon, see Desmet; Shohet, "YouTube"; and O'Neill. For Twitter Shakespeare, see chapter 7.

9. For instance, when one listens to a podcast of the *Shakespeare's Restless World* series, one also watches a reel-to-reel tape recorder playing "live" what one is listening to, which is also an example of the mutual reframing of old and new media Bolter and Grusin call "remediation" (55). In the "Soundscapes" section of *myShakespeare*, a multimedia web project created for the 2012 World Shakespeare Festival that intends to measure "Shakespeare's digital heartbeat" (n.pag.), and which includes commissioned work and amateur performances, sound files are often graphically represented. Interestingly, the website includes a tool for data visualization called Banquo, with data from Twitter, Flickr, and eBay. It explains that Banquo is "a ghost, a character created by Shakespeare who appears in *Macbeth*," and that this name is used "to draw parallels between the way social media leaves a lasting impression of our comments, ideas, thoughts and activity that remain in cyberspace long after they initially existed" (*sic*) (n.pag.).

10. In the course of an extremely lucid analysis, Geoffrey Winthrop-Young points out that "it is highly questionable whether a computer is a medium, given the ways in which it violates, annuls, or supersedes notions of communication,

remediation, and intermediality that are presupposed by most conventional definitions of medium" (186). He refers to work by media theorists Friedrich A. Kittler and Arjen Mulder as emblematic of opposing trends in media theory as regards the "nature" of computers—respectively, computers as essentially hardware configurations versus computers as essentially software configurations—to show that the "the end result" is the same: "to move *beyond media*" (195). To Winthrop-Young, these debates on computers as hardware or software take places against the background of the finitude of human "wetware," "the embattled area that the computer must yet master in order to render humans obsolete" (192).

11. One of the many interesting points that Greg Semenza makes in his "Introduction" to this special issue is that "only the death of the medium will validate the medium as an unequivocally worthy subject of academic study" (19). In this sense, Shakespeare on film may aspire to become canonical in Shakespeare studies precisely as a result of the proliferation of Shakespeares in new media, a proliferation that may mark the disappearance of Shakespeare on film. Some of the chapters of *Spectral Shakespeares* are more concerned with how early twenty-first-century Shakespeare on film is already after *itself*, and not only in a chronological sense.

12. For Lanier, "one of the many achievements of the nineties was to bring Shakespeare in line with late twentieth-century visual culture and in the process loosen the equivalence between Shakespeare and text" (106). Other "recalibrations" of Shakespeare that occurred in the 1990s (and that still shape the contours of our current Shakespearean mediascape) include "the practice of resituating Shakespearean narrative in a new setting or time period" (107), and the engagement with "the concerns and screen styles of youth culture, still the most lucrative market segment for film producers" (108).

13. In the same special issue Thomas Cartelli offers a polemical *and* nuanced assessment of the status of cinematic Shakespeare in the new millennium ("Slant Shakespeare").

14. For Bolter and Grusin, the "two seemingly contradictory logics [of immediacy and hypermediacy] not only coexist in digital media today but are mutually dependent" (6), so that the simulation of immediacy is only ever the re-emergence of hypermediacy. See also Mitchell: "Every medium constructs a corresponding zone of immediacy, of the unmediated and transparent, which stands in contrast with the medium itself" (*What Do Pictures Want?* 214).

15. On the mediatization of liveness, see Auslander.

16. Technophobia often combines with iconophobia. Thomas Cartelli and Katherine Rowe underline the extent to which iconophobia shapes responses to filmic adaptations of Shakespeare (32–34). For Shakespearean spin-offs as "the realm of bastard, deformed, or wayward children of the Bard," see Lanier, "Virtues of Illegitimacy" 132–37.

17. On the paradoxical emergence of "medium-specific rubrics" in Shakespeare studies "precisely at the moment when Shakespeareans are grappling with the phenomenon of media convergence in our daily lives" (36), a phenomenon that

is thus not unrelated to the policing of disciplinary and institutional boundaries, see Rowe, "Medium-Specificity."

18. For the proliferation of terms that describe the afterlife of a text, see, for instance, Sanders 3. For the *"will to taxonomize"* as itself a significant phenomenon, especially in relation to "how the field [of adaptation studies] has tried to mark out its own territory," see Cartmell and Whelehan (2). Adaptation is of course a "cultural process" (Cartelli and Rowe 25–26). But it is perhaps important to retain the "biological" meaning of adaptation, and also see adaptations as "living organisms." Almereyda sees his adaptation of *Hamlet* (2000) as follows: "While sharing essential vital organs, cell tissues and a patchy epidermal layer with Shakespeare's *Hamlet*, [my] adaptation is a separate creature, a mutation" (Almereyda xvi, qtd. in Harrison 15). This "biological" meaning also emerges in some critical discussions of adaptations (see Sanders 24; Lehmann, "Film Adaptation" 74–75; and of course Stam 1–3), and is fully exploited in Spike Jonze's highly self-reflexive film *Adaptation* (2002), a film obsessed with ghosts of various kind. (For an analysis of this film, see Calbi, "Adapting.") There is, perhaps, a "life" (and love) of adaptations just as there is "life" (and love) of images, as wonderfully explained by Mitchell, *What Do Pictures Want?* 201–21. As he suggests in one of his "ten theses on media," *"Images reside within media the way organisms reside in a habitat"* (his emphasis), and this, to Mitchell, is much more than a metaphor or a vague analogy (211, 216).

19. "Sweet" replaces the word "weak" of the original (*Rom.* 2.2.23–24). Whenever I cite from *Such Tweet Sorrow*, I reproduce tweets from the Twitter accounts of the characters, with date and time of delivery, checked against the timeline of the production's official website (<www.suchtweetsorrow.com>) and the "unofficial" archive put together by Bleys Maynard (Twitter username: @citizenbleys), one of the followers, soon after the end of the performance.

20. Cartelli and Rowe's notion of adaptation as cultural process is exemplary in this respect, both in terms of the theorization of the phenomenon and the interpretation of individual examples of screen Shakespeare. See esp. 25–37. For a lucid critique of various theoretical models of adaptation, including the one-to-one transpositional model, see esp. Leitch.

21. For the spectrality of cinema, see also Derrida, "Le cinéma" esp. 77–78.

22. See also Worthen, *Shakespeare*, esp. 1–27; and "Shakespeare 3.0."

23. On Salman's *Mad Dawg*, see chapter 6, note 26; on Abel's *In Othello*, see Burnett, *Filming* 129–57; on Boyd's *My Kingdom*, see Lehmann, "Postnostalgic"; on Avikunthak's *Dancing Othello*, see Calbi, "Entanglements"; on Tabish's short YouTube films, see Cimitile, "Cinema."

24. This book then often reformulates W. B. Worthen's approach. It insists on the odd temporality of adaptation as performance: adaptation is both effect *and* cause of a "Thing" that does not necessarily precede it. It also underlines the hybridity and impurity of adaptation as a construct, while casting doubts upon interpretations of the process of surrogation as absolute transfiguration or utter consumption without remains. For instance, in W. B. Worthen's reading of Baz Luhrmann's *William Shakespeare's Romeo + Juliet* as an emblematic example of

the potentially productive rephrasing of the relationship between text and performance, the shift from the word "long sword" (*Rom.* 1.1.72) to "Longsword" as the visualized brand name of Capulet's automatic rifle shows that the text "is instantly replaced by performance; re-figured;... *consumed*" (1104, emphasis added). I would want to underline, instead, that here and elsewhere in the film the "textual" and the "visual" stand in an irresolvable dialectical tension with each other, each haunting the other. As I try to show in the course of the book, this is by no means a return to a text-based understanding of performance/adaptation whereby the text precedes, directs, or informs performance/adaptation.

25. For Derrida, "autoimmunity" names the "strange illogical logic by which a living being can spontaneously destroy, in an autonomous fashion, the very thing within it that is supposed to protect it against the other, to immunize it against the aggressive intrusion of the other" (*Rogues* 123). He frequently uses this term in his latest work, especially in connection with the interrelated questions of politics, religion, and "tele-technoscience." See "Faith and Knowledge" esp. 44–54; Borradori 84–135; *Beast II* esp. 75–83. For exemplary readings of autoimmunity, see Mitchell, "Picturing"; Bennington; Naas. For a reading of autoimmunity in relation to *Coriolanus*, see Calbi, "States."

26. The category "foreign Shakespeare" often shores up the ideological fantasy that there *is* a "native Shakespeare," and that the latter is clearly identifiable as such, and separable from the former. In the realm of Shakespeare on film, how "native" is an English-speaking film such as Michael Almereyda's *Hamlet*, a film that conducts intense conversations with Kurosawa's *The Bad Sleep Well* and Kaurismaki's *Hamlet Goes Business*, and in fact "emerges from a filmic dialogism that is mostly non-Anglophone"? (Harrison 1). (Keith Harrison concludes his lucid analysis of this dialogism by claiming that Almereyda "articulates his *Hamlet* as a foreign language film [15]). Or, conversely, how "foreign" is a Nigerian video film such as Tunde Kelani's *Thunderbolt (Magun)* once it is released internationally in DVD format, with cover notes stating that it is "in a sense a retelling of the Othello story," and comparable to "any standard Western melodrama"? Once remediated in this way, it (spectrally) re-emerges as "foreign" but not quite. For Courtney Lehmann, *Thunderbolt* is an example of oppositional Shakespearean adaptation. In the film the jealous Othello-like character Yinka places the sexual curse of "Magun" upon the innocent Desdemona-like character Ngozi, a curse with deadly consequences. (In Yoruba "magun" is literally "a person forbidden from mounting," and the woman affected by this curse cannot have sex with any man without that man dying [Barrot 70]). For Lehmann, this allegorizes the "neglect that defines the policy of the West toward the AIDS crisis in Africa" ("Introduction" 77). The film is based on *The Whore (With Thunderbolt Aids)* (1998) by Adebayo Faleti, and the author himself plays the part of a traditional healer in the film, a chief herbalist who is strongly opposed to western medicine. (In the end traditional methods prevail). The film dialogue is mostly in English. English also functions practically and symbolically to bridge the gap between different ethnic communities: Yinka is a

Yoruba and Ngozi is a Igbo. Yet, it is this ethnic difference that raises the specter of jealousy. On the film, see also Barrot 70–71; Kelani, "In Spite."

27. See Cartelli and Rowe 151; Burnett, *Filming* 126–27.

28. Throughout the book, I use extensively Richard Burt's self-deconstructive and "impure" dialectic of "Shakespeareccentricity" and "Shakespearecentricity" because of its flexibility and its being context-bound: "every performance or citation reproduction of what counts as Shakespeare has a centrifugal pull on the text, is eccentric"; on the other hand, "citations and adaptations of Shakespeare return us to Shakespeare as a center, even if the Shakespeare imagined as central proves to be a fantasy. Something always counts as Shakespeare, and its gravity exerts a centripetal pull on other materials toward it" (5).

29. "Smooth," as opposed to "striated," is of course a reference to Deleuze and Guattari 474–500. For one of the most compelling treatments of the digital image as that which "*explodes* the frame," and thus as an entity that cannot be accounted for by having recourse to "the cinematic metaphor (even in the broad sense)," see Hansen, *New Philosophy* (34). For a phenomenological approach such as Hansen's, the explosion of the (cinematic) frame results in the *empowerment* of the body: "with the advent of digitization ..., the body undergoes a certain empowerment, since it ... *enframe[s]* something (digital information) that is originally formless" (11). Indeed, "the digital calls on us to invest the body as that 'place' where the self-differing of media gets concretized" (31). Hansen's stress on the inadequacy of the cinematic metaphor for an understanding of the digital is a critique of aspects of Lev Manovich's approach in *The Language of New Media*.

30. In this sense, it is a film that does not wait for its release into DVD format to cross into "posthistorical time" (Burt and Boose, "Editors' Cut" 4).

31. The reference here is to Derrida's analysis of the *pharmakon* (*Dissemination* 61–171).

32. One of the book's concerns is thus with the ways in which this age-old fantasy re-presents itself in connection with the emergence of new media configurations such as the one the film simulates and engages with. The theoretical background here is work by critics who emphasize, in various ways, that the interface of humans and media/ information technologies is a form of embodiment that should also prompt reconsiderations of the "human." The bibliography is extensive, but see especially Hayles; Hansen, *New Philosophy*; Latour, *We Have* and *Aramis*; and extremely lucid work by Wolfe. These are of course in addition to groundbreaking work by Haraway.

33. Many adaptations of *Macbeth*, from Roman Polanski's *Macbeth* (1971) to Geoffrey Wright's Australian version of the Scottish play (2006), from Greg Salman's *Mad Dawg* (2004) to Tom Magill's *Mickey B* (2007), foreground hallucinogenic substances, and perhaps not just in order to explore the semantic and cinematic potential of the "metaphysical" substances to which the play refers—the "insane root / That takes the reason prisoner" (1.3.82–83); the "vap'rous drop ... distilled by magic sleights" (3.5. 24, 26)—and/or as a

result of the transposition of the play into environments, often urban environments, marked by crime. Knoesel's film also obliquely associates the circulation of updated versions of ecstasy within the rave club with the circulation of mediatized Shakespeares in a variety of formats within the global "scene": both ecstasy and mediatized Shakespeares are addictive substances (see chapter 6).

34. This understanding of mediality resonates with work by Bernard Stiegler. Stiegler, one of Derrida's students, often insists on the essential correlation of the human and technics as well as the historically specific articulations of *différance* and the supplement through technologies of storage, production and transmission (including media) that mediate *and* constitute experience. For Stiegler, human life is "fundamentally exteriorized—as life by means other than life" ("Memory" 71). He stresses that "technicity," including the technicity of media, is "constitutive of life as ex-sistence" (72). See also Stiegler, *Technics 1* and *Technics 2*; and "Derrida and Technology." My understanding of mediality is also indebted to Cary Wolfe's work. In *What Is Posthumanism?*, for instance, Wolfe refers to Derrida to underline "the fundamental exteriority and materiality of meaning and communication itself..., of any form of semiotic marking and iterability to which both humans and nonhuman animals are subject in a trace structure that...exceeds and encompasses the human/ animal difference and indeed 'the life/death relation' itself" (xxviii).

35. W. T. J. Mitchell and Mark B. N. Hansen also underline, perhaps more problematically, that media "names an ontological condition of humanization"; and that "media critics who focus on the medium—and media in the plural— without regard to this ontological dimension run the risk of positivizing the medium": they run the risk, that is, of reducing the medium or the media to "a narrowly technical entity or system" (xiii), as is the case with "hardware-driven" media theories à la Friedrich Kittler. (On the definition of "hardware-driven" media theories, see Winthrop-Young, esp. 192–95). Interestingly, the "Index" to this collection of essays, which includes contributions by leading figures in the field of media theory, shows that Jacques Derrida is mentioned and/or cited in the volume more often than Marshall McLuhan, or any other critic (Mitchell and Hansen 331–53).

36. For a largely positive review of Kidnie's book, see Cartelli. Yet he also points out that there are problems with Kidnie's use of the notion of interpretive community. He draws attention to "Kidnie's occasional failure to resist what she...terms the 'potentially misleading' impulse 'to conceive of the work as a single or unified thing' [8] in whatever specific slice of time or space it prevails, as if only one interpretive community at a time can dictate what a work is and what it signifies" (224).

37. For Derrida's skepticism about the "identitarian" notion of community, and the latter's connection with the largely phallogocentric notion of fraternity and brotherhood, see especially *Politics of Friendship* 297–306 and *Rogues* 59–61. For an exploration of online communities, including the phenomenon of Twitter "followers" whose contradictory responses to the performance of *Such*

Tweet Sorrow can be seen as a debate about "what constitutes the essential or authentic Shakespeare" (Lanier, *Shakespeare* 9), see chapter 7.

38. On the impact, or lack of impact, of information culture on the text/performance dichotomy, see Worthen, "Shakespeare 3.0." For acute reflections on the interface between Shakespeare and information theory, see Galey.

39. On countersigning, see, for instance, Derrida "Strange Institution" 67–70. To reemphasize the complex temporality of the transactions between the work and adaptation, signature and countersignature, from a slightly different angle, one could argue that what adaptation responds to takes the form of an "absolute pastness" (70). But this "absolute pastness" is "already the demand for... and the expectation of" a countersignature. As Derrida succinctly puts it, "the first only inaugurates from after," which produces "an incalculable scene, because we can't count 1, 2, 3, or the first before the second" (70).

40. Discussing film adaptations of Shakespeare, and referring to Heminges and Condell's emphasis on Shakespearean "remains" in the prefatory material to the First Folio, Courtney Lehmann suggests that "a legacy comprised of remains is nothing less than an invitation to participate in an adaptation process that... is always unfinished" ("Film Adaptation" 75). She also proposes that we "shift our critical gaze from 'who' to 'what'" in order to "avoid the pitfall of paternity" (75). My approach to Shakespearean adaptation is indebted to these insights.

41. In the film *Ghost Dance* Derrida claims that "the modern technology of the image like cinematography... *enhances* the power of ghosts and their ability to haunt us" (emphasis added).

42. For Derrida, the "sur-" of "survivance"—a middle voice he prefers to "survival"—is "without superiority, without height, altitude or highness, and thus without supremacy or sovereignty" (130–31). He also underlines that "survivance" exceeds, and is heterogeneous to, both life and death as they are commonly understood: it is "neither life nor death pure and simple"; it is "not thinkable on the basis of the opposition between life and death" (130). The context of Derrida's remarks is the question of the survival of *Robinson Crusoe* (and survival *in Robison Crusoe*), a text he reads alongside various texts by Heidegger. For Derrida, "Like a trace, a book, the survivance of a book, from its first moment on, is a living-dead machine" (131). However, this (spectral) "living-dead machine" of survivance not only concerns "books, or... writing, or... the archive in the current sense" but also "everything from which the tissue of living experience is woven, through and through" (131). One may want to suggest that it also concerns the media as prosthetic technologies of archiving, production, and transmission that make and unmake the "tissue of living experience" of the human. In *Ecographies of Television* Derrida more explicitly connects the "living-dead" structure of survivance with the question of the media. In particular, he argues that media images always-already mark "a disappearance [*une disparition*]" but this disappearance "promises and conceals in advance another magic 'apparition,' a ghostly 're-apparition'" (Derrida and Stiegler 117).

1   The State of the Kitchen: Incorporation and "Animanomaly" in *Scotland, PA* and the BBC *Shakespeare Retold Macbeth*

1. Derrida uses the masculine pronoun because this subject is a "*schema* or image" based on "the virile strength of the adult male, the father, husband, or brother," a structure of exclusion(s).

2. Referring to Benveniste's etymological *Le vocabulaire des institutions européens*, Derrida often relates ipseity to power, which is also the supposedly indivisible power of the self-same: "The sovereign, in the broadest sense of the term, is he who has the right and strength to be and be recognized as *himself, the same, properly the same as himself*" (*Beast I* 66).

3. This problematization is already at work in the interview with Nancy. It is part of the larger question of "the ethics and the politics of the living" (117), which is in turn related to the question of the reinscription of language "in a network of possibilities" that "*are themselves not only human*" (116)—what Derrida variously calls the mark in general, the trace or iterability (116). But see also "The Animal"; "And Say"; and *Beast I*. In the latter seminar, the French philosopher clarifies that the problematization of the boundary between the human and the nonhuman animal concerns "the immense question of the living...the living in life itself" (176). For a cogent reading of this fundamental aspect of Derrida's work, and its connection with the problematics of iterability and the trace, see Wolfe, "Introduction," and *What Is Posthumanism?*, esp. 99–168. For a sample of the interest in the problematics of human exceptionalism in Shakespeare studies, see esp. Shannon. For Shannon, who also refers to Derrida's "The Animal," Shakespeare uses the word "animal" "when critically posing what we might well call 'the question of the human' rather than when humanity is asserted." She adds that "in the anti-Cartesian instances of Shakespearean usage, *animal* comes most into service when humanness is least secure and cross-species likeness are most evident" (477).

4. The BBC *Shakespeare Retold* series was broadcasted in the autumn of 2005. It also included adaptations of *Much Ado about Nothing, The Taming of the Shrew,* and *A Midsummer Night's Dream*.

5. In *Joe Macbeth* Big Dutch, an omnivorous mob character, meets his death by eating poisoned crêpe Suzettes. *Men of Respect* functions as a clearer antecedent, with so many scenes, including the initial scene, insisting on the interconnection of eating and murder. In one scene this takes the form of a nightmarish sequence, as the Macbeth-like character, Mike Battaglia (Joe Turturro), dreams of being dispatched by Bankie Como and his son during a barbecue: the hand that cooks meat turns into the hand that kills, which is one of the matrices of the logic this chapter explores. In another scene we are shown the female witch watching a TV cookery program in which a *capo d'agnello* (lamb's head) is being cooked. As we shall see, TV cookery programs are among the most significant intertexts of the BBC *Shakespeare Retold Macbeth*.

6. This sequence, originally in color, was reused in the opening titles of later episodes, which emphasizes even more its status as a repeat, as endlessly recyclable material.

7. However, there is also an ironic inversion here, as the "original" McCloud is a rustic detective with an odd accent, and is thus, in this respect, unlike the urban McDuff of *Scotland, PA*. In the DVD "Director's Commentary," Billy Morrissette claims that the aspect of *Macbeth* that mostly caught his attention when he first read it was the presence of the patronymic "Mac."

8. As Cartelli and Rowe point out, music is another crucial form of remediation (116–19). One only needs to think of the pervasive presence of music by Bad Company. For instance, the track "Bad Company" by Bad Company allows Mac to pose as someone who "was born 6-gun in [his] hand" and is "always on the run"; as someone, in short, who *is* "bad company" ("They call me bad company / And I can't deny / Bad company / Till the day I die"). The track accompanies Mac in his peregrination into the Fair playground, just before his meeting with the witches. It thus somehow also prepares him to be in the "bad company" of the witches. This is Morrissette's witty critical contribution to one of the crucial questions regarding the relationship between the witches and Macbeth in Shakespeare's play: do the witches act upon somebody who is already predisposed to act in a certain way? On the question of agency in *Macbeth* and *Scotland, PA*, and especially its relation to the construction of masculinity, see Shohet 190–93.

9. Surplus-enjoyment is a reference to Zizek's reading of Lacan's *jouissance*. See esp. Zizek, *Sublime*: "surplus-enjoyment...is not a surplus which simply attaches itself to some 'normal,' fundamental enjoyment, because *enjoyment as such emerges only in this surplus*, because it is constitutively an 'excess'" (52); see also *Plague* 48–50.

10. In Bolter and Grusin "remediation" also has the meaning of improvement on, and reform of, a previous medium (see, for instance, 19, 56).

11. According to Shohet, he is "too absorbed by the didactic *image* of effective policing to *act* as a police officer" (190).

12. Once we are inside Duncan's restaurant, incorporation re-presents itself. We are faced with an extreme close-up of a half-eaten burger on a tray, and then we see a waitress who picks up the tray and, on her way to the kitchen, takes a bite of the leftover burger. This clearly recalls the witches' consumption of fried chicken and Shakespeare. See also Shohet 189.

13. On the more general theoretical problematics of waste, see Scanlan.

14. This is "filthy air" (1.1.12) indeed. The location recalls the rubbish dump in which Macbeth, like an actor who has used up his role, is flung at the end of Michael Bogdanov's Channel 4 version of Shakespeare's play (1998). Also, it cannot fail to evoke the rubbish tip that appears at the end of Pier Paolo Pasolini's *Cosa sono le nuvole?* (1967). For a reading of Pasolini's striking adaptation of *Othello*, see Massai.

15. One of the garbage men is having a sandwich with corned beef and anchovies. In the film food clearly operates as a heavily charged symbolic marker of class distinctions.

16. The figure of the pig may have been suggested by the following exchange between two of the weird sisters: "Where has thou been, sister?"; "Killing swine"

(1.3.1–2). It is worth recalling in this context Andrzej Wayda's *The Siberian Lady Macbeth (Sibirska Ledi Magbet)* (1962), based on Nikolai Leskov's novel *Lady Macbeth of the Mtsensk District* (1865), with music by Dmitry Shostakovich, a film in which the pig also plays a prominent symbolic role. In the film the Lady Macbeth-like figure, Katarina, begins an affair with Sergei, a traveling swineherd, while her husband Zinovi is away on business. After poisoning her father-in-law Boris, she helps Sergei kill her returned husband. They then throw a banquet that recalls the banquet the Macbeths host after the murder of Banquo, where the guests repeatedly recoil from Sergei because of his lower-class status. As Sergei is about to cut and serve a roasted pig's head, he runs away as if in terror. Joined by Katarina, he expostulates: "We are eating him. The master." (They have previously buried Zinovi in the pigsty). Moreover, while in bed together, Katarina tells Sergei a nightmare she had: she dreamt of "a huge swine gnawing away at my threshold," a swine that "kept on tearing at the threshold." On this film, see Lanier "Spin-Offs" 204 (entry 833).

17. For Derrida, "The animal is a word, it is an appellation that men have instituted, a name they have given themselves the right and the authority to give to another living creature ..." ("The Animal" 392). The clear-cut distinction between "man" and "the animal"—a label under which a number of disparate nonhuman living organisms are lumped together—informs both common sense and a metaphysically inflected philosophical tradition. For Derrida, it is not a matter of replacing this rigorous distinction with a belief "in some homogeneous continuity between what calls itself man and what he calls the animal." Rather, it is a matter of asking oneself "what happens once the frontier [between man and what he calls the animal] no longer forms a single indivisible line but more than one internally divided line, once, as a result, it can no longer be traced, objectified, or counted as single and indivisible" (399). For similar observations, see *Beast I*: "one must not be content to mark the fact that what is attributed as 'proper to man' also belongs to other living beings if you look more closely, but also, conversely, that what is attributed as proper to man does not belong to him *in all purity and rigor*; and that one must therefore restructure the whole problematic" (56, emphasis added). This can be compared to Giorgio Agamben's notion of the "anthropological machine," the creation of "a zone of indifference," "a space of exception" in which decisions are continually made regarding the relationship between the human animal and the nonhuman animal. For Agamben, it is precisely because "the human is already presupposed every time" that the exclusion of the animal is "always already a capturing," and the inclusion "always already an exclusion" (*Open* 37–38). It can be argued that in *The Open* the animal becomes an emblem of what Agamben had earlier defined "bare life" (*Homo Sacer* esp. 1–12).

18. Later on in the film, he stresses that making a mistake in the kitchen hurts him; it causes him "actual physical pain."

19. In the DVD "Director's Commentary" Morrissette points out that he tried to use as many dead animals as he could, and that it was only after shooting the film that he became aware of the many references to animals in *Macbeth*.

20. The retroactive production of Duncan as a figure who "enjoys"—and perhaps enjoys too much—is far from being uncommon in filmic adaptations of *Macbeth*. Duncan's dance with Lady Macbeth in Roman Polanski's version (1971) points in this direction. An even more radical transformation can be found in Penny Woolcock's *Macbeth on the Estate* (1997). Other examples include Michael Bogdanov's Channel 4 *Macbeth* (1998), Greg Salman's *Mad Dawg* (2001), Geoffrey Wright's Australian *Macbeth* (2006), and Tom Magill's *Mickey B* (2007).

21. One may also be tempted to gloss the perturbing proximity between the "sovereign" head-chef Duncan and the nonhuman animal with Derrida's remarks on the "troubling resemblance" between the beast and the sovereign. Even though they seem "to be situated at the antipodes, at each other's antipodes" there is "a sort of obscure and fascinating complicity [between them], or even a worrying mutual attraction, a worrying familiarity, an *unheimlich*, uncanny reciprocal haunting" (*Beast I* 17): they are both "outside the law, at a distance from or above the laws" (17), "the beast ignorant of right and the sovereign having the right to suspend the right, to place himself above the law that he is, that he makes, that he institutes" (32); in this "spectacle of a spectrality" (17), if the animal is said *not* to respond ("And Say"), the sovereign similarly does not respond because he does not enter any contract or covenant, and is not responsible before the law. These references to sovereignty and the law's suspensions are part of Derrida's engagement with Carl Schmitt's *Political Theology*. On Schmitt, see also Derrida's *Politics* esp. 75–193.

22. The two Serbian immigrants Ella employs as kitchen-hands—they "come from the eleventh century," according to Ella, "also known as former Yugoslavia"—are blamed for the murder. I cannot explore here the significance of ethnic markings in the film, which is probably to be related to the panic about the inflow of refugees or migrants into Britain that constantly occupies the front pages of British popular press, and that could be read in terms of what Paul Gilroy calls postcolonial melancholia, the inability "to work through the grim details of imperial and colonial history and to transform paralyzing guilt into a more productive shame that would be conducive to the building of a multicultural nationality that is no longer phobic about the prospect of exposure to either strangers nor otherness" (108). Gilroy associates this "exposure to…otherness" with reworked forms of "conviviality" (133–68). Also worth further analysis in this context is the fact that at the moment of Duncan's murder we can hear a football fan outside his window screaming "En-gland, En-gland, En-gland," a scream that overlaps with Duncan's.

23. Doubling is pervasive in *Scotland, PA*, and this ranges from minor details to significantly repeated scenes. For instance, the owner of the beauty salon "When a Tan Loves a Woman" has a tanned son who is his exact replica; Donald's lover wears the same dressing gown as Donald; the two boys at the drive-through counter say goodbye to punters in exactly the same way, and they wear the same uniform.

24. Shohet argues that this is a "quite nuanced…, fragmented and subtle" version of the masque in the first scene of the fourth act of *Macbeth* (192). The masque's glass is replaced by a TV screen presenting a TV commercial which, by virtue of its endlessly iterable nature, can indeed "stretch out to th' crack of doom" (4.1.133).

25. The loss of a baby as some kind of emotionally devastating experience that lies at the basis of Lady Macbeth's murderous instincts is developed in many filmic versions of *Macbeth*, most notably Woolcock's *Macbeth on the Estate* and Wright's version of the Scottish play. In its initial phases, Wright's *Macbeth* goes as far as to show Lady Macbeth laying flowers and crying over the tomb of her deceased son in a cemetery that is also haunted by three devious schoolgirls who impersonate the witches.

26. On *Scotland, PA* as *noir*, see Lehmann, "Dislocating."

27. Royle's approach implicitly raises crucial epistemological questions about adapting *Macbeth*. What does it mean for an adaptation to adopt the original play's logic of reiteration and echo, a logic that, by its very nature, re-marks the lack of any clear-cut distinction between "before" and "after," "source" and "response"? Chapter 6 explores these questions more fully, in relation to another adaptation of *Macbeth*.

28. Billy/Banquo had previously attributed to this organ qualities that resemble those "mystical" characteristics Shakespeare's play confers on Duncan's body. According to Billy, who can be said to uphold a "corporatist" version of the kitchen's body politic, the liver is "the powerhouse: it stores stuff, it processes it, sends out what other parts of the body need, cleans the blood… It's an incredible worker. Yet, it is so delicate: ten seconds too long in the pan, and you've blown it, totally blown it." Leaving the liver "ten seconds too long in the pan" is exactly what will happen to Joe. In her excellent reading of the BBC *Shakespeare Retold* series, Margaret J. Kidnie shows how through "scriptwriting and camerawork" the series attempt "to reinvent for television not Shakespeare's words, but something like a convincing 'Shakespeare effect' that is available to be read by viewers as consistent with the work" (104). Yet this is arguably only the case with the BBC retelling of *Macbeth*. See also Cartelli, "Doing" 27, for a similar evaluation of the difference between the retelling of *Macbeth* and the retelling of other plays in the series.

29. Joe's is a crossing of boundaries from the "private" world of the kitchen to the sanitized "public" world of the restaurant over which Ella presides. It re-presents Ella's trajectory in an inverted form.

30. Derrida often plays on the double meaning of "*je suis*" in his ruminations on the subject of the animal: in French "*je suis*" is both "I am" and "I follow" ("The Animal"). To be is to be *after* the animal, in the sense of hunting and chasing it down, but also to come *after* the animal in a temporal sense. The feeling of belatedness in relation to the animal easily translates into the paranoid feeling of being pursued by the animal that one pursues. To a large extent, *Scotland, PA* illustrates this logic.

31. Mac points the gun at Banko in Birnam woods as if to shoot, but the witches dressed as deer stand in the way, perhaps to warn him that there are too many witnesses.

32. Pat cooks and serves the deer. She is so annoyed at Mac and his carnivorous friends' behavior at the table that she dubs them "you animals." The association between Banko and the infrahuman is also reemphasized by the following joke: "I'd swear he was thinking out there today. I could see those Banko brain cells moving." They all laugh at the joke, except Pat.

33. For one of the Lords in *Macbeth*, the restoration of order will be able to "give to our tables meat, sleep to our nights, / Free from our feasts and banquets bloody knives" (3.6.34–35). On hospitality in *Macbeth*, see Kottman.

34. The vegetarian not-of-woman-born Lt. McDuff starts making jokes about the unhealthy practices fostered by the drive-through as soon as he turns up at Duncan's wake with a vegetarian dish: "I envy you; by the time I get to my customers, they are usually dead. At least you get a chance to kill them…with that greasy food."

35. For many critics, the film shows that the "stain" of being "white trash" can never be deleted. See Deitchman; see also Brown. For the link between this "stain" and Pat's greasy burn, see especially Lehmann, "Out" 246.

36. In *Macbeth* Lady Macduff compares Macbeth to an "owl" (4.2.11); Macduff, after the news of the massacre of his family, implicitly refers to him as "hell-kite" (4.3.218). See also Keller 41.

37. Pat chops off her hand with a meat cleaver as the fight between the two men goes on. She also seem to be aware that she is acting within a field of powerful constraints, but decides to act nonetheless, even if the act leads to her death. It is one thing to die. It is quite another to die by "counter-signing" one's death. According to Lehmann's Lacanian reading, Pat "dies with a grin on her face," which shows her "identification with the *sinthome*" (i.e., the impossible conjunction of enjoyment and the signifier), "her liberating realization, having traversed the fantasy of her impossible class ambition, that there is nothing left for her but to identify with lack itself" ("Out" 246). Lehman's Lacanian "*sinthome*" is a reference to Zizek, *Sublime* 123.

38. Joe Macbeth ironically refers to himself as a "butcher" in a conversation with Ella.

39. Interestingly, when the garbage collectors meet Macbeth in the "dark alley" for the second time, the realm of leftovers they are able to "read" to foretell the future extends to include leftovers associated with activities of the "lower bodily stratum" (Bakhtin 303–436). These leftovers become emblems of a senseless reiterative structure: "The whole story is here…from thwarted sperm and banana-flavoured rubber right through to the yellow hacked-out gob of ancient drunks…all of life…and the special brew…dripping needles…all the great excitements that get us from cradle to the grave…the sound and the fury…it all ends with us…incinerated…obliterated…no more…yesterday's breakfast, yesterday's meat, yesterday's men…all our yesterdays…all our tomorrows" What can be heard here is thus an ingenious appropriation of Macbeth's "Tomorrow, and tomorrow, and tomorrow" speech (5.5.18–27). For

comments on how Moffat's script "*disrupts* viewer expectations of television dialogue to make the language sound in places self-consciously elevated," see Kidnie 118–19.

40. "Pig" is slang for policeman (OED Def. 6b).

41. These excerpts show Duncan, Macbeth and Malcom presenting the same recipe with some slight variation: rabbit stuffed with black pudding wrapped with Parma ham. This is a recipe, we learn earlier on, that none of the chefs can lay claim to. Joe tells Billy, who believes Duncan has stolen it from Joe, that it was an unidentified "old crone half-way up the mountains in Cumbria" who gave it to him. According to the OED, "crone" can refer to both a human and a nonhuman animal: it means "a withered old woman" (Def. 1) and "an old ewe" (Def. 2) and can therefore be associated with the witches qua liminal figures. It is a word of uncertain origin but was probably taken from the Old North French *carogne*, a carcass, a body in a stage of decomposition, and figuratively "a cantankerous or mischievous woman." What matters most here is that the posh restaurant's *pièce-de-resistance* does not *properly* belong. The (repeatedly) adapted recipe that does not belong may also be an allegorical reflection on adaptation as a process of surrogation that regularly evokes some spectral presence, some elusive ghostly "origin."

42. Many other filmic versions of *Macbeth*, including Welles's, Polanski's, and Woolcock's, are open-ended. In Orson Welles's *Macbeth* (1948), the youngish-looking legitimate heir looks up at Macduff, who has just cut off Macbeth's head, from a position that seems to indicate powerlessness: will he be able to pick up the crown that falls at his feet? Moreover, like in Welles's *Voodoo Macbeth*, the witches' "the charm's wound up" (1.3.35) is uttered at the very end, and this suggests that the "charm" may still be at work. At the end of Polanski's version we are shown Donalbain looking for the witches. At the end of *Macbeth on the Estate*, we see Donalbain jokingly making the gesture of shooting Malcom. As to Macduff, he does not join the celebration, and leaves the pub to comment on the political state of the country with lines borrowed from the original's 4.3.

43. The indeterminacy of the film's ending also has to do with the fact that McDuff shows some kind of unhealthy interest in the unhealthy addictive practices of the drive-through he ostensibly opposes. On this aspect, see Shohet esp. 188–89; and Keller 43–45.

44. Duncan as emblem of "Shakespeare" regularly falls asleep in his office. He is called "Norm" and keeps on vilifying what he calls Scotland's "white trash." Of course, another reason for this drowsiness is that he must embody "sleep" for Mac to be able to "murder sleep" (2.2.34).

45. On this scene, see Shohet 193; and Cartelli and Rowe 117.

2 Shakespearean Retreats: Spectrality, Survival, and Autoimmunity in Kristian Levring's *The King Is Alive*

1. "*Apprendre à vivre*" can mean both "to learn (how) to live" and "to teach (how) to live." In this "Exordium" Derrida stresses the overlapping and distinction

between the two meanings. The expression oscillates between "address as *experience* (is not learning to live experience itself?)" and "address as *education*…as taming* or *training* [*dressage*]." Address as "*taming* or *training*" arguably corresponds to ethics as a mere and predictable transmission of rules, "the one that goes most often from father to son, master to disciple, or master to slave ('I am going to teach you to live')" (xviii). Perhaps more poignantly, Derrida returns to the expression "to learn to live" in his last interview with *Le Monde* (*Learning* 23–26).

2. Rule number 9 of "The Vow of Chastity" states that "the film format must be Academy 35 mm." All the references to the rules included in the Dogme95 *Manifesto* are from Trier and Vinterberg. The budget for the film was almost $3 million, much more than previously certified Dogme95 films: Thomas Vinterberg's *Festen/The Celebration*, Lars von Trier's *Idioterne/The Idiots*, and Søren Kragh-Jacobsen's *Mifunes sidste sang/ Mifune's Last Stand*) (Roman 78). There has been much debate about the seriousness or playfulness of the ten rules of "The Vow of Chastity." For Levring's position, see Roman 74–75. For one of the most comprehensive and acute readings of the *Manifesto*, see Mackenzie, "Manifest Destinies." For an analysis of the extent to which the film abides by the rules, see Cartelli and Rowe 146–47.

3. Rule number 7 states that "Temporal and geographical alienation are forbidden. (That is to say that the film takes place here and now)." In an interview, Levring states that he was concerned with the characters' "demons" more than with "the survival of the body" ("Desert Dogme").

4. I'm borrowing the word "dis-adjustment" from Derrida (*Specters* 22), who is commenting on the "out-of-jointedness" that Hamlet articulates and its relationship with the "possibility of the other" (22) and justice. "Bare life" is a reference to Giorgio Agamben. For Agamben, "bare life remains included in politics in the form of an exception, that is, as something that is included solely through an exclusion" (*Homo Sacer* 11). One of the paradoxes of *Lear* is that Lear's decision in the abdication scene demonstrates the extent to which "the sovereign is, at the same time, outside and inside the juridical order" (15); and that the outcome of the sovereign decision is the inclusion as exclusion of the sovereign himself as "bare life," the kind of life that articulates itself in the liminality of the heath. It is worth mentioning that in the last of his posthumously published seminars, Derrida is extremely critical of Agamben's approach, especially of the (supposedly Aristotelian) distinction between *bios* and *zōē* on which the Italian philosopher bases his notion of bare life. This cannot be fully discussed here. For some pointers on this, see *Beast II* esp. 91–96 and 314–33.

5. On Kanana as choric function, see Burnett, *Filming* 124–25.

6. Many critics emphasize how the aesthetics of Dogme is based on the stripping down of (cinematic) excrescences, often associated with Hollywood. See, for instance, Gaut.

7. Many critics and reviewers have emphasized that this is a Dogme film about Dogme. *The Independent* reviewer Jonathan Romney observes that Henry's predicament "is exactly the situation of the film-maker working with Dogme's

sternly proscriptive rules" (n. pag.). See also Scott-Douglass 260. In an interview with Robert Blackwelder, Levring himself observes that the idea was that of "putting on a play without a theater, without props," and that *King Lear* was chosen because it is a play "about a man who loses everything, and that's very much what it's like when you're doing a Dogme film" (n. pag.).

8. In the 1608 quarto Edmund speaks of "death, dearth, dissolutions of ancient amities, divisions in state, menaces and maledictions against king and nobles" (*The History of King Lear. The Quarto Text*, Scene 2. 140–42).

9. One may add that even in the "uncompressed" quarto version, these lines are and are not Edmund's. They are, strictly speaking, Edmund's tongue-in-cheek dissimulative mimicry of his credulous father's assessment of the dire consequences of "these late eclipses" (Scene 2. 103).

10. In an interview with Richard Kelly, Levring states that his "biggest problem with Dogme" is the *Manifesto*'s condemnation of a director's "personal taste" (Kelly 216). For Levring's discussion of Dogme rules, see also Roman 74–75. On the range of opinions about whether Dogme is to be interpreted as an aesthetic or political project, see the collection of essays edited by Hjort and Mackenzie. In this collection, see esp. Hjort.

11. Although not specifically referring to *The King Is Alive*, Levring asserts that "to force the truth out of [the] characters and setting" remains one of the most interesting aspects of Dogme (Kelly 217).

12. Chapter 1 of the DVD version of the film defines the journey of the Western tourists as a "straight line to nowhere." Caroline Jess points out that in the Nama language, Namibia translates as an area where there is nothing, and thus "fittingly encapsulates the play's evocation of 'nothingness'" (6).

13. This "striptease act" becomes literal in the case of Gina and Liz (Janet McTeer). As is well known, Dogme rules insist on shooting on location with no imported props, extradiegetic music, or special lighting, including optical filters. According to Thomas Vinterberg, one of the founders of Dogme, "filmmaking must be linked to a certain degree of risk. Dogme 95 is my attempt to undress film, to reach the 'naked film'" (qtd. in Porter n. pag.) On the stripping down of the apparatus of Hollywood cinema, see esp. Cartelli and Rowe 144–46. What follows is heavily indebted to their understanding of how the film attempts to restore "a purer kind of cinematic experience that will get us back to human truth, 'the thing itself'" (144).

14. This is the implicit theoretical position of many interpreters of the film. According to Mark Thornton Burnett, the film "invites and frustrates efforts to fit and classify according to a Shakespearean paradigm" (118). Cartelli and Rowe make a similar point. They underline that "the characters 'acting' in Levring's film don't all play one Shakespearean role, nor do they ever play all of the role they variously quote, cite, or impersonate" (158–59).

15. Following the ten rules is this declaration: "I swear to refrain from creating a 'work,' as I regard the instant as more important than the whole" (Trier and Vinterberg n. pag.). This is also an implicit attack on the auteurism of the French New Wave.

16. The *Manifesto* points out the New Wave's inability to counter the "cosmeticiza-tion" of cinema in these terms: "In 1960 enough was enough! The movie had been cosmeticized to death, they said; yet since then the use of cosmetics has exploded" (Trier and Vinterberg n. pag.).

17. For Levring, this is a kind of director's in-joke, "the classic comment you get from actors" (Kelly 213).

18. In his conversation with Richard Kelly, and referring to this scene, Levring states that "Henry shows them that you have to find this [i.e., who the play's characters are] in the words…The answer is in the text" (Kelly 213).

19. Levring speaks of this as an "exorcism" of his cynicism (Kelly 211).

20. In a ground-breaking reading of both *Lear* and *The King Is Alive*, John Joughin insists on how they articulate a sense of life as belatedness, survival, and com-ing after, and in a way that is relevant to my approach here ("Afterlife"). For Joughin, "survival constitutes a type of haunting" (73). In one of the many pas-sages dedicated to the odd temporality of survival, Jacques Derrida argues as follows: "Survival structures every instant in a kind of irreducible torsion, that of a retrospective anticipation that introduces the untimely moment and the posthumous into what is most living in the living present, the rearview mirror of an expecting-death at every moment" (*Aporias* 55).

21. Amy Scott-Douglass underlines that "in a number of films as diverse in tone and genre as *Tea with Mussolini* (1999), *Shakespeare in Love* (1998), Godard's *King Lear*, and *The King is Alive* it is *because* of the American woman that the show goes on" (261).

22. Charles agrees to play Gloucester on condition that he "get[s] to fuck [Gina] until this madness ends."

23. For an interpretation of the emergence of Chronos in this context, see Burnett, *Filming* 122–23.

24. There is perhaps an implicit, ironic reference to the title here. Elvis imperson-ators reproduce the myth that "the King Is Alive" (cf. Burnett, *Filming* 111)

25. Not unlike the Gloucester of 1.2., he continuously abuses his son, while distrib-uting equal doses of pity and scorn onto his daughter-in-law Amanda. Paul's decision to take part in the play, and to take part as Edgar, only makes matters worse. Speaking of his son, and implicitly of his role as Edgar, Charles lashes out: "Your capability for self-degradation is quite formidable."

26. For Livingston, the primary target of Dogme is "the dominant cinema's reduc-tion of imaginative fiction to certain forms of fantasy" (103).

27. Cartelli and Rowe point out that Charles and Catherine sense that there is "something perverse and degrading in the very idea of [Henry's] project" (152). Likening *The King Is Alive* to a film *noir*, Carolyn Jesse observes that in the film "the 'detective' (Henry) discovers that he is part of the crime he is trying to solve" (13).

28. Amy Scott-Douglass argues that "Levring's film attempts to reclaim Shakespeare *for* Europe, *from* Hollywood" (260). Crucial to her argument is the interpreta-tion of the two Cordelias—Catherine, the self-styled quasi-intellectual French

woman, and Gina, the sexually connoted "dumb" American blonde—as alle-gories of, respectively, European and American Cinema. Yet, the film shows that there is no clear-cut opposition between these two Cordelias, and that each of these Cordelias is and is *not* Cordelia, which raises questions about their functioning as emblems of geographically and culturally distinct forms of cinema. *The King Is Alive* lends itself to allegorical interpretations. See also Simons 59–61. Referring to game theory, Jan Simons also emphasizes the ludic aspect of Dogme films: "*The King Is Alive* shares with *Idioterne* and *Mifune* a central concern for the game rather than the results. 'Spassing' is a continuous game with no real end" (60).

29. This recalls critical readings of Lear's abdication scene that underline the pres-ence therein of well-rehearsed folkloric themes. For a lucid account of this, see Garber, *After All* 653.

30. For another exploration of the Symbolic Father (i.e., the father of the Oedipus myth) and the Father-of-Enjoyment (i.e., the primal father of *Totem and Taboo*) as functions that overlap and supplement one another, see esp. Zizek, *Looking* 23–25.

31. This may be interpreted as the difference between an absent Symbolic Father as an agent of prohibition and the excessively present "Father-Enjoyment." "Father-Enjoyment" is another term Zizek uses to define this figure (*Enjoy* 143)

32. If one adopts the point of view offered by Gina's reiteration, Charles's statements after lovemaking such as "I'm flattered," or his eagerness for "love," retrospec-tively begin to sound like traits that assimilate him not only to Gloucester but also to Lear.

33. Given the sexual context of Gina's speech, they may also be an echo of the beginning of Faustus's proverbial address to Helen: "Was this the face that launched a thousand ships...?" (*Dr Faustus*, Scene 12. 81).

34. There is a "ghosting effect" in Gina's exploration. As she works through her naiveté, one cannot fail to hear an intertextual echo, namely the naiveté of the Cordelia-like character Caroline that Jennifer Jason Leigh interprets in Jocelyn Moorhouse's cinematographic version of *A Thousand Acres* (1997). In this film, Caroline refuses to accept that, like her sisters Ginny (Goneril) and Rose (Regan), she has been sexually abused as a child by her beloved father Larry.

35. See also chapter 1, note 21.

36. When we see him hanging from the ceiling we cannot fail to recall the words which describe *Cordelia's* fate in the "original": "My poor fool is hanged" (5.3.281).

37. While Henry tries to restore Ray's confidence, his wife Liz is flirting with Moses, so that Henry's "Forget about the rest of us" sounds ironic in this con-text. Yet the words Henry asks him to concentrate on ("This is nothing, fool") may also be interpreted as the way in which the *Lear* script tells Ray in advance that that there is nothing, or almost nothing, in Liz's flirting with Moses, and that to believe otherwise is foolish.

38. There is another "ghosting effect" here, as Lia Williams had just played Amanda, a self-effacing sister who finally decides to make a stand, in the popular British ITV series *Imogen's Face*. Janet McTeer brings to Liz's role her recent performance as a restless single mother in *Tumbleweeds*. She will play the leading role in Kristian Levring's next film *The Intended*, an adaptation of *Heart of Darkness*.

39. This "sound" is oddly juxtaposed to the "image" of a troubled Catherine who is concocting her plan to poison Gina.

40. On the black/white dichotomy in the film, see Bottinelli.

41. Throughout the scene, Liz as Goneril uses the quarto reading "arms" (*The History of King Lear. The Quarto Text*, Scene 12. 17) instead of the Folio "names" (4.2.17).

42. By walking into the desert, he does, indeed, "forget about the rest of us" (Henry's advice) to provide an effective performance as Kent.

43. The Folio has: "Now, good my lord, lie here and rest a while" (3.6.40); and "hard by here is a hovel...Repose you there while I to this hard house" (3.2.61, 63)

44. Jack's rules are as follows: "We get water, gather food reserves, build a shelter, remain visible, and keep our spirits up."

45. For Kristian Levring, Jack is, quite simply, "a joke" (Kelly 214).

46. The eighth rule states: "Genre movies are not acceptable" (Trier and Vinterberg, n. pag.). Levenson calls the film "an 'anti-adventure,' an exercise in doom and existential nothingness" (116).

47. On this aspect of *Lear*, see Joughin, "Afterlife," esp. 70–73. On survival/survivance, see also "Introduction" above, note 2 and 42.

48. Although they do not refer to this specific scene, Cartelli and Rowe observe that the "lapse into colloquial speech" reveals "the intellectual and emotional impoverishment of the characters, whose encounters and exchanges often operate at the level of the maudlin or soap operatic." This is in contrast with their delivery of lines from *Lear* in the film's last scene, which "comes closer to approximating the expressive intensity of the cinematography" (162).

49. Holman's review of the film hints at this.

50. Both Bennington and Mitchell ("Picturing") underline how often Derrida uses this concept in his latest work. Mitchell acutely observes the impossibility of establishing a literal meaning for "autoimmunity," and that this is exactly one of Derrida's points. Autoimmunity is part of both a sociopolitical discourse and a biological discourse, and they are inextricably bound up with each other: "the effect of the bipolar image...is to produce a situation in which there is *no literal meaning*, nothing but the resonances between two images, one bio-medical, the other political" (282). Derrida himself refers to autoimmunity as "something that might look like a generalization, without any *external* limit, of a biological or physiological model." He explains that if there is a generalization, this is part and parcel of a questioning of any clear-cut "separation of *physis* from its others, such as *technē*, *nomos*, and *thesis*" (*Rogues* 109). In "Faith and Knowledge"

Derrida speaks of a "general logic of auto-immunization," and argues that "it seems indispensable to us today for thinking the relations between faith and knowledge, religion and science, as well as the duplicity of sources in general" (75 n.). In subsequent work, it also becomes indispensable for thinking about the permeable boundaries of the body politic and the threat of terrorism, a threat that never quite comes from the outside. See Borradori esp. 94–109. On autoimmunity, see also "Introduction" above, note 25.

51. Interestingly, for Derrida, "the auto-immunitary haunts the community and its system of immunitary survival *like the hyperbole of its own possibility*" ("Faith and Knowledge 47, emphasis added). Lear's self-erasing "ab-solutism" may be seen as an example of this hubristic hyperbole. My understanding of absolutism in relation to *Lear* is indebted to Moretti. For an exploration of the usurpation of life as exemplary of belatedness and survival, see Joughin, "Afterlife." See also chapter 6 below for the interactions of autoimmunity and mediality.

52. "Imagined community" is of course a reference to Anderson's concept. In an interesting review of the film, which contains some inexactitudes, Martha Nochimson argues that "the vitality of 'the king' in the film is not the content of the Shakespeare play, but the play's ability to confer on the almost hopeless group a continuous, collaborative, spontaneous, humanizing *act* of narrative, the foundation of human community" (52). My approach to the notion of community in the film and to the role played by the "content of the Shakespeare play" is diametrically opposed to Nochimson's.

53. Hyphen added to the translation of "*la vie la mort*." "Life-death" (with an hyphen) perhaps makes clearer the aporia encapsulated in "*la vie la mort*" (Derrida, *La bête II* 192).

54. And if it brings death closer, this is not necessarily in the name of death, as shown by Ray's vicissitudes.

55. The Folio version of *Lear* reads: "By th' law of arms thou wast not bound to answer / An unknown opposite. Thou art not vanquished, / But cozened and beguiled (5.3.143–45).

56. The Folio reads: "What you have charged me with, that I have done, / And more, much more" (153–54).

57. The discourse of autoimmunity that the film incorporates and rearticulates undoubtedly points in the direction of Burnett's analysis. Derrida's development of the logic of the autoimmune is also an attempt to understand the so-called return of the religious ("Faith and Knowledge" 45) and, more generally, "the religiosity of religion" (51). For Derrida, a "new Enlightenment" (54) is not sufficient to account for this, as it would be unable, for instance, to shed light on how "religion today allies itself with tele-technoscience, to which it reacts with all its forces" (46).

58. See Cartelli and Rowe 151, and Burnett, *Filming* 126–27. This is also arguably a questioning of the colonialist modus operandi inscribed within the survival-narrative film.

3 Reiterating *Othello*: Spectral Media and the Rhetoric of Silence in Alexander Abela's *Souli*

1. They include the Montreal World Film Festival (2004), the Namur International French-Language Film Festival (2004), the Rio de Janeiro International Film Festival (2005), and the Monterrey International Film Festival (2006). The film was also nominated for the Grand Prix Award at the 2005 Paris Film Festival. My analysis of the film is indebted to Mark Thornton Burnett's groundbreaking study of Abela's Shakespearean production ("Madagascan"). It also owes much to personal conversations with the director conducted via email between 2009 and 2011. Alexander Abela also kindly provided me with a working copy of *Souli* in DVD format with English subtitles as well as with production stills.

2. As is well known, Shakespearean films do not often sell. Baz Luhrmann's *William Shakespeare's Romeo + Juliet* is an exception to this rule. To return briefly to *The King Is Alive*, Levring was told by the distributor of the film "not to talk too much about Shakespeare and theater because … that would turn off movie-goers" (Stevenson 117).

3. As Laura Marks observes apropos of intercultural cinema, "when verbal and visual representation is saturated, meanings seep into bodily and other dense, *seemingly silent registers*" (5, emphasis added). This cinema appeals to "nonvisual knowledge, embodied knowledge, and experience of the senses, such as touch, smell, and taste" (4). This is part of Marks's wider argument about haptic visuality whereby "the eyes themselves function like organs of touch" (162). Moreover, as she argues, "thinking of cinema as haptic is only a step toward considering the ways cinema appeals to the body as a whole" (163). In its *pars destruens*, the book is of course a critique of ocularcentrism, and especially the ways in which "ethnographic photography and film have objectified non-Western cultures and made a spectacle of them" (133). For one of the most interesting recent developments of this approach, which insists on the relationship of reversibility between film and viewer within shared tactile structures, and thus on the phenomenological, correlational aspect of cinematic experience, see Barker. Theories of haptic visuality are relevant to my reading of an example of "intercultural" cinema such as *Souli*, but they are often filtered, and rephrased, through Derrida's understanding of the haptic in *Touching*.

4. For a similar approach to the emergence of alterity out of compulsive reiteration, but in relation to a literary rewriting of *Othello*, Tayeb Salih's *Season of Migration to the North*, see Calbi, "Ghostly."

5. "Dis-adjustment" is a reference to Derrida, *Specters* 22–23. See chapter 2, note 4.

6. Subtitles modified. The French is: "*Écoutez la voix de cet homme qui parle avec la note.*"

7. In the latest cut of the film, the initial scene is missing: "The opening shot will show the protagonist, Souli (Othello), walking at night towards us along a narrow passage of cactuses. In voice over, he tells us that he is doing 'the dance of the passage'. In other words he is dead, and is waiting for the ancestors to accept

him to the other world." (Personal communication with Alexander Abela. 28 Dec. 2009).

8. Referring to the initial scene, Burnett comments as follows: "Despite his lived cultural confusions, Souli in death...enters a communicative third space which...may have the potential to involve other audiences beyond a strictly limited national and cultural purchase" ("Madagascan" 248). But this, of course, through the "friend" Abi. "Third space" is Homi Bhabha's expression (esp. 217–29).

9. See also the "Introduction" above, note 28.

10. One may want to add that "tell" is one of *Othello*'s first words (1.1.1), or that it ends with the word "relate" (5.2.382). Much has been written on this. See esp. Loomba, *Gender* 48–62; *Shakespeare* 1–21, 91–111; Neill; Parker. See also Calbi "Being a Guest."

11. In this scene with Buba, he also resembles Roderigo: by buying stale beer from him, he "put[s] money" in his "purse" (1.3.339).

12. This is an update and transformation of Iago's "She did deceive her father, marrying you" (3.3.210). Two of the veranda's supports enframe Yann and Souli as they speak. The mise-en-scène suggests citationality. On the reference to *Othello*, see also Costantini-Cornède n. pag.

13. This voyeuristic position is partially the result of self-inflicted marginality. In spite of being invited by Mona, Souli refuses to join the dance he feverishly observes from his remote location. This is a position that roughly corresponds to the one Othello occupies at the beginning of the fourth act of Shakespeare's play. For a classic study of voyeurism in early modern drama, see Maus. For a redeployment of Maus's argument in relation to non-Shakespearean Jacobean tragedy, see Calbi, *Approximate* 15–20, 27–31, 51–55.

14. My implied reference here is to Parker's investigation into the gendered cultural semantics of *Othello*, esp. 66–72.

15. For the mutual invagination of different kind of borders in films, new media, and critical apparatuses, see Burt, *Medieval* esp. 1–74.

16. Examples of this are his dialogue with Mona about discipleship: "I trust in fate. It'll tell me when the right man has come, and I'll wait for him the time it takes"; or his reflections on the dynamics of power as he talks to Yann on the veranda: "Today you're exploiting these fishermen, tomorrow someone else will."

17. Displacement is at work here once again, with Abi phantasmatically replacing Mona, which is a kind of translation of the merging of Bianca and Desdemona taking place most forcefully in 4.1. As a "city girl," and the sexual partner of a white man, Abi is also seen as an outsider in the remote village that provides the film's setting, and this facilitates her association with the courtesan Bianca.

18. It is also worth underlining that in Abela's film this episode is a "brawl" (2.3.165) and some kind of delayed effect of a previous "brawl": the charge of rape leveled at Carlos is a consequence of the fact that after fighting with one of the locals, he carries on drinking and dancing and ends up in a tent with Abi without remembering much.

19. See Loomba, *Gender* 57.

20. The brutality of the relationship between Yann and Abi is also a reinterpreta-tion of the relationship between Iago and Emilia in *Othello*, a reinterpretation that is not uncommon in filmic adaptations of *Othello*. An example of this from mainstream cinema is Oliver Parker's *Othello* (1995).

21. Singh analyzes Murray Carlin's *Not Now, Sweet Desdemona* and Tayeb Salih's *Season of Migration to the North*. (For a groundbreaking reading of Salih's novel, see Cartelli, *Repositioning* 147–68). In Murray Carlin's play, the charac-ters playing Othello and Desdemona, who are lovers in "real life," are rehears-ing lines from 3.3. when he strikes her, which in *Othello* happens in 4.1. The character playing Desdemona reacts as follows: "You're in the wrong part of the play...And you're over-acting" (*Not Now* 41). Then they start reminiscing about their "illegal" sexual relationship in apartheid South Africa. It is at this point that the character playing Desdemona becomes absorbed in her thoughts. After a long pause, her lover asks her: "What are you looking at?", to which she replies: "All the ghosts ..." (42), which is followed by another pause. These are the same "ghosts" that affect the relationship between Souli and Mona in Abela's film. In other rewritings of *Othello*, it is the reiteration of the *Othello* story that is emphasized, along with the deleterious consequences on the char-acters' life, and in a way that is also relevant to *Souli*. Emblematic is the very beginning of Djanet Sears's Africadian revision of *Othello*. The Desdemona-like character, simply called "She," addresses her partner (called "He") with the following words: "We keep on doing this, don't we?" ("Prologue" 21). Although my thinking in this section of the chapter is influenced by Jyotsna Singh, it can be argued that she makes a distinction between Western and African recep-tion of the Shakespearean text that may be too rigid: where could one locate, for instance, a passionate "reader"—and rewriter—of *Othello* such as the black British novelist Caryl Phillips? Caryl Phillips rereads *Othello* in *The European Tribe* and rewrites the play in *The Nature of Blood*. For the uncanny presence of *Othello* in Phillips's writing, see Calbi, "Ghosts." For a study of the theoretical problematic of writing *back* to Shakespeare as a form of (spectral) writing *with* Shakespeare, especially in connection with Derek Walcott's appropriation of *Antony and Cleopatra* in *A Branch of the Blue Nile*, see Calbi, "Writing."

22. It can be argued that this is also part of a writing back to *Othello*. Performing the murder in silence does not make Souli's act less violent but it partially undercuts Othello's magniloquent justification of the murder, especially his association of murder with a "sacrifice" (5.2.70) executed on behalf of (all) "men" (6). Othello's use of the word "men" in this context ("Yet she must die, else she'll betray more men") appeals to a universalistic construct that de facto excludes him. On this see Loomba, *Gender* 59–60.

23. Philosopher and cultural theorist Iain Chambers is here discussing the crisis of the Western anthropological gaze. He argues that "the interval of the unsaid, the shadows of the subaltern, of the dispossessed, are thrown across the trans-parency of a language accustomed to ignoring the ontology of silence" (174).

24. The film was also advertised as *Souli. The Last Breath* (*Souli. Le dernier souffle*).

25. For a study of cinema that adopts Levinas's understanding of ethics, see Girgus.

26. Levinas continues by emphasizing "a *despite myself* that is more me [*moi*] than myself: it is an election" (187), "election" being again an appropriate word to describe the inheriting/transmission of the tale in the scene. What I have called the "spectral" asymmetry of terms in the relationship between Souli and Abi builds on Levinas's emphasis on a temporal "*difference without simultaneity of unmatched terms*" (his emphasis) which is "a non-in-difference" (177), and which he calls diachrony.

27. The film often emphasizes touch and sexualizes it, and this can probably be related to the exchange between Othello and Desdemona concerning the latter's "hot, hot and moist...hand" in the original play (3.4.36–47). In the film touching hands is often a prologue to Souli and Mona's lovemaking. In this final scene, touching each other's hand is arguably a re-marking and displacement of these previous occurrences whose aim is that of interrupting and rephrasing what the film sees as the deleterious racial and sexual politics of *Othello*.

28. For a similar argument about tradition as transmission and translation to which I am indebted here, see Chow esp. 182–202.

29. In this sense, the relationship between Souli and Abi is a *partage*, an almost untranslatable French work that signifies "participation as much as irreducible partition." This relationship is "a sharing without fusion, a community without community, a language without communication, a being-with without confusion" (*Touching* 195). This is not the place to discuss Derrida's criticism of the metaphysics of touch, a criticism that also extends to contemporary theories of the haptic and haptic visuality (see note 3 above), including Deleuze and Guattari's (124–26). *On Touching*, which deals with all the major philosophers who elaborate on the problematics of touch, is also a reading of Jean-Luc Nancy, whose philosophical work is, to Derrida, exemplary in that it shows a "break with the immediacy or the continuity of contact" by repeatedly emphasizing the "interval of spacing [and] exteriority" even when it insists on "contiguity, touching, contact, and so forth" (119). The following excerpt, which is specifically from a reading of Husserl, gives an idea of Derrida's more general argument, and shows that spectrality and the *technē* of the prosthetic supplement are relevant to the experience of touch. The French philosopher asks "whether there is any pure auto-affection of the touching or the touched, and therefore any pure, immediate experience of the purely proper body, the body proper that is living, purely living. Or if, on the contrary, this experience is at least not already *haunted*, but *constitutively* haunted, by some hetero-affection related to spacing and then to visible spatiality—where an intruder may come through, a host, wished or unwished for, a spare and auxiliary other, or a parasite..., a *pharmakon* that already having at its disposal a dwelling in this place inhabits one's heart of hearts [*tout for intérieur*] as a ghost" (179–180).

30. Rey Chow's argument about the politically dubious reversal of the opposition between the West and its others is relevant here. For Chow, "there is a way in which contemporary cultural studies, in the attempt to vindicates the culture of the West's 'others,' end up revalorizing the 'original' that is the authentic history, culture, and language of such 'others'" (192). She insists, instead, that "critiquing the great disparity between Europe and the rest of the world means not simply a deconstruction of Europe as origin or simply a restitution of the origin that is Europe's others but a thorough dismantling of *both* the notion of origin and the notion of alterity as we know them today" (194). This is in the context of a discussion of translation and contemporary Chinese film. For a related understanding of the critique of binarisms, see Chakrabarty esp. 28–45, 237–55. On the question of whether Abela's film itself reproduces the ethnographic gaze, see Burnett, "Madagascan" 241–42.

31. Souli speaks Malagasy or French. In *Monolingualism of the Other*, Jacques Derrida argues that "the language called maternal is never purely natural, nor proper, nor inhabitable." He draws attention to the verb "to inhabit" as a verb that encapsulates "a value that is quite *disconcerting* and equivocal," and concludes that "there is no possible habitat without the difference of . . . exile and . . . nostalgia" (58). On the language called maternal, see also Derrida's long footnote (79–93). For Derrida, it is from out of this exile—what he also calls a constitutive "inalienable alienation" (25) in language—that there springs forth an irrepressible nostalgia for an uncontaminated origin. This is a desire for "a *first language . . .* , a *prior-to-the first* language" (61, Derrida's emphasis), a language that arguably recalls the "pure language" (*reine Sprache*) of Walter Benjamin's essay on translation ("Task" 80–81). Of course this language does not quite exist but its spectral effects are irreducible. The writer-protagonist of Abela's film is caught in this double bind.

32. Burnett underlines the "peripatetic" character of Abi's fate. He adds that "her status functions so as to recall and celebrate Souli's soul in passage, to assert a powerful equation between rest and mobility, and to declare the virtues of what Rosi Braidotti terms a 'nomadic subjectivity'" (253).

33. On the ambiguous fate of Yann, see Costantini-Cornède, n. pag.

4 "This Is My Home, Too": Migration, Spectrality, and Hospitality in Roberta Torre's *Sud Side Stori*

1. *Sud Side Stori* failed to achieve the critical acclaim of her first feature film, the mafia musical *Tano da Morire* (1997).

2. Roberta Torre prefers not to call it a musical, but a film in which music plays a fundamental role (Interview by Valerio Gualerzi).

3. Its idiosyncratic style within the Italian context can also be gauged by comparing the film to the current vogue for commercially driven adaptations of Shakespeare that appeal to the teen market, the most recent examples of which being Volfango De Biasi's *Come tu mi vuoi* (*The Way You Like Me*) (2007),

a remaking of *The Taming of the Shrew*, and *Iago* (2009), a romantic comedy loosely based on *Othello*. Both films were produced and distributed by Berlusconi-owned Medusa films.

4. The legendary British reggae artist Dennis Bovell, who contributed to the movie soundtrack, plays a Nigerian pimp. There is an effect of "ghosting" here, as he wrote the musical score for *Babylon* (1980), a groundbreaking British film directed by Italian-born Franco Rosso in which racial tensions and the fate of a reggae sound system combine in a depauperated South London.

5. For explorations of the more general relevance of Derrida's quasi-concept of spectrality to the analysis of Shakespearean adaptations, see Joughin (131–50). For a deft reading of the uncanny temporality of remainders in relation to notions of Shakespearean authorship and *auteurism avant la lettre*, a reading in which Derrida's *Specters of Marx* plays a significant role, see Lehmann (*Shakespeare Remains* 1–24).

6. This is a reference to a real-life event. In 1998 Mayor of Palermo Leoluca Orlando, in an effort to promote multiculturalism, strongly supported the celebrations in honor of Saint Benedict the Moor. See Cavecchi 95–96.

7. Unless otherwise indicated, translations from Italian are mine.

8. *Sbirra* is Italian slang for policewoman but of course she is hardly an emblem of Law and Order.

9. For a useful categorization of Shakespearean adaptations (conventional, transpositional, experimental, and oppositional) that is aware of the provisionality of categorizing, see Lehmann, "Film Adaptation" 75.

10. The three sisters recall the witches in *Macbeth* (Cavecchi 100).

11. In addition to *West Side Story* and *William Shakespeare's Romeo + Juliet*, they include *China Girl* (1987), *Bollywood Queen* (2002), *Pizza My Heart* (2005), and *Rome & Jewel* (2008). In recent years filmic adaptations of *Romeo and Juliet* have become more and more concerned with race and ethnic conflict, even more so than films based on *Othello*.

12. On visitation and invitation, unconditional and conditional hospitality, see also Borradori 128–30.

13. Alessandra Masolini points out that "if the inhabitants of the *Vucciaria* need to reinforce their sense of identity by projecting their own marginality on the Africans, also the Nigerian women must reject their white exploiters in order to avoid the pain of being absorbed as mere objects of desire" (228).

14. Derrida asks, in a way that is relevant to my argument here, "what is identity, this concept of which the transparent identity to itself is always dogmatically presupposed by so many debates on monoculturalism or multiculturalism, nationality, citizenship, and, in general, belonging?" (14). For Derrida there is only "the interminable and indefinitely phantasmatic process of identification" (28), a process that inevitably points to the traumatic trace of the "other" within a self that does not preexist this trauma.

15. The "America" that is "waiting for" Toni is perhaps an echo of the "America" the Puerto Rican girls ironically appropriate while singing and dancing on the roofs of Manhattan's West Side buildings in *West Side Story*.

16. Arguably, one of the defining characteristics of recent non-Anglophone (or not entirely English-speaking) Shakespearean films, is the mixing of material from more than one play. *Sud Side Stori*, with its references to *Othello* and *Macbeth* (e.g., Toni's three aunties resembling the witches in *Macbeth*), is not unique in this. For instance, in Roysten Abel's *In Othello* (2003), the white actor Barry quotes from *Macbeth*; Maqbool experiences an Othello-like jealousy toward Nimmi, the wife of the Duncan-like character, in Vishal Bhardwaj's adaptation of *Macbeth*, *Maqbool* (2003); Jeremy Wooding's *Bollywood Queen* (2002), a *Romeo and Juliet* spin-off, ironically quotes from *Macbeth*; Empress Wan is as much Gertrude as Lady Macbeth in Fen Xiaogang's *The Banquet* (2006), mostly an adaptation of *Hamlet*; *Romeo and Juliet* and *Othello* oddly combine in the recent teensploi Italian film *Iago*, directed by Volfango De Biasi (2008).

17. She first says: "*Amore va verso amore con cui è allontanato da amore come si vanno a scuola*," and then: "*Amore è allontanato da amore con la stessa tristezza come ragazzi che vanno a scuola.*"

18. "*Amore va verso amore come gli scolari scappano dai libri, ma amore si allontana da amore con la stessa tristezza con cui gli scolari vanno a scuola.*"

19. For Derrida, as shown in the Introduction, "the Thing, . . . like an elusive specter, *engineers* [*s'ingenie*] a habitation without proper inhabiting, . . . it inhabits without residing" (*Specters* 18).

20. In terms of style of delivery, tone and even content, this news report is "contaminated" by previous news reports on the exploits of the mafia by the same journalist. But it is also implicitly critical of the immediately antecedent style of doing TV, the "live" broadcasting of the murder of Toni, which is announced in voice-over as "breaking news."

21. One example is a news commentator caught off the record singing a stereotypical racist song about black people, and then going on air to expose the Mafia's racially motivated attack against the sculptor working on the statue of the Moorish saint.

22. This is perhaps an implied reference to the play's "she hangs upon the cheek of night / As a rich jewel in an Ethiope's ear" (1.5.44–45).

23. This is not to argue that the "Shakespeare" of Anglophone films, by contrast with the "Shakespeare" of non-Anglophone films, actually *belongs* and that it is not, in fact, always-already the "language of the other." In contemporary global media culture the distinction between Anglophone and non-Anglophone Shakespeare on film has become increasingly labile. For an argument that fully explores this, from a different perspective, see Burt: "Shakespeare film adaptation significantly blur if not fully deconstruct distinctions between the local and the global, original and copy, pure and hybrid, indigenous and foreign, high and low, authentic and inauthentic, hermeneutic and post-hermeneutic, *English and other languages*" ("Glo-ca1i-zation" 15–16, emphasis added). See also "Introduction" above (10).

24. In the chapter on the "Phenomenology of Eros" Levinas also underlines tenderness (*tendre*) as a movement toward, a tension (*tendre*), and associates it with "an extreme fragility, a vulnerability" (277). Douglas Lanier suggested that

"relation without relation" could be a definition of adaptation itself (personal communication).

25. Derrida further suggests that one should think hospitality "from the future" and "from death," and it is in this context that he mentions both *Romeo and Juliet* and *Antony and Cleopatra* (15). For a more extended reading of the hospitality of love as a theoretical problematic, and in relation to Shakespeare's *Othello*, see Calbi, "Being a Guest." On the "im-possible" in Derrida's work, see Carotenuto.

26. In a sense this parallels what happens to Toni toward the end of the first scene in the tavern, when the conflicting definitions of love in Shakespeare's play are remediated through the conflict between two icons of Italian popular culture who try to outshine one another: Mario Merola, a Neapolitan singer of the highly melodramatic *sceneggiata* who emerges from a volcano (probably standing for Vesuvius) and Little Toni, the emblem of the Italian version of rock'n'roll. On this, see Masolino 233. Merola's Neapolitan song *So'nnato carcerato* (*I Was Born in Jail*)) associates love with the sun (cf. "and Juliet is the sun," 2.1.45), and speaks of a very young "virginal" woman, as young as Juliet. Little Toni's performance is based on a more aggressive, Mercutio-like, approach to love and women.

27. When we next see Toni and Romea, they are in an undefined location outside the city, a kind of fair playground that reminds the viewer of the place where Romeo resides after his banishment in Luhrmann's film. It is, in a sense, a jungle, since a voice in the background repeatedly invites nonexistent customers to "Come to the magic world of Tarzan and Jane." They "consummate" their love as they spin around on a car inside the "Tunnel of Love." The style is still that of a silent film, and the music is the same as the one playing during the balcony scene. They look like fragile silhouettes intermittingly and precariously emerging from a dark background, while shots of a passport, of a number of black figures, and especially of one of the female procurers ("This is business, this is money," which is spoken in English) remind them and us of the "reality" outside this mobile and transient simulacrum of "home."

5 "Shakespeare in the Extreme": Ghosts and Remediation in Alexander Fodor's *Hamlet*

1. "Shakespeare in the Extreme" as a catchphrase for the film's *modus operandi* appears in the DVD booklet and the film's website: www.hamletmovie.co.uk.

2. Lines from this dialogue that are somehow related to future violent acts, as is the case with Laertes's "It may be death" (4.7.121), repeatedly conjure up fragments from the Ophelia scene. Fodor's montage, that is, works in an ironic way, since it suggests that there is an uncanny correlation between the pursuit of the cycle of revenge on Laertes's part and Ophelia's death.

3. For a development of Worthen's notion of "citational environment," see especially Cartelli and Rowe 29–34.

4. I am of course implicitly referring to Freud's classical formulation (*The Unconscious* 191). Freud's timelessness is arguably akin to Derrida's "*non-contemporaneity with itself of the living present*" (*Specters* xix, Derrida's emphasis), the time "without *certain* joining or determinable conjunction" (18) of anachrony. For an excellent reading of the "ghost room" as a device that shows "how new media can effect not only technical, but phenomenological changes in cinematic conventions," see Cartelli, "Slant Shakespeare." For Cartelli, the ghost room, which is "the staging ground for Hamlet's meeting with the ghost of his father, for Ophelia's suicide, and, more intriguingly, for several out-of-time sequences when (where?) Hamlet as a child interacts with his still-ghostly father," functions as the uncanny *locus* of "a stream of seemingly unauthored images and sounds" that displaces the conventional technique of flashback, in that it refuses any anchoring in an individual thinking subject (n. pag.).

5. The DVD booklet underlines the chess metaphors. There are red and white characters. Polonia, for instance, is the Red Queen, Laertes a Red Knight, Hamlet a white pawn, and so on. In this schematization, which is useful only to an extent, the Ghost is the Red King and the greatest manipulator. The ending of the film sanctions the victory of the Ghost. According to the booklet, "game set and match to the Ghost" (n. pag.). Given the absence of Fortinbras, it is the Ghost himself who may be said to reappear at the end to "claim [his] vantage" and his "rights of memory in this kingdom" (5.2. 344, 345).

6. The expression "toxic drive" appears in Ronell's wonderful study of addiction in/as literature (23).

7. For the distinction between "camp" and "revival" Shakespeare, see Cartelli and Rowe esp. 19–21, 34–37.

8. These children, who function as the ghost's dangerous emissaries, may be associated with the play's "eyre of children, little eyases" (2.2.340).

9. The party scene includes a compressed version of Claudius's speech, whose political meaning gets lost in the cacophony of voices, Laertes's advice to Ophelia, part of Polonia's scolding of Ophelia and the revelation of the ghost's apparition.

10. While on this "platform," he will not fail to express his annoyance at the fact that "the air bites shrewdly" (1.4.1).

11. On the contradictory injunction to remember *and* revenge, especially in terms of the different modalities of temporality involved therein, see Garber, *Ghost Writers* 147–53. See also Lehmann, *Shakespeare Remains* 107.

12. On female "matter," see Parker esp. 81. See also Calbi, *Approximate* 56–70, 83–100.

13. Jacques Lacan uses the expression "in-between-two-deaths" (*l'entre-deux-morts*) in his 1959–1960 seminar on *The Ethics of Psychoanalysis* (270–87).

14. "Archive fever" is a reference to Derrida, *Archive* esp. 91.

15. See Lomonico.

16. Of course, by "real life" Lanier means the real life of fictive characters.

17. I am here referring to Derrida's more general argument about the essential pros-theticity of language, a language "coming from the other, remaining with the other, and returning to the other" (*Monolingualism* 40).

18. In the film the grave-digger scene turns into slapstick comedy. The director plays the part of both the grave-digger and the priest. While doing so, he holds in his hand a copy of Shakespeare's *Complete Works*. One of the exchanges between Hamlet and the Gravedigger ("Whose grave's this, sirrah?" "*Mine*, sir" [5.1.115–16, emphasis added]) somehow allegorizes, in a comic way, Fodor's claim that *Hamlet* (or his remains) are *his*—*Fodor's* play. The ground that is being excavated is a minefield, and "mine" also turns out to be a mine that explodes, killing the other grave-digger and leaving only his hand behind.

6 "Restless Ecstasy": Addiction, Reiteration, and Mediality in Klaus Knoesel's *Rave Macbeth*

1. The main features of this *wunderkamera* is that it enhances the clarity of night scenes, essential to a film of this kind; it allows fewer interruptions between takes because of its 40-minutes digital tape; it boasts an HD monitor that shows exactly how the film will appear on the screen and offers digitally syn-ched audio and video. Because of all these features, although expensive in itself, the camera saves on postproduction costs. (A German company, Media! AG, provided the camera in exchange for a stake in the picture). See Roxborough; Wisehart; Jess-Cooke 169–70.

2. On rave culture see esp. Anderson and Reynolds.

3. Lanier cautiously speaks of "something 'in' Shakespeare" that products of pop-ular culture appropriate (97), with "in" in inverted commas, which seems to suggest, in terms of the argument developed in this book, that these aspects are simultaneously "in" Shakespeare *and* a retroactive effect of adaptation.

4. He cannot complain, as the character who bears the same name does in the original play, that he has not been "called to bear [his] part" (3.5.8).

5. To Dean's rhetorical question, "Nobody's freaking out, are they?", Marcus answers: "Nope," although we have already seen him falling prey to hallucinations.

6. Douglas Lanier points out that "several plays have seemed to fall inescapably into the gravitational pull of specific genres—in ways revealing about the inter-pretive predispositions audiences bring to these works." The "gangster saga" is the filmic template through which *Macbeth* is often experienced ("Spin-Offs" 134). Of course *Macbeth* is not the only Shakespearean play to be transposed to an urban environment marked by crime and the circulation of drugs. To refer to filmic adaptations of the new millennium, Don Boyd's *My Kingdom* (2001), a transposition of *Lear*, and James Gavin Bedford's *The Street King* (2002), a remake of *Richard III*, recall many of the themes that I will be exploring in this chapter. *My Kingdom*, in particular, can be seen as a trenchant exploration of the logic of the "white stuff" as *pharmakon*. Relatedly, it can also be seen as a compendium of the (deadly) working of autoimmunity, to which I will refer

later on in this chapter, as well as of the functioning of community as "auto-co-immunity" (see chapter 2). For a reading of these films see, respectively, Lehmann "Postnostalgic"; Burnett, *Filming* 129–57 and Cartelli and Rowe 103–5.

7. *Shakespeare's Ghost Writers* recirculated Mallarmé's essay in the field of Shakespeare studies. However, this essay is arguably even more uncanny than Garber believes it to be, in both "form" and "content." It is an uncanny essay about the uncanny in *Macbeth*. One only needs to mention how Mallarmé sets up the scene that leads to the exposition of his insight into the opening scene of *Macbeth* (after a detour through Thomas de Quincey's reading of the porter scene): while arranging some books on newly built shelves in his country house, the volume containing the complete works by Shakespeare falls open by chance at the very first scene of *Macbeth*, and this reminds him of the insight into the scene he had many years before. This is an insight, he tells us, that has been haunting him for a long time (*"L'aperçu que je signale, me hanta depuis son illumination lointaine,"* 346). See also Pearson esp. 136–39. Translations from the original French are mine. I am using the translation of the section of Mallarmé essay that appears in Garber (92–93) but I am modifying it whenever appropriate.

8. *"Les présenter, insisté-je, comment? Au seuil et qu'elles y règnent"* (349).

9. Mallarmé's essay is also a discussion of De Quincey's "On the Knocking at the Gate in *Macbeth*." For De Quincey, this knocking is notoriously "the recommencement of suspended life" (152). De Quincey speaks of the annihilation of time preceding this "recommencement," "the awful parenthesis" that suspended "the goings-on of the world in which we live"(153). In short, he underlines a sense of temporality as anachrony.

10. *"Le prodige, antérieur... n'eut lieu, du moins régulièrement ou quant à la pièce"* (350).

11. "One bore witness to it, the worse for that, it should have been ignored, like dark primordial antecedents not concerning anybody" (350). (*"On en fut témoin, tant pis, on le devait ignorer, comme primordiaux antécédents obscurs ne concernant personne"*).

12. Speaking of fan fiction, Douglas Lanier argues that these works "return Shakespeare's plays... to their place in a long tradition of imitation and adaptation from which their status as literary monuments has tended to isolate them" (*Shakespeare* 85). *Rave Macbeth* frames Shakespeare in a similar way while transferring the remains of the author function to Hecate.

13. See also "Media" esp. 59–62.

14. In the second volume of *The Beast and the Sovereign* seminars, Derrida clarifies: "What I call iterability, which repeats the same while displacing or altering it, is all at once a resource, a decisive power, and a catastrophe of repetition or reproduction (*Beast II* 75).

15. Among the many reflections on the notion of the event by Derrida, perhaps the clearest is in the collection of interviews *Negotiations* 85–116. In "The Deconstruction of Actuality," Derrida insists, on the one hand, on

"artifactuality," the extent to which "'reality'...reaches us through fictional constructions" (86); on the other, he underlines the necessity of vigilant critique, warning us against what he calls "the *delusion of delusion*, the denial of the event" which is a form of "critical neo-idealism" (88). Deconstruction is "a thinking of singularity—and thus of the event, and what it retains that is ultimately irreducible" (88).

16. One may also surmise that it is only from the "dominant" perspective of "master" Hecate (and the witches) that reiterations bear negative connotations.

17. Playing himself in *Ghost Dance*, Derrida asserts that "the experience of ghosts is not tied to a bygone historical period...but on the contrary, is accentuated, accelerated by modern technologies like film, television, the telephone. These technologies inhabit, as it were, a phantom structure." In *Ecographies of Television*, he points out that "we are spectralized by the shot, captured or possessed by spectrality in advance" (Derrida and Stiegler, 117), and that this always-already inscribes the promise of a comeback. See also *"Le cinéma et ses fantômes"* esp. 77–80 for an understanding of cinema as the art of specters. See also "Introduction" above on the interrelation of media and survivance in Derrida's work (note 42).

18. On windows from the perspective of media theory, see Mitchell, *What Do Pictures Want?* 214–15.

19. Hecate's reiterated phantasmagoric performance, in the course of which the "main" screen is often reduced to an optional "window," recalls the rhizomatic, "paratactic, and smooth space of digital compositing," the additive, nondialectical juxtapositions typical of a "post-cinematic" mode (cf. Shaviro 78). Shaviro opposes the "digital compositing" of the post-cinematic to the "classical," dialectical notion of montage *à la* Eisenstein (71–72).

20. See also Burt and Boose, "Introduction," esp. 1–4.

21. By convergence, Henry Jenkins notoriously means "the flow of content among multiple media platforms, the cooperation among multiple media industries, and the migratory behaviour of media audiences who would go almost anywhere in search of the kind of entertainment experiences they want" (2).

22. The interchangeability between English and German in the DVD version of the film as well as the inclusion of actors who have frequently taken part in both German- and English-speaking films, further contributes to the putting under erasure of medium specificity.

23. Nicholas Royle notes the "strange effect of the after before, of what comes later coming earlier," and stresses that this is "fundamental to [*Macbeth*] as a whole" (95).

24. See also the use of this uncanny temporal structure in Lehmann, *Shakespeare Remains* 19.

25. Part of my argument here is informed by W. J. T. Mitchell's call for a reconsideration of the question of visuality: "We need to reckon with not just the meaning of images but their silence, their reticence, their wildness and nonsensical obduracy" (*What Do Pictures Want?* 10).

26. The unsafe *hubris* of vision is also central to another twenty-first-century version of "Shakespeare in the Extreme," a "direct-to-video 'gangsta' adaptation"

of *Macbeth* (Lanier, *Spin-Offs* 214), Greg Salman's *Mad Dawg. Running Wild in the Streets* (2001). The DVD cover, which does not reference *Macbeth*, summarizes the plot of the film with the words: "It's a Dawg Eat Dawg World." Thus, like Shakespeare's play, the film shows that the "state of exception" is the rule, a state in which, according to Agamben, "everyone is bare life and a *homo sacer* for everyone else" (*Homo Sacer* 106). Repeated clips of a TV religious program punctuate the criminal activities of Dunkin's "clique" until the TV preacher himself appears to Mac and Banc. He tells the former that "he has moved up but doesn't know it yet," and that he will "move up again until there is no further up that [he] can go"; he tells the latter that Mac's money "is going to help get [his] son out of the ghetto." (This turns out to be true, as a sleep-deprived Lady M will give Banc's widow all the money they have accumulated after the murder of Dunkin, leaving Mac with only a 20-dollar bill.) The film somewhat sacrilegiously associates "the power of the Lord" with the supernatural power of the witches one finds in the "original." It continually juxtaposes the "equivocation of the fiend" (5.5.41) with the equivocation of a televised religious "truth" and, more generally, with a series of themes that have to do with vision. The TV preacher of the "Church of the Oracle" promises Mac "a charmed life"; he predicts that "no bullet shall pierce his skin" and that his "kingdom" will last until "the blind are cured." Mac's sense of security begins to waver when a TV news program announces that Stevie Wonder will undergo surgery. Subsequently, Duffy (i.e., the one "marked with a double cross," a tattoo on his neck) shoots Mac through the eye, which confirms the preacher's "equivocation" that "no bullet shall pierce [his] skin." This contrived ending suggests that the "power of the Lord" *does* work in mysterious ways. For Lanier, the film turns *Macbeth* into "a moralistic parable about the temptations of gangsta glamour, money, and violence" (214), with the televangelist becoming "the ethical chorus of the film." Yet, the televangelist's position is, to say the least, ambiguous, as is the restoration of order, which is performed by a character deeply involved in criminal activities. The "double cross" that marks Duffy shows that religion is itself a simulacrum, double and divided, in much the same way as religious symbols in Baz Luhrmann's *William Shakespeare's Romeo and Juliet* or James Gavin Bedford's *The Street King*. *Mad Dawg* also includes a scene from Carol Reed's *The Third Man* (1949), a film Banc and his wife are watching just before Banc is murdered. (Banc's wife manages to escape with their son Shorty.)

27. For Lacan's classical definitions of the mirror stage and the "imaginary," see *Écrits* 1–29.
28. Speaking to the Petry girls in a previous scene, Hecate defines Marcus "a man afraid," and declares that "a simple riddle will spell his end."
29. If one were to expand this analysis to the more general framing of the scene, one could argue that Marcus is himself the "picture" he has been given to complete also because he is an enlarged spectral spot on Hecate's supplementary screen.
30. When he kills Dean, Marcus emphasizes a sense of violence as an end unto itself: "I may not know what it is like to keep a kingdom, but I know how to get one."

31. In states of terror such as Macbeth's, one inevitably terrorizes oneself through acts of terror. On the autoimmune logic of terror, see Borradori.

32. Derrida's notion of autoimmunity is an ambitious attempt to redefine the boundaries between life and death, between *physis* and *nomos*, life and *tekhnē*, or at the very least "to situate the question of life and the living being, of life and death, of life-death" (*Rogues* 123)—"life-death" being Derrida's oxymoronic formulation that encapsulates the relationship of reciprocal haunting between life and death as well as the irreducibility of "death-in-life" and "life-in-death." For an exploration of the problematics of autoimmunity from a different angle, see chapter 2.

33. In the second volume of *The Beast and the Sovereign*, Derrida provides a definition of autoimmunity that emphasizes the extent to which this process takes place "in an irrepressibly mechanical and apparently spontaneous, auto-matic, fashion" (*Beast II* 83).

34. This is not to erase differences between contemporary teletechnologies and "traditional" archival technologies such as writing (in an extended sense), which is one of the recurring themes of the intense dialogues between Derrida and Stiegler in *Echographies of Television*.

35. Commenting on Derrida's work, Wolfe is here attempting "to reframe the question of the visual," "to cut it loose from its indexical relation to the human, to reason, and to the representational mastery of space itself" (133–34). This is part of a critique of human exceptionalism that points toward a sense of the posthuman as embodied interface, in biological and technical terms (esp. xv–xvi, xxv–xxvi).

36. From a Lacanian point of view, as shown earlier, this fantasy corresponds to the "geometral" dimension of vision, vision as the representation of space through perspective. As Lacan summarizes, whenever desire as displacement is involved, "I am not simply that punctiform being located at the geometral point from which the perspective is grasped" (*Four* 96). This is not to argue that Derrida and Lacan's thinking on the subject of vision are equivalent. It is only to underline some points of convergence.

37. As Derrida clarifies, "as soon as there is technology of the image, visibility brings night. It incarnates in a night body, it radiates a night light" (Derrida and Stiegler 115).

38. Of course this is not the only essay in which Derrida emphasizes this "technological condition" that affects the purity of the source and defers it, but it is worth quoting from an essay dealing with the issue of drugs, an issue that is central to *Rave Macbeth*. One may add that even for "traditional" Freudian psychoanalysis, the bodily ego is the projection of a surface, and thus inextricably involved in a field of mediality that displaces the ego's centrality as subject of vision. In a recent essay Bernadette Wegenstein reminds us that "the ego (body ego) *is* (the projection of self as) image and, as such, is particularly responsive to the world of images, which for the at least the past century have been created and manipulated by the media" (25).

39. This prostheticity is not exclusively or necessarily human. It is through this prostheticity that one can begin to rethink clear-cut distinctions between the human and the nonhuman, organic and inorganic, life and death. See, for instance, Derrida "The Animal" (esp. 397–401), where he repeatedly discusses the question of the limit by coining a word, "limitrophy" (397). Putting under erasure the distinction between "what calls *itself* man and what *he* calls the animal" (398), he speaks of "a heterogeneous multiplicity of the living, or more precisely...a multiplicity of organizations of relations between living and dead, relations of organization or lack of organization among realms that are more and more difficult to dissociate by means of the figures of the organic and inorganic, of life and/or death," in that they "do not leave room for any simple exteriority of one term with respect to another" (399). All these "relations of organizations" are subjected to technological supplementarity, the iterability and reproducibility of the structure of tracing (in an extended sense). This is not an erasure of differences. As Derrida argues, "the discussion becomes interesting once, instead of asking whether or not there is a discontinuous limit [between the human and the nonhuman animal], one attempts to think what a limit becomes once it is abyssal, once the frontier no longer forms a single indivisible line but more than one internally divided line, once, as a result, it can no longer be traced, objectified, or counted as single and indivisible" (399). On this, see especially Wolfe, who has most cogently pursued this Derridean line of analysis. In their "Introduction" to *Critical Terms for Media Studies*, Mitchell and Hansen insist on "a general mediality that is constitutive of the human as 'biotechnical' form of life" (ix) as well as on the "operation of exteriorization and invention" (xiii) that makes humans "'essentially' prosthetic beings" (xii). These reflections are important to my understanding of prostheticity and mediality here. See also the "Introduction" above and note 34 and 35 in the Introduction.

40. The track here is the same as the one used for the DVD root menu, which contributes to the idea that the characters are also potentially replayable actants.

41. Spectral coexistence also points to survival. Interestingly, in one of his quasi-aphoristic, endlessly citable statements, media theorist Friedrich A. Kittler juxtaposes media and spectrality: "Ghosts, a.k.a. media, cannot die at all" (130). This also articulates a logic of the uncanny permanence of media across time, what from the Derridean perspective developed in this chapter may be called the spectral *survivance* of media or spectral *survivance as* media(lity). Yet Kittler completes his statement by reasserting some kind of indivisibility of the boundary between one medium and another, which is what this chapter attempts to contest: "Where one [medium] stops, another somewhere begins" (130). And, of course, *Gramophone, Film, Typewriter* most famously begins with a bleak prediction of the future of media, a depiction of a scenario of digital convergence and absolute translatability in which "ghosts" have no place whatsoever: "The general digitization of channels and information erases the differences among individual media. Sound and image, voice and text are reduced to surface effects,

known to consumers as interface... Once optical fiber networks turn formerly distinct data flows into a standardized series of digitized numbers, any medium can be translated into any other. With numbers, everything goes... a total media link on a digital base will erase the very concept of medium" (1–2). But, as he ironically adds, "there are still media; there is still entertainment" (2).

7 "He Speaks... Or Rather... He Tweets": The Specter of the "Original," Media, and "Media-Crossed" Love in *Such Tweet Sorrow*

1. The five weeks roughly correspond to the five acts of the play (11 April–13 May 2010). Interestingly, given the Royal Shakespeare Company's involvement in the project, this Twitter adaptation took place in a period in which Rupert Gould's innovative production of the play was being staged at the Courtyard in Stratford-upon-Avon, a production, according to a reviewer, that attempted to recapture the spirit of the play: "This is a play that, rightfully, belongs to youth. And there is a headlong, impetuous quality about Rupert Goold's new RSC production that chimes exactly with the spirit of the play. I can't recall as exciting a revival since Zeffirelli stunned us with his *verismo* in 1960" (Billington). As reported by the blog of the producer, Charles Hunter, the original plan was as follows: "Anyone on twitter will be able to follow all or any of the characters, who will be 'played' by their RSC actors from the stage production. The 'script' will incorporate story-lines, ideas and language from the production too" (see Hunter, "Part 2" n. pag.).

2. They include performance artist Brian Feldman's *Twitter of the Shrew*, which presented a condensed version of each scene of the *Taming of the Shrew* for 12 days in 2009 (<www.facebook.com/events/54668665562>, accessed 10 June 2010); and a Twitter version of *Romeo and Juliet* (2009), with lines being tweeted at regular intervals of 15 minutes for just over a month from 15 different Twitter accounts (<http://labs.timesonline.co.uk/blog/2009/03/06/romeo-and-juliet-twitter>). The profile pictures of these Twitter accounts show the "characters" of the play as kittens.

3. As described by the production team's Twitter account the day after the end of the performance, these "missions" were "detailed daily schedules of motivation and story" (*Such Tweet Sorrow @Such_Tweet*, 14 Apr. 2010, 7.06 a.m.). The writing team also designed a "mastergrid," a schedule of the plot with all the characters' main actions for the whole performance. The actors and the writers, under the direction of Roxana Silbert, met each week and then tweeted from different locations using laptops or mobile phones.

4. For reflections on Twitter as a medium used for dramatic purposes, see Charles Hunter's blog: "Twitter is: 1. Now—instant. 2. Short (though it can be endless) 3. Quick (also infinite) 4. Unfurling /rolling 5. Different voices 6. Then—a record. 7. Diary/blog v. Conversation 8. Personal vs Public" (Hunter, "Part 1" n. pag.)

5. All the citations from *Such Tweet Sorrow* are from the Twitter accounts of the six characters, with date and time of feeds (British time), checked against the time-line of the production's official website (<www.suchtweetsorrow. com>) and the "unofficial" archive put together by Bleys Maynard (Twitter username: @citizen-bleys), one of the followers, soon after the end of the performance. The Twitter accounts are as follows: Romeo@romeo_mo (<https://twitter.com/romeo_mo>); Juliet@julietcap16 (<https://twitter.com/julietcap16>); Mercutio@mercuteio (<https://twitter.com/mercuteio>); Laurence Friar@LaurenceFriar (<https://twitter.com/LaurenceFriar>); Jess Capulet@Jess_nurse (<https://twitter.com/Jess_nurse>); Tybalt Capulet@Tybalt_Cap (<https://twitter.com/Tybalt_Cap>). As we shall see, there is an extra character, Jago, whose Twitter account is Jago Mosca@jago_klepto (<https://twitter.com/jago_klepto>). This character is also active on Tumblr (<http://kleptojago.tumblr.com>).

6. As the chapter develops, it will become clear that the notion of convergence is of limited use to analyze this Twitter phenomenon. For objections to Jenkins's approach that are based on a distinction between convergence and mashup, see Booth. For a case study of the project's strategies, execution, and results, which also includes statistics of visits to the official webpage, number of followers of each character, and visits to Juliet's own YouTube channel, see <www.figar-odigital.co.uk/case-study/Mudlark.aspx>.

7. See, for instance, Navas 158; see also Booth, and Kuhn.

8. As Deborah Cartmell recently reminded us, new technologies are always "greeted with suspicion" ("100+ Years" 1).

9. The title *Such Tweet Sorrow* is of course a medium-oriented transformation of a line Juliet speaks toward the end of the balcony scene. In the "original" this oxymoron applies to her "parting" from Romeo ("Parting is such sweet sorrow," 2.1.229). The line emerges at the end of a dialogue in which Juliet associates Romeo with a "bird" that a "wanton" boy (222) capriciously allows to "hop a little from his hand / Like a poor prisoner in his twisted gyves, / And with a silken thread plucks it back again" (223–25). In a way, this dialogue can be said to allegorize this Twitter play's bitter sweet departure from, and return to, Shakespeare, a "Shakespeare" that, like the "wanton's bird," is itself a "poor prisoner" in the "silken threads" of vociferous tweets. Moreover, this Shakespeareccentric "parting" can be said to be a paradoxical kind of "cherish-ing" (228), one that may "kill" (228) with kindness. For some reviewers of the performance, of course, this "cherishing" is nonexistent.

10. On the day of her birthday, for instance, Juliet mentions the brand new mobile phone she has just received as a present from her father and adds: "Its gna be soo good for tweeting from" (23 Apr., 12: 26 a.m.), which was duly retweeted by the production team's Twitter account *@Such_Tweet*. Moreover, some potential followers received a free phone so that they could connect on the move and react to the story. See, for instance, Orr.

11. The name of the café is probably a reference to Tom Wolfe's *Electric Kool-Aid Acid Test*.

12. For instance, Tybalt's tweets and videos often insist on the homoerotic relation-ship between Mercutio and Romeo. Mercutio reciprocates by calling Tybalt the "Prince of Pussy...the 'courageous' captain of cocks!" (13 Apr., 7:03 a.m.), and uploading YouTube videos of Tybalt as (literally) "Prince of Cats" (cf. 2.3.18–19).

13. Tim Wright's models for this character are also Nick Carraway, the unreli-able narrator of F. Scott Fitzgerald's *The Great Gatsby*, and Billy Fisher (Tom Courtenay) in John Schlesinger's *Billy Liar* (1963).

14. Jago defines his Tumblr pages as "a personal take on what goes on in this town." He adds: "and believe me I take what I like" (<http://kleptojago.tumblr.com>, accessed 8 June 2010). "Take" has at least two meanings here: first of all, it refers to the realm of photography—in the section "Who I am & What I'm About" of his Tumblr blog, he introduces himself as a "camera, a spy camera, a cold-eyed reporter"; second, "take" jokingly refers to the fact that he is a petty thief, a kleptomaniac, and perhaps allegorically hints at the appropriation of the "original." In one of his most self-reflexive moments, he states: "Sometimes I wonder if Jago's real at all, if he's just a nasty dream, insinuating his way into our consciousness" (*TM* 9 May, 4:22 p.m.). When I cite from Jago's Tumblr pages, date and time will be preceded by "*TM*"; when I cite from his Twitter account date and time will be preceded by "*TW*."

15. An example is the following tweet addressed to Tybalt, a tweet that is perhaps prosaic but effective in terms of plot development: "@Tybalt_Cap UR MUM IS DEAD. U WILL BE TOO #TEAMMONTAGUE" (30 Apr., 2:30 a.m.). Jago hates Mercutio, and this is part of his (Iago-like) plan to "poison[...] [his] delight" (*TW* 15 Apr., 4:41 p.m.) (cf. *Oth.* 1.1.68).

16. Given this invitation, the audience also feels free to ask metadramatic questions about the significance of his role vis-à-vis the *Such Tweet Sorrow* project as a whole. The Tumblr pages are thus a different, selective point of entry into the performance. The official *Such Tweet Sorrow* website does not mention Jago as a character.

17. The invitation to "talk to strangers" is also an invitation to talk to him and thus to partially bring him out of the state of invisibility he simultaneously enjoys.

18. Of course, this is itself part of a strategy to draw the audience into the perfor-mance. For instance, in spite of his disparaging comments on Romeo, he also says: "it might interesting to see who follows him" (*TM* 16 Apr., 12:46 a.m.).

19. As to himself, he asserts: "I have a life" (*TM* 13 Apr., 4:20 p.m.).

20. He appropriates words just as he appropriates other characters' belongings in his role as a petty thief. Answering a question by one of the followers regard-ing his role in the performance, he enigmatically states: "I am what I am," and provides a YouTube link to "I am What I Am" (<www.youtube.com/watch?v=FXWhj5CNG7U>), a video by Kid Creole & The Coconuts (*TM* 9 May, 3:39 p.m.). The lyrics of this track are a repeated refrain: "I am what I am what I am cause I am what I am I can only play my jam." They suggest that identity is a playful reiteration that endlessly defers essence, a matter of "jam"

and irreverent mashup, perhaps like the Twitter performance itself. Moreover, "I am what I am" also resembles Iago's enigmatic and opaque "Demand me nothing. What you know you know" (*Oth.* 5.2.309). Jago explicitly refers to these lines by the "original" Iago after reacting to Romeo's final tweets. He states, in a typical tongue-in-cheek fashion, that he is fed up with questions from the audience: "wot u kno u kno. 'nuff said" (*TM* 13 May, 11:15 a.m.), which is a mashup of Iago's lines and words from the track "I Know It's Over" by Mancunian band The Smiths. For an attempt to theorize mashups as embodying an "additive or accumulative" logic, a logic of the "*plural*" and the "*as well as*," see Sonvilla-Weiss 8–9. The follower asking questions about Jago's role in the performance, corambis2, happens to be the author of this chapter.

21. This was then reproduced in the blog post dated 15 April 2010, which included comments to the original review of *Such Tweet Sorrow* posted on 13 April 2010.

22. This is echoed in another blog: "When you take away the poetry, the language, the suspense and the characterisation, there's really not that much left to *Romeo & Juliet*, and *Such Tweet Sorrow* ends up as a bright idea, well done—but one that doesn't really work" (*Sans Taste* n.pag.).

23. As Wyver continues, "*Romeo and Juliet* played out in, say, East Enders is not Shakespeare. Just as *West Side Story*, 1957 and 1961, is not Shakespeare—although Baz Luhrmann's great movie *Romeo + Juliet*, 1996, most definitely is. And 'Deffo! I should really hop off to bed! School in the morning! xx', one of julietcap16's immortal tweets yesterday, probably isn't."

24. Specifically replying to Helen, Alan Turner underlines that "each time a new communication mode emerges," in this case Twitter, "dire predictions have been made in response" (15 Apr., 5:55 a.m.).

25. Another interesting example of responses to *Such Tweet Sorrow* is Nicklin. Her two blog posts also contain a considerable number of comments and links to other blog posts or reviews. They also include posts by Jason Hull, one of the coinvestors in the project (19 Apr., 8:44 p.m., 11:03 p.m.).

26. Part of Wyver's criticism may have to do with the fact that his post is an early review of this Twitter production. As the show develops, the characters use Shakespeare's language more and more. Or rather, as we shall see, they re-use and re-cite it. The presence of Shakespeare's language is a *spectral* presence. Its appearance is a re-appearance.

27. On "participatory culture" see Jenkins; see also Burgess and Green. Producer Charles Hunter is aware that the audience is "a purely virtual one, but is potentially infinite in size" (Hunter, "Part 1" n. pag.). On the top right side of the official website of *Such Tweet Sorrow*, one can find "What is Twitter?," which invites would-be users to sign up to Twitter to follow the characters' feeds.

28. In the interview with *The Stage*, she makes a similar point: "I think [Shakespeare] would have been delighted to see the play moving on" (qtd. in Woolman n. pag.).

29. An anonymous theater blogger ironically observes: "Not only is Silbert wrong in her perception of what does or doesn't make a production at the Globe (need I go any further than Lucy Bailey's current production of *Macbeth* to prove her assertion at best outdated, at worst lazy?) but Twitter being 'pure'? One of the joys of the medium is everything you can throw at it—all the twitpics, the audioboos, the YouTube links, the Spotify playlists, the blog links, the RTs, the memes" ("Musings").

30. My discussion of old new media here is indebted to Burt, *Film and Media* esp. 24–29. My reference to the "countertime" of anachrony is from Derrida, "Aphorism Countertime." This will be explored further later on in this chapter.

31. At the time of writing, she is still followed by 3,879 tweeple, who have decides not to "unfollow" her after the end of the show. For useful statistics on *Such Tweet Sorrow*, see the blog post on Tumblr by thejives ("#Such Tweet" n. pag.).

32. Blog posts, sometimes by followers, often address the question of the conventions of this Twitter performance, and underline that *Such Tweet Sorrow* is treading new ground. See the blog post by a follower, thejives, which stresses how this "twitter drama," because of its novelty, "make[s] its own conventions" ("Thoughts" n. pag.); and the anonymous "Parting," which is critical of the lack of dramaturgy and proper planning on the part of the production team (n. pag.). On the question of the public/private dichotomy, see "Musings" n. pag.

33. As he shouts after the death of the two lovers: "ALL MY FAULT" (12 May, 5:40 a.m.).

34. The webpage is here: <http://lfek.wordpress.com>.

35. We have also already heard him snoring when Mercutio uploads an audio file on Audioboo.

36. This may be an attempt to rewrite the lines with which the "original" Romeo addresses the "original" Mercutio regarding a different medium: "You have dancing shoes / With *nimble* soles, I have a soul of *lead* / So stakes me to the ground I cannot move" (1.4.14–16, emphasis added).

37. For a critique of the gender stereotypes this Twitter play reproduces, see Nicklin: "The level of gender stereotyping that has been occurring in #suchtweet has been painful to behold. The boys tweet pictures of girls breasts, make fun of the 'ginger mingers' they pull by accident, and generally fight and swear. The female characters moan, cry, and go shopping to relieve their tension" (19 Apr., n. pag.). The blogger also discusses the issue of when and how, given the interactive nature of the performance, it is appropriate to deliver criticism in the hope of influencing its development. She had already tweeted her dissatisfaction with the gender stereotyping "in character," an example of which is the following, perhaps ironically retweeted by Jess Nurse: "@Jess_nurse cooking, shopping, weeping, nursing. Do you girls do anything intelligent, interesting? Get angry? Active? Just a thought" (17 Apr., 6:02 a.m.).

38. Donaldson continues by arguing that this makes these films "media fables or media allegories as well Shakespeare adaptations" (23).

39. Hansen's observations are set against the background of what he sees as a bifur-
cation in the function of media in contemporary culture. For Hansen, media
no longer solely perform their "traditional" role of exteriorizing "human experience in durable, repeatable, and hence transmissible form"; they also "mediate
for human experience the…computational processes that increasingly make
up the infrastructure conditioning all experience in our world today," some
kind of "'transcendental technicity' underlying real experience in our world
today" (180) that nonetheless "remain[s] fundamentally unfathomable by us"
(179). (For this unfathomability, cf. Derrida and Stiegler 57). Social media Web
2.0 companies "colonize" the gap between media and technics. They "operate
precisely by collapsing the dissociation between media and technics: they give
us a new functionality—massive connectivity—by transmitting familiar media
forms *in ways that avoid drawing attention to* the new 'transcendental technicity' of computational networks" (181). And yet they also obliquely reveal the
gap they simultaneously suture, "to the precise extent that connectivity emerges
as an end in itself" (181, emphasis added). Of course this article relates back to,
and expands, Hansen's fundamental analyses in the field of media theory. See
esp. *Bodies* and *New Philosophy*.

40. Manovich also uses Michel de Certeau's *The Practice of Everyday Life* to show
that the latter's well-known distinction between strategies and tactics no longer
fully obtains. To a large extent tactics are built into the strategies of institutions
and power structures: "strategies and tactics are now often closely linked in an
interactive relationship, and often their features are reversed." On the one hand,
in contemporary "born-digital industries and media, such as software, computer games, web sites, and social networks…products are explicitly designed
to be customized by users" (323). More generally, companies "have developed
strategies that mimic people's tactics of bricolage, reassembly, and remix" (324).
On the other hand, social networking sites often show that "what was ephem-
eral, transient, unmappable and invisible"—in short, what de Certeau would
associate with the realm of tactics—has become "permanent, mappable, and
viewable" (324). The tendency is "towards constant capture and broadcasting" of one's (customized) everyday life" (325). For a compelling reading of the
undermining of the distinction between producers and consumers, senders and
receivers, in what he calls the "participative technology" of the Internet age, see
Stiegler, "Memory." This undermining paves the way for a "a new economy of
memory" (83).

41. For Manovich, these scenarios do not simply foreground the emotive and/or
phatic communication functions of language as described in Roman Jakobson's
well-known and influential essay "Linguistics and Poetics." He argues that
a thorough investigation of these conversations could show that they are "a
genuinely new phenomenon" (327). For a recent study of "the latency of the
media concept" in Jakobson's model, a model that still relies on a face-to-face
exchange, see Guillory esp. 356–59.

42. In the course of the performance a number of followers pretended to be characters with Twitter names such as BenVoli0, boyparis, romeo_mon (rather than

the romeo_mo of the "original" Twitter Romeo). The production team was forced to issue a statement declaring that Benvolio, one of the most active of these avatars, was not a real character. (Interestingly, Benvolio's profile picture reproduced an image of Baz Luhrmann's Benvolio). However, some followers played the game by continuing to interact with these "fake" characters. On the blurring of boundaries between characters and followers, see Nicklin. See also Dibdin, "Review Week 2."

43. This can still be found at <http://tweetmare.tumblr.com/>.

44. After his (fictional) death Tybalt *increased* his number of followers, in spite of Jesse Nurse's request to the followers, issued from her brother's Twitter account, that they should "unfollow" him so as to respect the family's grief: "Please ignore all tweets from this account and unfollow. Thank you. Please respect the Capulet family's privacy at this time" (5 May, 7:19 a.m.). Tybalt's account will become active one more time when old Capulet manages to access it to send a message about his missing daughter Juliet (12 May, 3:17 a.m.).

45. My reference is to W. B. Worthen, who sees Baz Luhrmann's *William Shakespeare's Romeo + Juliet* as exemplary of contemporary modes of cultural production that "constitute their authority through the surrogation of Shakespeare," and underlines how the Shakespearean text emerges in the film as "a ghostly 'origin' of a contemporary process of surrogation" ("Performativity" 1104).

46. Interestingly, for Lovink, one of the forms of resistance to this obsessive "identity management" (38) within the "walled garden" (17) of social media, a kind of "management" that is an attempt to perform a flattened out and hyperbolic version of the Self, is to frankly admit: "'I am not who I am'" (44). Although Lovink does not refer to Shakespeare, this is clearly a statement that recalls the words of the Shakespearean villain. This statement is repeated, as shown earlier, by Iago's Twitter equivalent when he introduces himself (*TM* 9 Apr., 12:06 p.m.). See also note 20 above.

47. As argued in chapter 3 in relation to Alexander Abela's *Souli*, the analysis of the rhetoric of silence vis-à-vis the hypotext, a silence that is not necessarily lack, needs to become more central to the theoretical problematics of adaptation studies, and to the study of Shakespearean adaptation in particular.

48. "Sweet flower" replaces "weak flower" (cf. 2.2.23–24).

49. The title of the blog refers to the lyrics of the YouTube video Mercutio posts just before he dies, Jack Hylton's version of "Life Is Just a Bowl of Cherries" by George Gershwin.

50. In this very funny post Mercutio is said to be "a special favourite of Queen Elizabeth the First who... was so distraught, following the play's first performance, that she penned a personal letter to the Bard, demanding script changes, on pain of death." In this lost version, as reported by the article, Mercutio does not say "Ask for me tomorrow and you shall find me a grave man." (cf. 3.1.97–98). He flees the scene, and makes an aside to the audience: "Ask for me tomorrow and you will find me at Gravelly Hill." As a result of this, the report continues, "residents of Gravelly Hill, a much maligned suburb of Birmingham, are celebrating."

51. "So I was a drug dealer. So what? I'm a reformed character now. 10 years of cleaner living. 10 years of making up for mistakes gone by" (13 Apr., 6:42 p.m.). He adds: "The Friar of old dealt in grass, he smuggled it tight up his ass, mistakes he did make & risks he did take, but now he's much cleaner at last!" (6:48 p.m.).

52. Parody perhaps remains the dominant mode of the presence of Shakespeare in the world of social media, from YouTube videos with Shakespearean content to Sara Schmelling's more sedate, tongue-in-cheek Facebook Shakespeare, samples of which find their way in a book that attempts to confer cultural legitimacy on the world of social media, *Ophelia Joined the Group Maidens Who Don't Float*. See esp. Desmet on parody as defining characteristic of YouTube Shakespeare; and O'Neill on the question of the importance of the specificity of YouTube as a medium when analyzing Shakespeare's afterlife.

53. To Lanier, "the tension between reverence and resistance is characteristic of Shakespop's ambivalent use of Shakespeare" (55). The often parodic revisiting of Shakespeare's language in this Twitter play symptomatizes the production team's attempt to come to terms with what Lanier aptly and lucidly identifies as one of the most challenging and "perhaps ultimately intractable" issues haunting Shakespop in the twentieth century, and that keeps on haunting, one may add, social media Shakespeare at the beginning of the twenty-first century—the issue of "how to lay claim to Shakespeare's cultural authority, so intimately connected to his verbal style, while keeping faith with pop's commitment to contemporaneity and relevance" (80–81).

54. As noted earlier, this Shakespearean line is also a reaction to Romeo's assertion that "Twitter is for twats," as reported by Mercutio (15 Apr., 8:02 a.m.).

55. "Going 2 chat to Tybalt about responsible drug use, moderation & giving up skunk" (25 Apr., 11:32 a.m.), he announces, and yet this precedes a long smoking session. He extols the qualities of "recreational cannabis" (22 Apr., 12:46 p.m.) but he seems to be mixing cannabis and alcohol at every available opportunity, which produces deleterious effects in the morning.

56. Juliet is the character who first associates following with stalking (11 Apr., 5:13 a.m.).

57. "Twexting" has a variety of meanings in Twitterland: it can mean tweeting while walking; using Twitter (improperly) as if it was a text messaging service; or, which is closer to Romeo's meaning, as an equivalent to "sexting" (i.e., texting in the hope of having sex with strangers one follows on Twitter) (cf. <www.urbandictionary.com>).

58. Before mentioning Sonnet 129, Mercutio opts for the much more prosaic: "Blimey—yesterday I was sat with my mate who had cojones and am now he's turned into a little girl" (24 Apr., 4:44 p.m.).

59. These interpretations are ruled by "a philosophical logic which would like accidents to remain what they are, accidental," a logic that also "throws out into the unthinkable an anachrony of structure, the absolute interruption of history as deployment of *a* temporality, of a single and organized temporality" ("Aphorism Countertime" 420).

60. Just as the system of marks or codes to which Derrida refers, social media platforms avoid *and* "produce misunderstandings [and] accumulate opportunities for false steps or wrong moves" (419).

61. It is perhaps not by chance that at the end of the performance a new (old) medium appears in the streets of this provincial town: a painting by Montague that commemorates the death of the two "media-crossed" lovers, and that implicitly inscribes the latter as a reiteration of the death of a previous irresistible love between a Capulet and a Montague. Seeing this painting in the street, Jesse Capulet comments with a revision of the final words of the "original" Prince: "A gloomy peace this painting with it brings. With it, a Father I was taught to hate shows more love to me than my own...Thank you" (13 May, 5:30 a.m.) (cf. 5.3.304).

62. "@mercuteio what do i do merc everything has turned to death....TELL ME WHAT TO DO MERCUTIO!!!!!" (12 May, 11:56 p.m.).

63. Working from and against Shannon and Weaver's "classical" theory of information, and referring to Michel Serres's *The Parasite*, Bruce Clarke draws attention to noise as "unexpected information" (164). He observes, in a way that is relevant here, that "from the standpoint of art forms instantiated in informatic media (aural sounds, visual images, linguistic signs), the noise *is* the art." He adds that "media arts remediate information in the form of meaningful noise" (164).

Bibliography

Adaptation. Dir. Spike Jonze. Screenplay by Charlie Kaufman. Columbia Pictures, Intermedia Films, Magnet and Clinica Estetico Productions. 2002. Film.

Agamben, Giorgio. *Homo Sacer. Sovereign Power and Bare Life.* Trans. Daniel Heller-Roazen. Stanford: Stanford UP, 1998.

———. *The Open. Man and Animal.* Trans. Kevin Attell. Stanford: Stanford UP, 2004.

Almereyda, Michael. *William Shakespeare's Hamlet Adapted by Michael Almereyda.* London: Faber and Faber, 2000.

Anderegg, Michael. "James Dean Meets the Pirate's Daughter: Passion and Parody in *William Shakespeare's Romeo + Juliet* and *Shakespeare in Love.*" Burt and Boose 56–71.

Anderson, Benedict. *Imagined Communities. Reflections on the Origins and Spread of Nationalism.* London and New York: Verso, 1983.

Anderson, Tammy. *Rave Culture: The Alteration and Decline of a Philadelphia Music Scene.* Philadelphia: Temple UP, 2009.

Attridge, Derek, ed. *Jacques Derrida. Acts of Literature.* New York and London: Routledge, 1992.

Auslander, Philip. *Liveness: Performance in a Mediatized Culture.* London: Routledge, 2008.

Babylon. Dir. Franco Rosso. Diversity Music and National Film Finance Corporation, 1980. Film.

The Bad Sleep Well (Warui yatsu hodo yoku nemuru). Dir. Akira Kurosawa. Kurosawa Production and Toho Company. 1963. Film.

Bakhtin, Mikhail. *Rabelais and His World.* Trans. Hélène Iswolsky. Cambridge, MA: MIT P, 1968.

The Banquet. Dir. Feng Xiaogang. Applause Pictures and MediaCorp Raintree Pictures. 2006. Film.

Barker, Jennifer M. *The Tactile Eye. Touch and the Cinematic Experience.* Berkeley, Los Angeles and London: U of California P, 2009.

Barrot, Pierre et al., eds. *Nollywood: The Video Phenomenon in Nigeria.* Oxford: James Currey; Bloomington: Indiana UP; Ibadan, Nigeria: HEBN, 2008.

Benjamin, Walter. "The Task of the Translator. An Introduction to the Translation of Baudelaire's *Tableaux Parisiens*." Trans. Harcourt Brace, *Illuminations*. New York: Random House, 1968. 69–82.

Bennington, Geoff. "Foundations." *Textual Practice* 21 (2007): 231–49.

Best, Michael and Eric Rasmussen, eds. *Internet Shakespeare Editions*. University of Victoria, n.d. Web. 14 Jan. 2013. Available at: <http://internetshakespeare.uvic.ca/>.

Bhabha, Homi K. *The Location of Culture*. London and New York: Routledge, 1994.

Billington, Michael. Rev. of *Romeo and Juliet* by Rupert Goold. Royal Shakespeare Company, Courtyard Theatre, Stratford-upon-Avon. *The Guardian,* March 19, 2010. Web. 15 Aug. 2010. Available at: <www.guardian.co.uk/stage/2010/mar/19/theatre>.

Billy Liar. Dir. John Schlesinger. Vic Films and Waterfall Productions. 1963. Film.

Blackwelder, Rob. "Desert Dogme." Rev. of *The King Is Alive*. Dir. Kristian Levring. *Spliced Wire*, n.d. Web. 14 Aug. 2011. Available at: <www.splicedwire.com/01features/klevring.html>.

Bollywood Queen. Dir. Jeremy Wooding. Arclight Films, Dream Fish Production, and Redbus Films. 2002. Film.

Bolter, Jay David and Richard Grusin. *Remediation: Understanding New Media*. Cambridge, MA and London: MIT P, 1999.

Bonetti, Mahen and Prerana Reddy, eds. *Through African Eyes: Dialogues with the Directors*. New York: African Film Festival, 2003.

Booth, Paul J. "Mashup as Temporal Amalgam: Time, Taste, and Textuality." Ed. Francesca Coppa and Julie Levin Russo, Spec. issue of *Transformative Works and Cultures* 9 (2012): n. pag. Available at: <http://journal.transformativeworks.org/index.php/twc/article/view/297>.

Borough of Kings. Dir. Elyse Lewin. Paragon Film Group, Avenue R Films / Chris Brinker Patrick Newall Production. 2000. Film.

Borradori, Giovanna. *Philosophy in a Time of Terror. Dialogues with Jürgen Habermas and Jacques Derrida*. Chicago and London: U of Chicago P, 2004.

Bottinelli, Jennifer J. "Watching *Lear*: Resituating the Gaze at the Intersection of Film and Drama in Kristian Levring's *The King Is Alive*." *Literature/Film Quarterly* 33.2 (2005): 101–9. *Literature Online*. Web. 15 Aug. 2011. Available at: http://lion.chadwyck.com/.

Brown, Eric C. "Shakespeare, Class, and *Scotland, PA*." *Literature/Film Quarterly* 34.2 (2006): 147–53.

Burgess, Jean and Joshua Green. *You Tube. Online Video and Participatory Culture*. Cambridge: Polity, 2009.

Burnett, Mark Thornton. "Applying the Paradigm: Shakespeare and World Cinema." Semenza, 114–24.

———. *Filming Shakespeare in the Global Marketplace*. Houndsmill: Palgrave, 2007.

———. "Madagascan Will: Cinematic Shakespeares / Transnational Exchanges." Holland, *Sound* 239–55.

Burnett, Mark Thornton and Ramona Wray, eds. "Introduction." Burnett and Wray 1–12.

———. *Screening Shakespeare in the Twenty-First Century.* Edinburgh: Edinburgh UP, 2006.

Burt, Richard. "Shakespeare, 'Glo-cali-zation', Race, and the Small Screens of Post-Popular Culture." Burt and Boose 14–36.

———. "Introduction: Shakespeare, More or Less? From Shakespeareccentricity to Shakespearecentricity and Back." Burt, *Shakespeares* 1–9.

———. *Medieval and Early Modern Film and Media.* New York: Palgrave Macmillan, 2008.

———. "*Hamlet*'s Hauntographology: Film Philology, Facsimiles and Textual Faux-rensics." Ed. Deborah Cartmell, *A Companion to Literature, Film, and Adaptation.* Oxford: Wiley-Blackwell, 2012. 216–40.

Burt, Richard, ed. *Shakespeares after Shakespeare. An Encyclopedia of the Bard in Mass Media and Popular Culture.* Vol. 1. Westport and London: Greenwood P, 2007.

Burt, Richard and Lynda Boose, eds. "Introduction: Editors' Cut." Burt and Boose 1–13.

———. *Shakespeare, the Movie II: Popularizing the Plays on Film, TV Video and DVD.* London and New York: Routledge, 2003.

Calbi, Maurizio. "Adapting…to Lidia: The *vol* of the Ghost." Ed. Anna Maria Cimitile, Serena Guarracino, and Marina Vitale, *Sfida e passione. Dagli studi culturali agli studi delle donne.* Naples: Università degli Studi di Napoli "L'Orientale," 2007. n. pag. DVD-ROM.

———. *Approximate Bodies: Gender and Power in Early Modern Drama and Anatomy.* London and New York: Routledge, 2005.

———. "Being a Guest But Not Quite…White: *Othello* and Hybrid Hospitality in the Mediterranean." *Anglistica* 6.2–7.1 (2002–3): 27–42.

———. "'The Ghosts of Strangers': Hospitality, Identity and Temporality in Caryl Phillips's *The Nature of Blood.*" *Journal for Early Modern Cultural Studies* 6.2 (2006): 38–54.

———. "*Othello*'s Ghostly Remainders: Trauma and (Post)Colonial 'Dis-ease' in Tayeb Salih's *Season of Migration to the North.*" Ed. R. S. White, Christa Jansohn, and Richard Fotheringham, *Shakespeare's World/World Shakespeares.* Newark: U of Delaware P, 2008. 342–57.

———. "Postcolonial Entanglements: Performing Shakespeare and Kathakali in Ashish Avikunthak's *Dancing Othello.*" Cimitile and Rowe 27–32.

———. "States of Exception: Autoimmunity and the Body Politic in Shakespeare's *Coriolanus.*" Ed. Maria Del Sapio, Maddalena Pennacchia, and Nancy Isenberg, *Questioning Bodies in Shakespeare's Rome.* Gottingen: Vandenhoeck & Ruprecht, 2010. 77–94.

———. "Writing with Ghosts: Shakespearean Spectrality in Derek Walcott's *A Branch of the Blue Nile.*" Ed. Mélanie Joseph-Vilain and Judith Misrahi-Barak, *Postcolonial Ghosts / Fantômes Post-Coloniaux.* Montpellier: Presses universitaires de la Méditerranée, 2009. 195–212.

Carlin, Murray. *Not Now, Sweet Desdemona. A Duologue for Black and White within the Realm of Shakespeare's Othello.* Nairobi, Lusaka, and Addis Ababa: Oxford UP, 1969.

Carotenuto, Silvana. "Editorial: Im-possible Derrida. Works of Invention." *Im-Possible Derrida.* Ed. Silvana Carotenuto. Spec. issue of *Dark Matter. In the Ruins of Imperial Culture* 8 (18 May 2012): n. pag. Web. 3 Aug. 2012. Available at: <www.darkmatter101.org/site/category/journal/issues/8-impossible-derrida>.

Carson, Christie, ed. *Designing Shakespeare: An Audio-Visual Archive 1960–2000.* Royal Holloway and Shakespeare Birthplace Trust, n.d. Web. 10 Feb. 2010. Available at: <www.arts-humanities.net/ node/2119>.

Cartelli, Thomas. "Doing it Slant: Reconceiving Shakespeare in the Shakespeare Aftermath." Semenza 25–36.

———. *Repositioning Shakespeare. National Formations, Postcolonial Appropriations.* London: Routledge, 1999.

———. Rev. of *Shakespeare and the Problem of Adaptation*, by Margaret Jane Kidnie. Semenza 218–24.

———. "Shakespeare in Pain: Edward Bond's *Lear* and the Ghosts of History." Holland, *King Lear* 159–69.

Cartelli, Thomas, and Katherine Rowe. *New Wave Shakespeare on Screen.* Cambridge: Polity, 2007.

Cartmell, Deborah. "100+ Years of Adaptations, Or, Adaptation as the Art Form of Democracy." Ed. Deborah Cartmell, *A Companion to Literature, Film and Adaptation.* Oxford: Blackwell, 2012. 1–14.

Cartmell, Deborah and Imelda Whelehan. "Introduction—Literature on Screen: A Synoptic View." Ed. Deborah Cartmell and Imelda Whelehan, *The Cambridge Companion to Literature on Screen.* Cambridge: Cambridge UP, 2007. 1–12.

Cavecchi, Mariacristina. "Shakespeare in the Vucciria: 'Fair Verona' in Roberta Torre's *Sud Side Stori.*" Ed. Carla Dente and Sara Soncini, *Across Time and Space: Shakespeare Translations in Present-Day Europe.* Pisa: Plus/Pisa UP, 2008. 89–106.

The Celebration (Festen). Dir. Thomas Vinterberg. Nimbus Film, Danmarks Radio, Nordisk Film and TV-Fond. 1998. Film.

Chakrabarty, Dipesh. *Provincializing Europe. Postcolonial Thought and Historical Difference.* Princeton and Oxford: Princeton UP, 2000.

Chambers, Iain. *Culture after Humanism. History, Culture, Subjectivity.* London and New York: Routledge, 2001.

———. *Mediterranean Crossings. The Politics of an Interrupted Modernity.* Durham and London: Duke UP, 2008.

Chan, Adrian. "Social Media: Paradigm Shift?" *Gravity7*, n.d. Web. 3 Aug. 2011. Available at: <www.gravity7.com/paradigm_shift_1.html>.

Charnes, Linda. *Hamlet's Heirs: Shakespeare and the Politics of a New Millennium.* London and New York: Routledge, 2006.

China Girl. Dir. Abel Ferrara. Great American Films, Streetlight Films, and Vestron. 1987. Film.

Chow, Rey. *Primitive Passions. Visuality, Sexuality, Ethnography, and Contemporary Chinese Cinema.* New York: Columbia UP, 1995.

Cimitile, Anna Maria and Katherine Rowe, eds. "Introduction. Shakespeare: Overlapping Mediascapes in the Mind." Cimitile and Rowe i–iii.

———. *Shakespeare in the Media: Old and New.* Spec. issue of *Anglistica* 15.2 (2011): 1–104. Web. 15 Aug. 2012. Available at: <www.anglistica.unior.it/content/shakespeare-media-old-and-new>.

A Cinematic Translation of Shakespearean Tragedies. Dir. Liz Tabish. 2008. YouTube Film. 10 Sept. 2012.

Clarke, Bruce. "Information." Mitchell and Hansen 157–71.

Come tu mi vuoi (The Way You Like Me). Dir. Volfango De Biasi. Medusa Film. 2007. Film.

Coriolanus. Dir. Ralph Fiennes. Hermet of Pictures, Magna Films, Icon Entertainment International. 2011. Film.

Cosa sono le nuvole? (What Are Clouds Like?) Dir. Pier Paolo Pasolini. Dino De Laurentiis Cinematografica. 1968. Film.

Costantini-Cornède, Anne-Marie. "Horizons nouveaux, *Souli* (Alexander Abela) et *Stage Beauty* (Richard Eyre): deux versions d'*Othello* en marge, à l'horizon du texte." *La Clé des Langues.* Lyon: ENS LYON/DGESCO, 5 Dec. 2011. Web. 2 Jan. 2012.

Croteau, Melissa, and Carolyn Jess-Cooke, eds. *Apocalyptic Shakespeare: Essays on Visions of Chaos and Revelation in Recent Film Adaptations.* Jefferson, NC and London: McFarland, 2009.

Dancing Othello (Brihnnlala Ki Khelkali). Dir. Ashish Avikunthak. Perf. Arjun Raina. 2002. Film.

Deitchman, Elizabeth A. "White Trash Shakespeare: Taste, Morality, and the Dark Side of the American Dream in Billy Morrissette's *Scotland, PA.*" *Literature/Film Quarterly* 34.2 (2006): 140–46.

Deleuze, Gilles and Felix Guattari. *A Thousand Plateaus: Capitalism and Schizophrenia.* Trans. Brian Massumi. Minneapolis: U of Minnesota P, 1987.

De Quincey, Thomas. "On the Knocking at the Gate in *Macbeth.*" Ed. Frederick Burwick, *The Works of Thomas De Quincey.* Vol. 3. London: Pickering and Chatto, 2000. 150–54. 7 vols.

Derrida, Jacques. "The Animal That Therefore I Am (More to Follow)." Trans. David Wills. *Critical Inquiry* 28.2 (2002): 369–418.

———. "Aphorism Countertime." Trans. Nicholas Royle. Attridge 414–34.

———. *Aporias.* Trans. T. Dutoit. Stanford: Stanford UP, 1993.

———. *Archive Fever.* Trans. Eric Prenowitz. Chicago and London: U of Chicago P, 1995.

———. *The Beast and the Sovereign. Volume I.* Trans. Geoffrey Bennington. Chicago and London: The U of Chicago P, 2009.

———. *The Beast and the Sovereign. Volume II.* Trans. Geoffrey Bennington. Chicago and London: The U of Chicago P, 2011.

———. "Des Tours de Babel." Ed. and Trans. Joseph F. Graham, *Difference in Translation*. Ithaca and London: Cornell UP, 1985. 165–207.

———. *Dissemination*. Trans. Barbara Johnson. Chicago: Chicago UP, 1981.

———. "'Eating Well,' Or the Calculation of the Subject: An Interview with Jacques Derrida." Ed. Eduardo Cavava, Peter Connor, and Jean-Luc Nancy and trans. Peter Connor and Avital Ronell, *Who Comes after the Subject?* London and New York: Routledge, 1991. 96–119.

———. "Faith and Knowledge: The Two Sources of 'Religion' at the Limits of Reason Alone." Ed. Jacques Derrida and Gianni Vattimo and trans. Samuel Weber, *Religion*. Cambridge: Polity, 1998. 1–78.

———. "Hostipitality." Trans. Barry Stocker with Forbes Morlock, *Angelaki* 5.3 (2000): 3–18.

———. "Le cinéma et ses fantômes." Interview with Antoine de Baecque and Thierry Jousse. *Cahiers du cinéma* 556 (2001): 75–85.

———. *Learning to Live Finally: The Last Interview*. Interview with Jean Birnaum. Basingstoke: Palgrave Macmillan, 2007.

———. *Margins of Philosophy*. Trans. Alan Bass. Brighton: Harvester P, 1982.

———. *Memoirs of the Blind: The Self-Portrait and Other Ruins*. Trans. Pascale-Anne Brault and Michael Naas. Chicago: Chicago UP, 1993.

———. *Monolingualism of the Other; Or, the Prosthesis of Origin*. Trans. Patrick Mensah. Stanford, CA: Stanford UP, 1998.

———. *Negotiations. Interventions and Interviews, 1971–2001*. Trans. Elizabeth Rottenberg. Stanford, CA: Stanford UP, 2002.

———. *On Touching—Jean-Luc Nancy*. Trans. Christine Irizarry. Stanford, CA: Stanford UP, 2005.

———. *Parages*. Paris: Galilée, 1986.

———. *Politics of Friendship*. Trans. George Collins. London: Verso, 1997.

———. "The Principle of Reason: The University in the Eyes of Its Pupils." Trans. Jan Plug et al., *Eyes of the University: Rights to Philosophy 2*. Stanford, CA: Stanford UP, 2004. 129–55.

———. "The Rhetoric of Drugs." Trans. Michael Israel. *Differences: A Journal of Feminist Cultural Studies* 5.1 (1993): 1–24. Rpt. in *Points...Interviews, 1974–1994*. Stanford, CA: Stanford UP, 1995. 228–54.

———. *Rogues. Two Essays on Reason*. Trans. Pascale-Anne Brault and Michael Naas. Stanford, CA: Stanford UP, 2005.

———. "And Say the Animal Responded?" Ed. Cary Wolfe and trans. David Wills, *Zoontologies: The Question of the Animal*. Minneapolis and London: U of Minnesota P, 2003. 121–46.

———. *Séminaire. La bête et le souverain. Volume II (2002–2003)*. Paris: Galilée, 2010.

———. *Specters of Marx. The State of the Debt, the Work of Mourning and the New International*. Trans. Peggy Kamuf. London and New York: Routledge, 1994.

———. "'This Strange Institution Called Literature': An Interview with Jacques Derrida." Trans. Geoffrey Bennington and Rachel Bowlby. Attridge 33–75.

Derrida, Jacques and Anne Dufourmantelle. *Of Hospitality*. Trans. Rachel Bowlby. Stanford, CA: Stanford UP, 2000.

Derrida, Jacques and Safaa Fathy. *Tourner les mots: au bord d'un film*. Paris: Galilée, 2000.

Derrida, Jacques and Bernard Stiegler. *Echographies of Television. Filmed Interviews*. Trans. Jennifer Bajorek. Oxford: Polity and Blackwell, 2002.

Desmet, Christy. "Paying Attention in Shakespeare Parody: From Tom Stoppard to YouTube." Holland, *Sound* 227–38.

Dibdin, Thom. "Review—*Such Tweet Sorrow. Annals of Edinburgh Stage*," Apr. 16, 2010, n.pag. Web. 20 May 2010. Available at: <http://thomdibdin.co.uk/review-such-tweet-sorrow>.

———. "Review—*Such Tweet Sorrow Week 2. Annals of Edinburgh Stage*," 25 Apr. 2010, n.pag. Web. 20 May 2010. Available at: <http://thomdibdin.co.uk/review-such-tweet-sorrow-week-2>.

Donaldson, Peter S. "Bottom and the Gramophone." Holland, *Sound* 23–35.

———. "'In Fair Verona': Media, Spectacle, and Performance in *William Shakespeare's Romeo + Juliet*." Ed. Richard Burt, *Shakespeare after Mass Media*. New York: Palgrave, 2002. 59–82.

———. "The Shakespeare Electronic Archive: Collections and Multimedia Tools for Teaching and Research, 1992–2008." Galey and Siemens 250–60.

Donaldson, Peter S., Alexander C. Y., Huang et al., eds. *Shakespeare Performance in Asia*. MIT, n.d. Web. 12 Jan. 2013. Available at: <http://web.mit.edu/shakespeare/asia/>.

Faleti, Adebayo. *The Whore (With Thunderbolt Aids)*. Monatan—Ibadan: Laolu Press, 1998.

Fernie, Ewan. "Introduction: Shakespeare, Spirituality and Contemporary Criticism." Ed. Ewan Fernie, *Spiritual Shakespeares*. London and New York: Routledge, 2005. 1–27.

Freud, Sigmund. *Totem and Taboo* [1913]. Ed. Albert Dickson and trans. James Strachey, *The Origins of Religion: Totem and Taboo, Moses and Monotheism and Other Works*. Penguin: Harmondsworth, 1990. 43–224. Vol. 13 of *The Penguin Freud Library*. 15 vols.

———. *The Unconscious* [1915]. Ed. Angela Richards and trans. James Strachey, *On Metapsychology. The Theory of Psychoanalysis: Beyond the Pleasure Principle, The Ego and the Id and Other Works*. Penguin: Harmondsworth, 1984. 159–222. Vol. 11 of *The Penguin Freud Library*. 15 vols.

Galey, Alan. "Networks of Deep Impression: Shakespeare and the History of Information." Rowe, ed. 289–312.

Galey, Alan and Ray Siemens, eds. *Reinventing Digital Shakespeare*. Spec. issue of *Shakespeare* 4.3 (2008): 201–350.

Garber, Marjorie. *Shakespeare After All*. New York: Anchor Books, 2004.

———. *Shakespeare's Ghost Writers. Literature as Uncanny Causality*. London: Methuen, 1987.

Gaut, Berys. "Naked Film: Dogma and Its Limits." Hjort and Mackenzie 90–101.

Ghost Dance. Dir. Ken McMullen. Looseyard LTD, Channel Four TV, ZDF. 1983. Film.

Gilroy, Paul. *After Empire. Melancholia or Convivial Culture?* London and New York: Routledge, 2004.

Girgus, Sam B. *Levinas and the Cinema of Redemption: Time, Ethics, and the Feminine.* New York: Columbia UP, 2010.

Grigely, Joseph. *Textualterity: Art, Theory, and Textual Criticism.* Ann Arbor: U of Michigan P, 1995.

Griggs, Yvonne. *Screen Adaptations. Shakespeare's King Lear. The Relationship between Text and Film.* London: Methuen Drama, 2009.

Grusin, Richard. "DVDs, Video Games, and the Cinema of Interactions." Ed. James Lyons and John Plunkett, *Multimedia Histories: From the Magic Lantern to the Internet.* Exeter: Exeter UP, 2007. 209–21.

Guillory, John. "Genesis of the Media Concept." *Critical Inquiry* 36.2 (2010): 321–62.

Hall, Jason. "All the World's a Stage." *Screen WM,* 13 Apr. 2010. Web. 5 May 2010.

Hamlet. Dir. Kenneth Branagh. Castle Rock, Columbia. 1996. Film.

Hamlet. Dir. Michael Almereyda. Miramax and Double A Films. 2000. Film.

Hamlet. Dir. Alexander Fodor. Zed Resistor and Soho Films, 2006. Film.

Hamlet Goes Business (Hamlet liikemaailmassa). Villealfa Filmproduction. 1987. Film.

Hamlet X. Dir. Herbert Fritsch. Web. 12 Feb. 2010. Available at: <www.hamlet-x. de/>.

Hansen, Mark B. N. *Bodies in Code: Interfaces with Digital Media.* New York: Routledge, 2006.

———. "New Media." Mitchell and Hansen 172–85.

———. *New Philosophy for New Media.* Cambridge, MA and London: MIT P, 2004.

Haraway, Donna. *Simians, Cyborgs and Women: The Reinvention of Nature.* London and New York: Routledge, 1991.

Harrison, Keith. "Kurosawa, Kozintsev, and Almereyda: *Hamlet* and Transnational Dialogism." *Shakespeare Association of America Annual Meeting.* Chicago: Unpublished paper, Apr. 2010. 19.

Hayles, Katherine N. *How We Became Posthuman. Virtual Bodies in Cybernetics, Literature, and Informatics.* Chicago and London: U of Chicago P, 1999.

Henderson, Diane H., ed. *Alternative Shakespeares 3.* London and New York: Routledge, 2008.

Hjort, Mette. "Dogma 95: A Small Nation's Response to Globalisation." Hjort and Mackenzie 31–47.

Hjort, Mette and Scott Mackenzie, eds. *Purity and Provocation: Dogma 95.* London: BFI, 2003.

Holland, Peter, ed. *King Lear and Its Afterlife.* Spec. issue of *Shakespeare Survey* 55. Cambridge: Cambridge UP, 2002.

———. *Shakespeare, Sound and Screen*. Spec. issue of *Shakespeare Survey* 61. Cambridge: Cambridge UP, 2008.

Holman, Curt. "Melancholy Dane. *The King Is Alive* stages *Lear* in the Desert." Rev. of *The King Is Alive*, Dir. Kristian Levring. *Creative Loafing*. 15 Aug. 2001, n. pag. Web. 10 Aug. 2011. Available at: <http://clatl.com/atlanta/melancholy-dane /Content?oid=1232634>.

Horkheimer, Max and Theodore W. Adorno. *Dialectic of Enlightenment. Philosophical Fragments*. Trans. Edmund Jephcott. Stanford, CA: Stanford UP, 2002.

Huang, Alexander C. Y. *Chinese Shakespeares: Two Centuries of Cultural Exchange*. New York: Columbia UP, 2009.

Hunter, Charles. "Such Tweet Sorrow Epilogue and Chronicle Pt 1." Mudlark, May 26, 2010. Blog Entry. Web. 10 June 2010. Available at: <http://wearemudlark .com/blog/suchtweet-chronicle-part-one>.

———. "SuchTweet Chronicle Part Two." Mudlark, June 8, 2010. Blog Entry. Web. 10 June 2010. Available at: <http://wearemudlark.com/blog/suchtweet-chronicle -part-two>.

Hutcheon, Linda. *A Theory of Adaptation*. London and New York: Routledge, 2006.

HyperMacbeth. Dir. dlsan. Web. 12 Feb. 2010. Available at: <www.dlsan.org/mac-beth/the_mac.htm/>.

Iago. Dir. Volfango De Biasi. Medusa Film. 2009. Film.

The Idiots (Idioterne). Dir. Lars von Trier. Zentropa Entertainments, Danmarks Radio, Liberator Productions. 1998. Film.

Imogen's Face. Dir. David Wheatley. TYRO Production, Independent Television Channel (ITV), New Films International. 1998. 3 episodes. Television.

In Othello. Dir. Roysten Abel. ANB Pictures and Can and Abel Theatres. 2003. Film.

The Intended. Dir. Kristian Levring. Parallax Projekt (Innocence), Produktionsselskabet, Southeast Asia Film Location Services. 2002. Film.

"It's the Berries@mercutio." #mercutiosgroupies. Web. 3 June 2010. Available at: <http://mercuteiosgroupies.blogspot.it>.

Jameson, Fredric. *Postmodernism, or, the Cultural Logic of Late Capitalism*. Durham: Duke UP, 1991.

Jenkins, Henry. *Convergence Culture: Where Old and New Media Collide*. New York: New York UP, 2006.

Jess, Carolyn. "New-Ness, Sequelization, and Dogme Logic in Kristian Levring's *The King Is Alive*." *New Cinemas: Journal of Contemporary Film* 3.1 (2005): 3–15.

Jess-Cooke, Carolyn. "The 'Promised End' of Cinema: Portraits of Apocalypse in Post-Millennium Shakespearean Film." Croteau and Jess-Cooke 216–28.

———. "Screening the McShakespeare in Post-Millennial Shakespeare Cinema." Burnett and Wray 163–84.

Joe Macbeth. Dir. Ken Hughes. Columbia Pictures. 1955. Film.

Joughin, John J. "*Lear*'s Afterlife." Holland, *King Lear* 67–81.

———. "Philosophical Shakespeares: An Introduction." Ed. John J. Joughin, *Philosophical Shakespeares*. London and New York: Routledge, 2000. 1–17.

————. "Shakespeare's Genius: *Hamlet,* Adaptation and the Work of Following." Ed. John J. Joughin and Simon Malpas, *The New Aestheticism.* Manchester: Manchester UP, 2003. 131–50.

Kelani, Tunde. "In Spite of Modernity." Interview with Dorothy Désir. Bonetti and Reddy 105–16.

Keller, James R. *Food, Film and Culture. A Genre Study.* Jefferson and London: McFarland, 2006.

Kelly, Richard. *The Name of This Book Is Dogme95.* London: Faber, 2000.

Kennedy, Al. "Tweet Dreams…Our Top 50 Twitter Feeds for the Arts." *The Observer,* 18 Apr. 2010. Web. 10 June 2010. Available at:<www.guardian.co.uk/ technology/2010/apr/18/twitter-and-the-arts>.

Kidnie, Margaret J. *Shakespeare and the Problem of Adaptation.* London and New York: Routledge 2009.

The King Is Alive. Dir. Kristian Levring. Newmarket and Good Machine International, Zentropa Entertainments. 2000.

King Lear. Dir. Peter Brook. The Royal Shakespeare Company and Filmways. 1971. Film.

King Lear. Dir. Jean-Luc Godard. Bahamas and Cannon Films. 1987. Film.

Kittler, Friedrich A. *Gramophone, Film, Typewriter.* Trans. Geoffrey Winthrop-Young and Michael Wutz. Stanford, CA: Stanford UP, 1999.

Kottman, Paul. "Hospitality in the Interval: *Macbeth*'s Door." *Oxford Literary Review* 18.1 (1996): 87–115.

Kuhn, Virginia. "The Rhetoric of Remix." Ed. Francesca Coppa and Julie Levin Russo, *Fan/Remix Video.* Spec. issue of *Transformative Works and Cultures* 9 (2012): n. pag. Available at: <http://journal.transformativeworks.org/index.php/ twc/article/view/358/279>.

Lacan, Jacques. *Écrits: A Selection.* Trans. Alan Sheridan. London: Tavistock, 1977.

————. *The Four Fundamental Concepts of Psycho-Analysis.* Trans. Alan Sheridan. London: The Hogarth P, 1977.

————. *The Seminar of Jacques Lacan. Book VII: The Ethics of Psychoanalysis 1959–1960.* Trans. Dennis Porter. New York and London: Norton, 1992.

Lanier, Douglas. "Film Spin-Offs and Citation: Entries Play by Play." Burt, *Shakespeares* 138–365.

————. "Introduction. On the Virtues of Illegitimacy: Free Shakespeare on Film." Burt, *Shakespeares* 132–37.

————. "Recent Shakespeare Adaptation and the Mutations of Cultural Capital." Semenza 104–13.

————. *Shakespeare and Modern Popular Culture.* Oxford: Oxford UP, 2002.

Latour, Bruno. *Aramis or, the Love of Technology.* Trans. Catherine Porter. Cambridge, MA: Harvard UP, 1996.

————. *We Have Never Been Modern.* Trans. Catherine Porter. Cambridge, MA: Harvard UP, 1993.

Lehmann, Courtney. "Introduction, 'What Is a Film Adaptation? Or 'Shakespeare Du Jour.'" Burt, *Shakespeares* 74–80.

————. "Out Damned Scot: Dislocating *Macbeth* in Transnational Film and Media Culture." Burt and Boose 231–51.

————. "The Postnostalgic Renaissance: The 'Place' of Liverpool in Don Boyd's *My Kingdom*." Burnett and Wray 72–89.

————. *Shakespeare Remains. Theater to Film, Early Modern to Postmodern*. Ithaca, NY: Cornell UP, 2002.

Leitch, Thomas. "Adaptation and Intertextuality, or, What Isn't an Adaptation, and What Does it Matter?" Ed. Deborah Cartmell, *A Companion to Literature, Film, and Adaptation*. Oxford: Wiley-Blackwell, 2012. 87–104.

Lessard, Bruno. "Hypermedia *Macbeth*: Cognition and Performance." Ed. Nick Moschovakis, *Macbeth: New Critical Essays*. New York and London: Routledge 2008. 318–34.

Levinas, Emmanuel. *God, Death, and Time*. Trans. Bettina Bergo. Stanford, CA: Stanford UP, 2000.

————. *Totality and Infinity*. Trans. Alphonso Lingis. Pittsburg: Duquesne UP, 1969.

Levring, Kristian. "Desert Dogme." Interview by Rob Blackwelder. *Splicedwire. Film Reviews, News, & Interviews*. Web. 12 Aug. 2011. Available at: <http://splicedwire.com/01reviews/kingisalive.html>.

Livingston, Paisley. "Artistic Self-Reflexivity in *The King Is Alive* and *Strass*." Hjort and Mackenzie 102–13.

Lomonico, Michael. "Haunting Hamlet Shot For Halloween." *News on the Rialto*. 30 Oct. 2006. n. pag. Blog. Web. 2 Apr. 2008. Available at: <http://shakespea-remag.blogspot.it/2006/10/haunting-hamlet-shot-for-halloween.html>.

Loomba, Ania. *Gender, Race, Renaissance Drama*. Manchester and New York: Manchester UP, 1989.

————. *Shakespeare, Race, and Colonialism*. Oxford: Oxford UP, 2002.

Lovink, Geert. *Networks without a Cause. A Critique of Social Media*. Cambridge: Polity, 2011.

Macbeth. Dir. Orson Welles. Mercury Productions for Republic Pictures. 1948. Film.

Macbeth. Dir. Roman Polanski. Playboy Productions, Caliban Films. 1971. Film.

Macbeth. Dir. Michael Bogdanov. Channel Four UK and The English Shakespeare Company. 1998. Film.

Macbeth. Dir. Mark Brozel. Screenplay by Peter Moffat. BBC ONE, UK and Acorn Media UK. 2006. Screened on BBC ONE. 14 Nov. 2005. Television.

Macbeth. Dir. Geoffrey Wright. Revolver Entertainment, Film Finance Corporation Australia, Film Victoria, Arclight Films, Mushroom Pictures Production. 2006. Film.

Macbeth on the Estate. Dir. Penny Woolcock. BBC TWO, UK. 1997. Film.

McKernan, Luke, ed. *Bardbox: Shakespeare and Online Video*, n.d. Web. 1 Sept. 2012. Available at: <http://bardbox.wordpress.com/>.

Makibefo. Dir. Alexander Abela. Blue Eye Films, 1999. Scoville Film, 2008. DVD.

Mad Dawg: Running Wild in the Streets. Dir. Greg Salman. Leo Films and Fusion Films. 2001. Film.

Mackenzie, Scott. "Manifest Destinies: Dogma 95 and the Future of the Film Manifesto." Hjort and Mackenzie 47–58.

Mallarmé, Stéphane. "*La fausse entrée des sorcières dans Macbeth.*" *Oeuvres complètes.* Ed. Henri Mondor and G. Jean-Aubry. Paris: Gallimard, 1945. 346–51.

Manovich, Lev. *The Language of New Media.* Cambridge, MA and London: MIT P, 2001.

———. "The Practice of Everyday (Media) Life: From Mass Consumption to Mass Cultural Production?" *Critical Inquiry* 35.2 (2009): 319–31.

Maqbool. Dir. Vishal Bhardwaj. Kaleidoscope Entertainment. 2003. Film.

Marks, Laura U. *The Skin of the Film. Intercultural Cinema, Embodiment, and the Senses.* Durham and London: Duke UP, 2000.

Marlowe, Christopher. *Dr Faustus.* Ed. Roma Gill. London: Black; New York: Norton, 1989.

Masolini, Alessandra. "Rometta's Roaming and Giulietto's Swing: (Ho)Staging Shakespeare on Screen." *Anglistica* 6.2–7.1 (2002–3): 223–38.

Massai, Sonia. "Subjection and Redemption in Pasolini's *Othello.*" Ed. Sonia Massai, *World-Wide Shakespeares. Local Appropriations in Film and Performance.* London and New York: Routledge, 2005. 95–103.

Maus, Katharine E. "Horns of Dilemma: Jealousy, Gender, and Spectatorship in English Renaissance Drama." *English Literary History* 54 (1987): 561–83.

Maynard, Bleys, comp. "*Such Tweet Sorrow* Archive". Version 0.4.2. 2010. Web. 1 Sept. 2010. Available at: <www.bleysmaynard.net/suchtweet/>.

Men of Respect. Dir. William Reilly. Central City Film, Arthur Goldblatt Productions, and Grandview Avenue Pictures. 1990. Film.

Meza, Ed. "US Spin for Teuton 'Rave'." *Daily Variety.* 5 Nov. 2001, n. pag.

Mickey B. Dir. Tom Magill. Educational Shakespeare Company Production. 2007. Film.

Mifune's Last Song (Mifunes sidste sang). Dir. Søren Kragh-Jacobsen. Nimbus Film. 1999. Film.

Mitchell, W. J. T. "Picturing Terror: Derrida's Autoimmunity." *Critical Inquiry* 33 (2007): 277–90.

———. *What Do Pictures Want? The Lives and Loves of Images.* Chicago and London: Chicago UP, 2005.

Mitchell, W. J. T. and Mark B. N. Hansen, eds. *Critical Terms for Media Studies.* Chicago and London: Chicago UP, 2010.

Modenessi, Alfredo Michel. "(Un)doing the Book 'Without Verona Walls': A View from the Receiving End of Baz Luhrmann's *William Shakespeare's Romeo + Juliet.*" Ed. Courtney Lehmann and Lisa S. Starks, *Spectacular Shakespeare: Critical Theory and Popular Cinema.* Madison, NJ: Fairleigh Dickinson UP, 2002. 62–85.

Moretti, Franco. "The Great Eclipse: Tragic Form as the Deconsecration of Sovereignty." Trans. Susan Fischer, David Forgacs, and David Miller, *Signs Taken for Wonders: Essays in the Sociology of Literature.* London and New York: Verso, 1988. 42–82.

"Mudlark: 'Such Tweet Sorrow.' Case Study." *Figaro Digital*, n.d. Web. 15 June 2010. Available at: <www.figarodigital.co.uk/case-study/Mudlark.aspx>.

"Musings in More Than 140 Characters on Such Tweet Sorrow." *Blogging by Numbers: Writing, Making, and Blogging Theatre*, 14 May 2010. Web. 5 June 2010. Available at: <http:// writebynumbers.wordpress.com/2010/05/14/musings-in-more-than-140-characters-on-such-tweet-sorrow>.

My Kingdom. Dir. Don Boyd. Close Grip Films, Primary Pictures, and Sky Pictures. 2001. Film.

myShakespeare. Royal Shakespeare Company, n.d. Web. 16 Jan. 2013. Available at: < http://myshakespeare.worldshakespearefestival.org.uk/>.

Naas, Michael. *Miracle and Machine. Jacques Derrida and the Two Sources of Religion, Science, and the Media.* New York: Fordham UP, 2012.

Navas, Edoardo. "Regressive and Reflexive Mashups in Sampling Culture." Ed. Stefan Sonvilla-Weiss, *Mashup Cultures.* Vienna: Springer Vienna Architecture, 2010. 157–77.

Neill, Michael. "Unproper Beds: Race, Adultery, and the Hideous in *Othello.*" *Shakespeare Quarterly* 40 (1989): 383–412.

Nicklin, Hannah. "Such Tweet Sorrow, a Blog Post in Two Acts." 19 Apr. 2010, 25 Apr. 2010. Web. 26 Apr. 2010. Available at: < www.hannahnicklin.com/2010/04/such-tweet-sorrow-a-blog-post-in-two-acts/>.

Nochimson, Martha P. Rev. of *The King Is Alive.* Dir. Kristian Levring. *Film Quarterly* 55.2 (2001–2): 48–54. *ProQuest.* Web. 20 May 2010.

O'Neill, Stephen. "Uploading *Hamlet*: Agency, Convergence and YouTube Shakespeare." Cimitile and Rowe 63–75.

Orr, Jake. "Such Tweet Sorrows: Such a Let Down." *A Younger Theatre. Theatre through the Eyes of the Younger Generations.* 6 May 2010. Web. 10 June 2010. Available at: <www.ayoungertheatre.com/such-tweet-sorrows-such-a-let-down>.

Osborne, Laurie. "iShakespeare: Digital Art/Games, Intermediality, and the Future of Shakespearean Film." Semenza: 48–59.

Othello. Dir. Oliver Parker. Castle Rock, Dakota Films, Imminent Films. 1995. Film.

The Oxford English Dictionary. 2nd ed. 1989.

Parker, Patricia. "*Othello* and *Hamlet*: Dilation, Spying, and the 'Secret Place' of Woman." *Representations* 44 (1993): 60–95.

"Parting with Such Tweet Sorrow." *Open Source Theatre*, 23 May 2010. Web. 5 June 2010. Available at: < http://opensourcetheatre.wordpress.com/2010/05/23/parting-with-such-tweet-sorrow>.

Pearson, Roger. *Mallarmé and Circumstance: The Translation of Silence.* Oxford: Oxford UP, 2004.

Phillips, Caryl. *The European Tribe.* London: Faber and Faber, 1987.

———. *The Nature of Blood.* London: Faber and Faber, 1997.

Pilcher, Tim. *E: The Incredibly Strange History of Ecstasy.* Philadelphia: Running Press, 2008.

Pizza My Heart. Dir. Andy Volk. GWave Productions, Walt Disney Studios, and ABC Family. 2005. Film.

Porter, Steven. "Dogme Eat Dog." *The New Review.* Laura Hird, n. pag. Web. 12 Aug. 2011. Available at: <www.laurahird.com/newreview/dogmeeatdog.html>.

The Postman. Dir. Kevin Costner. Tig Productions, Warner Bros. Pictures. 1997. Film.

Raskin, Richard, ed. *Aspects of Dogma.* Spec. issue of *p.o.v. Filmtidsscrift. A Danish Journal of Film Studies* 10 (2000): n. pag. Web. 10 Jan. 2013. Available at: <http://pov.imv.au.dk/Issue_10/POV_10cnt.html>.

Rave Macbeth (Nacht der Entscheidung). Dir. Klaus Knoesel. 2K Filmproduktion, Falcon Films, and Framewerk Produktion. 2001. Film.

Reynolds, Simon. *Energy Flash: A Journey Through Rave Music and Dance Culture.* London: Picador, 1998.

Richmond, Hugh, ed. *Shakespeare's Staging.* U of California, Berkeley, n.d. Web. 13 Jan. 2013. Available at:<http://shakespearestaging.berkeley.edu/>.

Roman, Shari. *Digital Babylon: Hollywood, Indiewood & Dogme '95.* Los Angeles: Lone Eagle, 2001.

Rome & Jewel. Dir. Charles T. Kanganis. Rome & Jewel LLC and Emerging Pictures. 2008. Film.

Romney, Jonathan. Rev. of *The King Is Alive,* dir. Kristian Levring. *The Independent.* 13 May 2001, n. pag. Web. 14 Aug. 2011.

Ronell, Avital. *Crack Wars: Literature, Addiction, Mania.* Lincoln: U of Nebraska P, 1992.

Roxborough, Scott. "Rave Focus." *Hollywood Reporter* 364.23 (22 Aug. 2000): 20.

Rowe, Katherine. "Medium-Specificity and Other Critical Scripts for Screen Shakespeare." Henderson 34–53.

Rowe, Katherine, ed. *Shakespeare and New Media.* Spec. issue of *Shakespeare Quarterly* 61.3 (2010): 289–440. *Literature Online.* Web. 3 Mar. 2011.

Royle, Nicholas. *How to Read Shakespeare.* London: Granta Books, 2005.

———. *In Memory of Jacques Derrida.* Edinburgh: Edinburgh UP, 2009.

Salih, Tayeb. *Season of Migration to the North.* Trans. Denys Johnson-Davies. Oxford: Heinemann, 1969.

Sanders, Julie. *Adaptation and Appropriation.* London and New York: Routledge, 2006.

Scanlan, John. *On Garbage.* London: Reaktion Books, 2005.

Scheib, Ronnie. Rev. of *Souli,* dir. Alexander Abela. *Variety* 6–12 Sept. 2004: 34–35.

Schmelling, Sarah. *Ophelia Joined the Group Maidens Who Don't Float. Classic Lit Signs on to Facebook.* London: Plume Book, 2009.

Schmitt, Carl. *Political Theology: Four Chapters on the Concept of Sovereignty.* Trans. George Schwab. Chicago: Chicago UP, 2006.

Scotland, PA. Dir. Billy Morrissette. US Abandon Pictures, Paddy Wagon Productions, and Veto Chip Productions. 2001. Film.

Scott-Douglass, Amy. "Dogme Shakespeare 95: European Cinema, Anti-Hollywood Sentiment, and the Bard." Burt and Boose 252–65.

Sears, Djanet. *Harlem Duet.* Winnipeg, MB: Shillingford, 1997.

Semenza, Greg, ed. *After Shakespeare on Film.* Spec. issue of *Shakespeare Studies* 38 (2010): 1–285. *Literature Online.* Web. 15 Dec. 2012.

Serres, Michel. *The Parasite*. Trans. Lawrence R. Schehr. Minneapolis: U of Minnesota P, 2007 [1982].

The Seventh Seal (Det sjunde inseglet). Dir. Ingmar Bergman. Svensk Filmindustri. 1957. Film.

Shakespeare, William. *William Shakespeare: The Complete Works*. 2nd ed. Ed. Stanley Wells and Gary Taylor. Oxford: Clarendon P, 2005.

Shakespeare, William. *King Lear*. Ed. Kenneth Muir. The Arden Shakespeare. London and New York: Methuen, 1972.

The Shakespeare Quartos Archive. British Library, Folger Shakespeare Library, U of Maryland, et al., n.d. Web. 15 Dec. 2012. Available at: < www.quartos.org/>.

Shakespeare's Restless World. The British Museum and BBC Radio 4. 16 Apr.–11 May 2012. 20 episodes. Podcast (Radio and Web). 15 June 2012. Available at: <www.bbc.co.uk/programmes/b017gm45>.

Shannon, Laurie. "The Eight Animals in Shakespeare; Or, Before the Human." *Publications of the Modern Language Association* 124.2 (2009): 472–79.

Shaviro, Steven. *Post-Cinematic Affect*. Ropley: O-Books, 2010.

Shohet, Lauren. "The Banquet of *Scotland (PA)*." *Shakespeare Survey* 57 (2004): 186–95.

———. "YouTube, Use, and the Idea of the Archive." Semenza 68–76.

The Siberian Lady Macbeth (Fury Is a Woman or Sibirska Ledi Magbet). Dir. Andrzej Wajda. Altura Films International, Avala Films. 1962. Film.

Simons, Jan. *Playing the Waves: Lars Von Trier's Game Cinema*. Amsterdam: Amsterdam UP, 2007.

Singh, Jyotsna. "Othello's Identity, Postcolonial Theory, and Contemporary African Rewritings of *Othello*." Ed. Margo Hendricks and Patricia Parker, *Women, "Race," and Writing in the Early Modern Period*. London and New York: Routledge, 1994. 287–99.

Sinfield, Alan. *Faultlines. Cultural Materialism and the Politics of Dissident Reading*. Oxford: Clarendon P, 1992.

Sonvilla-Weiss, Stefan. "Introduction. Mashups, Remix Practices, and the Recombination of Existing Digital Content." Ed. Sonvilla-Weiss, *Mashup Cultures*. Vienna: Springer Vienna Architecture, 2010. 8–23.

Souli. Dir. Alexander Abela. Gondwana Dreams, Red Island Productions, Nori House. 2004. Working Copy. DVD.

The Space. Arts Council England and BBC, n.d. Web. 10 Sept. 2012. Available at: <http://thespace.org/>

Stam, Robert. "Introduction: The Theory and Practice of Adaptation." Ed. Robert Stam and Alessandra Raengo, *Literature and Film. A Guide to the Theory and Practice of Film Adaptation*. Oxford: Blackwell, 2005. 1–52.

Stevenson, Jack. *Dogme Uncut. Lars Von Trier, Thomas Vinterberg, and the Gang That Took on Hollywood*. Santa Monica: Santa Monica P; London: Turnaround, 2004.

Stiegler, Bernard. "Derrida and Technology: Fidelity at the Limits of Deconstruction and the Prosthesis of Faith." Ed. Tom Cohen, *Derrida and the Humanities: A Critical Reader*. Cambridge: Cambridge UP, 2002. 238–70.

———. "Memory." Mitchell and Hansen 64–87.

Technics and Time, 1. The Fault of Epimetheus. Trans. Richard Beardsworth and George Collins. Stanford, CA: Stanford UP, 1998.

———. *Technics and Time, 2. Disorientation.* Trans. Stephen Barker. Stanford, CA: Stanford UP, 2009.

The Street King. Dir. James Gavin Bedford. Mistral Pictures. 2002. Film.

Such Tweet Sorrow. Dir. Roxana Silbert. Mudlark, Royal Shakespeare Company, and 4iP. 11 Apr.–13 May 2010. Web. (Twitter) 1 Sept. 2010. Available at: <www.suchtweetsorrow.com>.

Such Tweet Sorrow @Such_Tweet. A Mudlark and RSC Production. Romeo & Juliet live, via Twitter. Web. (Twitter) 14 May 2010. Available at: <https://twitter.com/Such_Tweet>.

Rev. of *Such Tweet Sorrow*, Mudlark/RSC. *Sans Taste. A London Theatre Blog*, 28 Apr. 2010. Web. 17 June 2010. Available at: < www.sanstaste.com/2010/04/28/review-such-tweet-sorrow-mudlarkrsc/>.

Rev. of *Such Tweet Sorrow. This Is My Blog. After a Fashion, Anyway.* 12 Apr. 2010. Available at: <http://batsgirl.blogspot.it/2010/04/such-tweet-sorrow.html>.

Sud Side Stori. Dir. Roberta Torre. Gam Film and Istituto Luce, 2000. Film.

Tano da Morire. Dir. Roberta Torre. ASP Productions and Lucky Red, 1997. Film.

thejives. "#Such Tweet by the #S." 14 May 2010. Web. (Tumblr) 1 June 2010. Available at: <http://thejives.tumblr.com/post/598924672>.

———. "Thoughts on Suchtweet Critiques." 26 Apr. 2010. Web. (Tumblr) 1 June 2010. Available at: <http://thejives.tumblr.com/post/551151297>.

A Thousand Acres. Dir. Jocelyn Moorhouse. Beacon Communications, PolyGram Filmed Entertainment, Prairie Film. 1997. Film.

Thunderbolt (Magun). Dir. Tunde Kelani. Mainframe. 2000. Film.

Torre, Roberta. Interview by Barbara Palombelli. *MyMovies.It.* Web. 17 Apr. 2010. Available at: <www.mymovies.it/critica/persone/critica.asp?id=37906&r=7450>.

———. Interview by Valerio Gualerzi. *KWVenezia2000. 57. Mostra internazionale di arte cinematografica di Venezia*. Web. 28 May 2010. Available at: <www2.kwcinema.kataweb.it/venezia2000/p_torre_gualerzi.html>.

von Trier, Lars, and Thomas Vinterberg. *The Dogma 95 Manifesto and Vow of Chastity*. Raskin n. pag.

Tumbleweeds. Dir. Gavin O'Connor. Spanky Pictures, Solaris, River One Films, 1999. Film.

Wegenstein, Bernadette. "Body." Mitchell and Hansen 19–34.

Wells, Stanley, and Gary Taylor, eds. *William Shakespeare: The Complete Works.* 2nd ed. Oxford: Clarendon Press, 2005.

West Side Story. Dir. Robert Wise and Jerome Robbins. US Mirisch Pictures, Seven Arts Productions, and United Artists, 1961. Film.

Wiens, Birgit. "Hamlet and the Virtual Stage: Herbert Fritsch's Project hamlet_x." Ed. Freda Chapple and Chiel Kattenbelt. *Intermediality in Theatre and Performance*. Amsterdam and New York: Rodopi, 2006, 223–36.

William Shakespeare's Romeo + Juliet. Dir. Baz Luhrmann. US Bazmark Productions, 1996. Film.

Wilson, Richard. *Shakespeare in French Theory. King of Shadows*. London and New York: Routledge, 2007.

Winthrop-Young, Geoffrey. "Hardware/Software/Wetware." Mitchell and Hansen 186–98.

Wisehart, Cynthia. "Rave On." *Video Systems* 27.4 (Apr. 2001): 58.

Wolfe, Cary. "Introduction." Ed. Cary Wolfe, *Zoontologies: The Question of the Animal*. Minneapolis and London: U of Minnesota P, 2003. ix–xxiii.

———. *What Is Posthumanism?* Minneapolis and London: U of Minnesota P, 2010.

Woolman, Natalie. "RSC to 'stage' Twitter Romeo and Juliet." *The Stage News*. 12 Apr. 2010. Web. 10 May 2010. Available at: <www.thestage.co.uk/news/2010/04/rsc-to-stage-twitter-romeo-and-juliet>.

Worthen, W. B. "Drama, Performativity, and Performance." *Publications of the Modern Language Association* 113.5 (1998): 1093–1107.

———. *Shakespeare and the Force of Modern Performance*. Cambridge: Cambridge UP, 2003.

———. "Shakespeare 3.0: Or Text Versus Performance, the Remix." Henderson 54–76.

Wray, Ramona. "Shakespeare on Film in the New Millennium." *Shakespeare* 3.1–3 (2007): 270–82.

Wyver, John. "Tweets, Tweets, Tweets [Update]." *Illuminations*. 15 Apr. 2010, n. pag. Web. (Blog) 1 June 2010. Available at: < www.illuminationsmedia.co.uk/blog/?news_id=662>.

Zizek, Slavoj. *Enjoy Your Symptom. Lacan in Hollywood and Out*. New York and London: Routledge, 1992.

———. *Looking Awry. An Introduction to Jacques Lacan Through Popular Culture*. London and Cambridge, MA: MIT P, 1991.

———. *The Plague of Fantasies*. London and New York: Verso, 1997.

———. *The Sublime Object of Ideology*. London and New York: Verso, 1989.

Index

BBC *Shakespeare Retold Macbeth*, see
  Macbeth (Moffat)/BBC *Shakespeare
  Retold*
Bedford, James Gavin
  The Street King, 193n6
Bennington, Geoff, 59
Berlusconi, Silvio, 91–2
Bhardwaj, Vishal
  Maqbool, 118
Boyd, Don
  My Kingdom, 193n6
Brook, Peter, 43
Brozel, Mark, 22
Burnett, Mark Thornton, 41–3, 63–4,
  68, 70, 73
  on Abela's films, 77
  *Filming Shakespeare in the Global
  Marketplace*, 84
  on metadramatic films, 111
Burt, Richard, 10, 18, 66, 135
  "Shakespearecentric", 109
  on "Shakespeares", 2

Carlin, Murray
  Not Now, Sweet Desdemona, 186n21
carnivorous culture, 33–4
carno-phallogocentric subject, 25–6
Cartelli, Thomas, 7, 23, 41, 48, 58, 102
Chambers, Iain, 76, 94–5
Chan, Adrian
  from media to social media, 151
Channel 4's 4iP, 137
Charnes, Linda
  Hamlet, a noir text, 103–4
  patriarchal fantasy of cloning, 107
Chow, Rey, 188n30
cinema
  intercultural, 184n3
  cinematic techniques, 109–10
Cinema-verité, 110
Clarke, Bruce, 207n63
cloning, 107, 109
coming back from the dead, *133*
connectivity, 15–16, 150–1, 204n39

consumption
  conspicuous consumption, 24–5
  of flesh, 21–3, 26, 33–4
conversations
  on social media, 151–2
Corfield, Lu, 138

Derrida, Jacques, 6, 11
  on anachrony, 6, 16, 18, 134, 146,
  161, 170n39
  on the animal, 25–6, 171n3, 173n17,
  174n21, 198n39
  on autoimmunity, 56, 182n50; *see
  also* autoimmunity
  on hospitality, 86, 94
  on hos(ti)pitality, 88
  on the human subject, 21–2, 25–6
  on identity, 189n14
  and the logic of iterability, 134
  on the messianic, 60
  Specters of Marx, 1–2, 18, 39–40,
  43–4, 82, 123
  on spectrality, 66, 131–2, 134
  "system of marks", 160–1
  on "teletechnologies", 2, 13, 129–31,
  195n17
  on touch, 76
  On Touching, 187n29
digital Shakespeare, 164n8
disempowerment, 71
displacement, 185n17
  economic and sexual, 68–9
  see also migration
documentary film, 110
  conventions of, 84–5
Dogme95/Dogme films, 5, 40, 42–4,
  47, 55–6, 179n13
  see also The King is Alive (Levring)
Donaldson, Peter, 11, 14, 122
  Shakespearean films: and media
  regimes and practices, 109
drugs, 13, 101–2, 115–16, 168n33,
  197n38
  addiction to, 157–8